Praise for *LAZARUS AND THE HURRICANE*

"Young Lazarus will win your heart and the Hurricane will inspire you. This book vividly illustrates the pain of a dream deferred and the joy of opportunity fulfilled."

Coretta Scott King

"The Hurricane Carter case is one of [the twentieth] century's most important legal sagas. . . . Spellbinding, a must-read for anyone interested in justice and human drama."

F. Lee Bailey

"This book represents all the future possibilities of good old down-home human relationships. Power. The ability to define, know and realize the phenomena of corrupt power structures . . . then, in a committed, dedicated, caring way, make the phenomena act in a desired manner. Literally powerful!"

Bobby Seale, co-founder of the
Black Panther Party

"This book is like me—floats like a butterfly, stings like a bee."

Muhammad Ali

"The first book [*The Sixteenth Round*] was a heartbreaker. This one is a mind-breaker, abolishir

Bob Dylan

"My grandmother said   l and the force of good out there. And my   give good a hard time, but good will alwa,. .... This wonderful story bears that out."

Roberta Flack

"Rubin Carter lost twenty years of his life to justice gone wrong. He rose from the living dead of false imprisonment, in part because *Lazarus and the Hurricane* is what real justice is all about—truth in action. The moral energy of Carter, and the authors, in righting a monstrous misdeed of the system is a real inspiration."

Michael Harris, author of *Justice Denied*

"A legal thriller . . . amazing . . ."

Peter Gzowski, "Morningside," CBC Radio

"Thrilling and appalling . . . A Canadian tale of triumph."

The Toronto Star

"Superbly written . . . fast-reading . . . sensitive . . . moving . . ."

Quill & Quire

"*Lazarus and the Hurricane* takes the reader on a shocking and often frustrating roller-coaster ride through the American legal system."

Coles Booktalk

"Determination, desire and compassion [are] the heart and soul of the book. If a book about the triumph of the human spirit interests you, *Lazarus and the Hurricane* is definitely worth reading."

The Leader Post (Regina)

"Carter is plainly an extraordinarily tough and resilient man, his mind even quicker than his fists. . . . A real-life thriller about wrongful imprisonment and the crusading spirit."

The Globe and Mail

"The feel-good book of the year."

The Toronto Sun

"A double-fisted tale of liberation."

The Vancouver Sun

LAZARUS
and the
HURRICANE

THE FREEING OF
RUBIN "HURRICANE" CARTER

Sam Chaiton and Terry Swinton

St. Martin's Griffin ✺ New York

To
Jumping Mouse,
who was not stopped by fear,
and to
John Eagleshield,
for whom walking through mountains
is walking through mountains

ISBN 0-312-25397-4

First published in Canada by Penguin Books Canada Limited.

First St. Martin's Griffin Edition: January 2000
10 9 8 7 6 5 4

CONTENTS

ACKNOWLEDGMENTS

This book would not have been a reality without the aid of many people over many years who contributed to the freeing of Rubin Carter.

For their friendship and invaluable legal expertise, principal thanks go to Leon Friedman, who has also supported this book with boundless enthusiasm and time, to Myron Beldock and to Lewis Steel—all indefatigable, tenacious and generous lawyers.

To other attorneys who lent their assistance: Edward Graves, Larry Levine, Elliott Hoffman, Richard Bellman, Ronald Busch, Louis Raveson, Jeff Fogel, Harold Cassidy, William Perkins, Robert Utsey, James Myerson, Benjamin Hooks, Charles Carter, Grover Hankins, Nancy Baxter, Kathleen Wresien, Cynthia Rollings, Elliott Sagor, Karen Dippold, Evan Steinberg, David Korzenik, Stanley Van Ness, John Noonan, Michael Blacker, John Flynn, Jack Doran, Raymond Brown, Arnold Stein, William Kunstler, Ron Kuby, Florence Kennedy, Russell Grayson, Seymour Wishman, Alfred Slocum, Irene Hill-Smith, Governor William Cahill, Donald Belsole, N.J. Attorney General Carey Edwards, U.S. Rep. John Conyers, Cedric Hendricks, Edward Bennett Williams.

To the investigators: the "indispensable" Fred Hogan, Herb Bell, Mims Hackett, Brenda Wilkes. Others who helped with the investigation: Ed Carter, Shahid Ali, Henry Wimberly, Norman "Lush" Brown, Rudy Davis, Glenn Carlos, Barbara Samad, Cephas Phillips, Luther Wallace, Violet Fells, Rebecca Roach, Alvin Moses, Reverend William Sloan Coffin, Father Luis Gigante, Reverend Neil Connally, Archie McCabe, Linda Pitney, Cornbread Givens, Reginald Poe, Chris Norwood, Tony Liccione, Thom Kidrin.

To the dedicated legal support staff at Beldock, Levine and Hoffman: Amanda George, Stephanie Jacobs, Sandi Gonski, Jill Levy, Ancilla Black, Diego Caldron.

Thanks also to Bob Dylan, Muhammad Ali, Joe Frazier, Angelo Dundee, Charmaine Carter, Dave Anderson, Selwyn Raab, Dr. K. Chen and Michael Murnaghan for their responsiveness.

Thanks to the entire Martin family in New York and the Carter family in New Jersey.

A special acknowledgment to John Artis.

We also salute those who have waited and those who are still waiting in New Jersey: Jimmy Blake, A.J. Hawk, Glen Turner, Johnny D'Amico, Watasi, Louie Van Dyne, Tommy Trantino, Arnette Thomas (Tayu), Rockfish, Ray Cieslak, Smalls, Mobutu, Nicola Chalet, Nick the Greek, Brother Franklin, Jap Wilder, "New York," Smurf and Li'l Bit, Fred "Bugsy" Siegle, Chuck Carter, "Hey Baby," Jomo, Big Muhammad, "Honky Tonk" Bud, John Hall, Omar Mathis, Sugar Earl Best, Rick Rowe, Quadi, The Rose and Rosemary, Zig and Sheila, Isabell Carter, Saifuddin and Marion, Lenny Hinson, "Sweet Al," Gamu, Misra, "Top" Choice, Luis Diaz, "Swamp Man" Smitty, Tony "Baby Bull" Ayala, Fox, Country, Money, Sam Jennings, Vickie and Snookie, Dawson, Shaky Brown, Tariq Darby and Belinda, Billy "Red" Smith and Loretta, Mr and Mrs Jimmy Landano, Brother Dozier, Captain Dick and his entire family including Jahad, Tyrone Parker, Ricky and Anne Roots, Malone, Jim-Jim Rainey, "Homeboy," Charlie Chandler, Goldie and Marie, Tony D'Amato, The Undertaker, Wolf, Brother Kamau, Danny and Sheila, Malik, Brownie and Connie, Trish and Greg, Steve and Donna, Dave and Brianne Collins, Greg and Belinda, Dagu Abdul Wasi, Gerald Stewart, Carole, Joyce, Bill and Pat, Earl Doyle, Werton, Brother Lilly, Mr Richter, Joe Arnez, Brother Battle, Joe Wright, John Redding, Carson Edwards, Larry Ianuzzi, Dwight Mason, Sam Clark, Willy Ham, Alfonse Leake, Todd McCuaig, Samad, Robert Holmes, Esther Eves, Zeke and Rena, Thomas and Sis, Patty and "Ricky" Nelson, Jeanette and Zeke, Barbara and Lonnie, Dave and Doris, Brown, Diane and Rocky, Rajan, Hillard Phillips, Tommy Tyson, Jose Velez, "Butterfly," Melvin, Jimmy Mack, Bob Jolley, Omar Shabazz, George Jacques, Bob Parrish, Jamil, Brother Middleton, Brother Ali, Royster, Frederick, Nate, Richard, Frank, Julio, Jack, Barry, Walter, David, Oscar, Sekou, Hassan, Basir,

Stokes, Joseph, Royal, Tony Puchalski, Jeffrey, William Gebhardt, Leroy "Duke" Snyder, Robert Woodley, Wannamaker, Charles, Donald, James Wattlington, Giles Williams, Lawrence, Clarence, Clemmins, Kareem, Larry Pease, Sam Vanderhorst, Cooper, Mareno, Bobby Martin, Jerry Lucas, John Rafferty, Johnson, John Julian, and others whose names may not be mentioned but who will never be forgotten.

We'd like to thank our Canadian agent, David Johnston, for his inspired suggestion of the book's title and for directing our proposal to the best editor for us, Iris Skeoch, at Penguin Books Canada Limited. Thanks to Iris for her co-operative spirit, thoughtful inputs, refreshing sense of humour, and trust. Thanks to Cynthia Good for her high-energy participation, commitment and care. To Catherine Marjoribanks for her incisive editing suggestions, warmly given. To others at Penguin—Brad Martin, Christeen Chidley-Hill, Lori Ledingham, Bruce Bond, Pat Cooper, Karen Cossar, Scott Sellers, Wilf Clarke, Jeff Boloten, Jacqueline Rothstein—thanks for welcoming the story and welcoming us.

Likewise to the folks at St. Martin's Press in New York. Special thanks to Michael Denneny for his unflagging enthusiasm and support over the years, to Christina Prestia for her thoughtfulness and thoroughness, and to Paul Sleven for his good advice.

And, of course, without Lazarus and the Hurricane, there would have been no book to write.

AUTHORS' NOTE

Unless attributed otherwise, the information about the Carter case recounted in this book has its source in the voluminous record of the case, comprising in the tens of thousands of pages: transcripts of grand jury hearings, evidentiary hearings and two full trials; police statements, investigative reports and notes; affidavits, depositions, exhibits, briefs and court opinions.

Over the years, the prosecution has advanced many arguments and accusations that have been legally or factually discredited by the courts. These meritless contentions do not appear here except to the extent that they relate to the freeing of Rubin "Hurricane" Carter. A complete rehashing of the twenty-two-year case would be neither practical nor fruitful, nor is it the story of this book.

For the reader's convenience and ease of reference, a chronology of the Carter case is included as an appendix.

PEACE BRIDGE

They exited the highway at Porter Avenue under a sign that read "Peace Bridge to Canada." Only a trace of snow remained on the ground—unusual for the beginning of March—but it was cold. The brisk night air glowed red in the exhaust surrounding the tail-lights streaming up ahead; inside, the smell of the car's heater mixed with that of well-worn leather. The old Mercedes still had a lot of life left as it hummed along that Buffalo street, past a row of Victorian clapboard houses, and made the hard right turn toward the bridge. After a long ordeal they were finally coming home, and they were elated.

They paid the toll, crossed the bridge where the Stars and Stripes and the red Maple Leaf waved side by side, and waited their turn at Canada Customs.

"Where do you live?"

"Toronto."

"Toronto."

"New Jersey."

"Your citizenship?"

"Canadian."

"Canadian."

"American."

"May I see your passports or birth certificates, please."

The customs officer quickly inspected the documents, then focused his attention on the American in the front passenger seat.

"The purpose of your visit?"

"I'll be visiting with my friends here. In Toronto."

"How long do you intend to remain in Canada?"

"I'm not sure. A few weeks."

"Do you intend to work in Canada?"

"No, sir. I'm . . . on vacation."

The American was handed a coloured slip of paper and told to present himself to the Manpower and Immigration office located across the parking lot. The three men were nervous as they pulled up to the building and climbed the few steps leading in.

Under the glare of fluorescent lights inside, the office was typically governmental, but quiet since it was an off hour. The trio went up to the counter, and the American handed the slip of paper to a grey-haired man in his late forties.

"What can I do for you?" the immigration officer asked. After taking stock of the American's impeccable grooming, the natty, tweed sports coat, its suede elbow patches matching a wool turtleneck sweater, he looked down at the form.

"Did you tell them at Customs that you planned to work in Canada?"

"No," answered the American.

"What is the purpose of your visit?"

"Visiting friends," he said. "And travelling."

"Well, how come they sent you in here?"

The American shrugged his shoulders and shook his head. Maybe it was something in his movement that prompted the next question.

"Have you ever been arrested?"

The African-American hesitated for a moment, then answered, "Yes." Here we go again, he thought. And the Canadians stood by helplessly, as the officer hit upon the very questions they had hoped he would not ask.

"Have you ever been convicted of a crime?"

"Yes . . ."

"You know that makes you inadmissible to enter this country."

"B-b-b-but . . ." The threat of being turned away after having come so far reawakened a long-dormant stutter.

The officer continued; his questioning remained routine, his voice formal.

"Did you serve time in prison?"

"Yes."

"How long?"

Pause. "Twenty years."

"What was the crime?"

"Homicide."

"So you served your full term and then were released and now you want to come to Canada. As I said . . ."

"No. That wasn't my full term"

"No? Well just how long did you have?"

"Triple life."

"So you were paroled and barring any unforeseen circumstances . . ."

"No. I was exonerated."

"Oh, someone finally came forward and confessed to the crime?"

"No."

"Then how did you get out of prison?"

"My conviction was overturned."

"Where?"

"In court . . . federal court . . . three federal courts. The United States District Court in Newark, the Third Circuit Court of Appeals in Philadelphia and the United States Supreme Court."

"Hmmm."

"And then the State of New Jersey dropped all charges."

"Say, what's your name?" demanded the officer.

"Rubin Carter."

"Didn't I just see you on TV? On 'Good Morning America' or something like that?" he probed.

Rubin nodded.

"I *thought* you looked familiar!" He turned to another immigration officer at the back of the office. "Hey, Joe!" he shouted, his voice now loud and excited. "This is him! The guy I was tellin' you about! Rubin 'Hurricane' Carter! The prizefighter! The guy who was just cleared! He spent twenty years in prison for a crime he didn't commit!"

Turning back around, he grabbed hold of Rubin's hand and shook it heartily. "Congratulations, Mr Carter!" he said. "And welcome to Canada!"

As Rubin, Sam and Terry left the building, the tears that filled their eyes were not only the result of meeting that crisp night air.

"What brings him to Canada of all places?" the immigration officer asked Joe before the door had closed behind the three men. His question was self-deprecating in a characteristically Canadian way: not that he wasn't flattered that Rubin "Hurricane" Carter would want to come to his country—he was puzzled.

Rubin would have told him, but neither he nor his Canadian friends would have known how to begin. It would mean going back about a decade, at least to 1979. They would have to go from Lazarus to the Hurricane, because that was the way it happened. And it was a story so full of unlikely meetings, curious parallels and Dickensian twists that even if the officer had had the time to listen, he probably wouldn't have believed it anyway.

PART ONE

TAKING AN ELL

To use his own words, further, he said, "if you give a nigger an inch, he will take an ell. . . . Learning will spoil the best nigger in the world . . ."

—Frederick Douglass
My Bondage and My Freedom

1

It was a sunny day in September 1979 when a group of friends gathered at the arrivals gate at Toronto International Airport. There were eight of them, most in their early thirties. Scots, English, Austrian, German, Jew—their ethnic backgrounds blended well into the multinational mosaic of Canada, where they had grown up and prospered.

The overhead monitor indicated that Air Canada flight 709 from New York had landed on time. The excitement in the group was palpable, and tinged with apprehension over the responsibility they were about to assume. They knew they could count on one another, all good friends, to share the weight. They could scarcely have imagined, though, just how their combined resources would be needed and put to use in the years ahead.

Most of them had met as students at the University of Toronto in the sixties, and all shared a general dissatisfaction with things as they were. Some had been anti-Vietnam War activists who assisted American draft-dodgers. Others had been involved in the performing arts. Several had done social work, some with the mentally handicapped, others with drug abusers. They were Kathy and Michael and Lisa and Terry and Marty and Gus and Mary and Sam: the children of wealth and privilege and the WASP Establishment and the offspring of poor immigrants; the nephew of a Nazi SS officer and the son of survivors of Bergen-Belsen. Having their parents even sit in a room together was unthinkable; no doubt it would have inspired World War III. Yet, the group had been living together in harmony for almost ten years, and working together on many different projects and business enterprises.

"There he is!" Kathy called out, as a stocky black kid ran toward them at full tilt. His hair was cut close to his head, and he was wearing shiny, unhemmed black pants with a red stripe down the outside seams, a cerise polyester T-shirt and pointed grey shoes a couple of sizes too big. Clutched in his hand was a paper shopping bag containing all his worldly possessions.

"Hi, all y'all!"

"Lesra!" they shouted back. "You made it!"

Lesra burst into a huge, jagged smile that was missing half a front tooth. They grabbed him and hugged him.

"What happened to your hair?" asked Terry. "Where's the afro?"

"Whatchootalkinbout?" came the retort. "Ev'ybody have a Caesar!" And Terry and the others all laughed, realizing how glad they were to see him.

Most of the group had met Lesra in New York that summer while researching a new business venture at the Environmental Protection Agency (EPA) lab in Brooklyn. Lesra and another black youth, William, had been hired at the lab as part of a government-funded make-work summer program for inner-city youth.

Although both Lesra and William were fifteen years old, together they made a comic Mutt and Jeff team: Lesra was barely five feet tall and William over six. Their "work" consisted of napping, guzzling Coca Cola by the quart, chasing and punching each other and generally hanging out. Although they tried their best to be quiet when others were present, they both exhibited a certain creativity in playfully cursing out each other's momma when they thought no one else was listening. It was obvious they were not familiar with generally accepted good work habits, nor did it seem they were being taught any.

Just before the Canadians arrived, the boys had been given the task of hosing down one of the vans used for testing emission levels of New York City taxi cabs, but that assignment ended abruptly when their hosing turned to roughhousing, and Lesra hit his head so hard against the pavement that he had to be taken to the hospital. They were later relegated to playing with the phones in the air-conditioned office, which was Lesra's favourite activity, not only because of the air-conditioning but because he didn't have the luxury of a telephone at home.

The boys gravitated toward the white people who said they were from somewhere called "Canada" and who talked funny and liked to joke around and ask a lot of questions. Lesra and William trailed them around the EPA facilities, from the offices to the garages to the computer area. "Dere go Canada!" the boys would shout, poking their heads through doorways, under car hoods and over the water cooler, trying not to get in the way but wanting to be part of the action. Despite their best intentions, they would easily get distracted and start inciting each other.

Lesra was the more outgoing of the two; William hardly spoke at all. On one occasion, after Lesra greeted Michael with a "Yo, Canada, wha's up?" Michael let him in on a secret: "You know, Lesra, people from Canada are called *Canadians.*" From then on, "Dere go Canadians!" was the familiar refrain.

Lesra's speech was almost impossible for the Canadians to understand, but they managed to decipher that Lesra lived with his family in the Bushwick section of Brooklyn. He had a mother and a father at home, as well as seven brothers and sisters.

One day Terry, Michael and Lisa offered Lesra a ride home. But Lesra didn't know how to get there, except by the one subway route he took to work every day. "No problem," they said. "We'll get the map." They produced a street map of Brooklyn and, sure enough, were able to trace a route to Linden Street from the EPA lab in the Greenpoint section of Brooklyn.

But there was much that the map didn't tell them. It didn't indicate that they had to drive through a wasteland of desolate neighbourhoods, past block after block after block of abandoned, burnt-out, run-down shells of buildings strewn with broken bottles, discarded mattresses and months of uncollected garbage, and populated by people (not a white face among them) whose bearing tragically reflected the neglect of their environment. Nor did the map show topography. Where apartment houses had collapsed, their guts were spilled out onto the sidewalks in hills, as if a petulant giant had stepped on the building and booted the resulting debris out of his way and into the street. People simply walked around or over the mounds that had become a permanent part of the landscape.

The three Canadians felt overwhelmed by the immensity of the ghetto and the sense of claustrophobia it induced. This was no small pocket of poverty; the misery stretched on forever. Once in, they were afraid they'd never get out. They finally turned down Linden Street, one of the many identical streets running off Broadway, and pulled up to Lesra's address. Michael remarked that the building next door was all boarded up, and Lesra informed him matter-of-factly that it was used as a crash pad for junkies and winos.

The Canadians felt conspicuous. Scores of curious eyes in doorways and behind windows, puzzled by the rare appearance of whites in their neighbourhood, concluded that they must be probation officers bringing home a wayward child. Feeling important but keeping his cool, Lesra hopped out of the car. The Canadians also tried to look nonchalant, as though for them, too, this drive through hell was nothing unusual.

Even after they'd returned to Toronto, the group found it difficult to forget Lesra and William. The annual Caribana festival, a dazzling celebration of West Indian culture, was approaching, and Kathy suggested they invite the boys up for that long weekend. The idea was enthusiastically received and discussed. Wonderful as it would be to have Lesra and William see Toronto and enjoy the steel drums and unbelievable costumes in the Caribana parade, would it be fair, they wondered, to expose them to a way of living that was so far beyond their experience and their prospects that they might justifiably become frustrated when they returned to their dead-end Brooklyn streets? After deliberating carefully, the group decided that, on balance, the potential benefits of the experience outweighed any possible drawbacks. Ignorance was definitely not bliss: seeing another world might stimulate the boys' curiosity, might enable them to extend their reach.

Arranging the trip required some complicated logistics (not having a telephone, Lesra's parents were difficult to get in touch with) but both sets of parents gave their consent. The boss at the lab, a sympathetic Hungarian-American, had sent Lesra and William home with notes vouching for the Canadians and endorsing the proposed trip.

The plane tickets were waiting for the boys at the Air Canada counter at LaGuardia in New York, but Lesra didn't believe they'd be there. He thought it was too good to be true; the trip had to be some kind of scam. His scepticism, however, did not prevent him from taking that crucial first step—getting to the airport. He'd never been to an airport, he rationalized, so even if the tickets weren't there, so what? He and William could have fun watching planes come and go. That the tickets *were* there set the tone for a visit full of surprises for Lesra and William.

Of course, there were the usual attractions for young American teenagers: being away from home for the first time, the excitement of a first airplane ride, the weirdness of foreign paper money that was colourful instead of drab green. But it was other mundane, everyday stuff the Canadians took for granted that really intrigued the boys.

The Canadians lived in a house perched on a wooded ravine. Although it was in downtown Toronto, it felt like the country. This was no urban landscape, certainly not for Lesra and William. So foreign was it to them to walk on grass that they stumbled constantly, and climbing up even the tiniest hill was a challenge. It was as though sod or bare earth underfoot was as insubstantial as walking on putty. "Please walk on the grass" signs in parks were invitations to disaster. Yet at home, negotiating rooftops and mounds of rubble, these boys were adept and graceful.

Trees were strange obstacles never encountered on Brooklyn rooftops or "real" city streets. William, in particular, was fascinated by a silver birch that grew behind the house. He would lean up against it, touching its papery bark with delight, trying to figure out what it was and how it got to be that colour. Eventually he solved the mystery: someone must have painted the tree white and now the paint was peeling off in strips!

Mysterious for Lesra was the source of the scary shadows that, at night, moved across the windows facing out onto the ravine. It's amazing how terrifying the combination of moon, wind and tree can be when you are used to only the wailing of sirens, the crack of gunshots, the scurrying of rats and the whining and fighting of junkies and winos.

To lessen the culture shock, several of the group drove the boys down Yonge Street one night at about eleven o'clock, to the seedy section that at least somewhat resembled New York's 42nd Street. The traffic was stop and go. The boys began to feel comfortable when they passed a building that had some graffiti sprayed on its side. "Dere go New Yawk!" shouted Lesra, one arm pointing out the window, the other elbowing William in the ribs. The boys settled back into their seats, basking in familiar neon, crowded sidewalks, topless bars.

Suddenly they both leaned forward, eyes wide and mouths agape, and their heads slowly turned from the front to the rear of the car. The Canadians searched for what had so completely seized the boys' attention. All they saw was a kid, about eleven or twelve, peddling an ice-cream-vending bicycle-cart up the street.

"Try dat in New Yawk!" yelled William out the window, and he and Lesra howled at the absurdity. Composing himself for a moment, Lesra explained the obvious: in Brooklyn, it "wouldn't take but a second" for that kid to get ripped off for his cart, his bike, his money and anything else he had. "Lest he got a big-assed gun!" chimed in William. And they laughed till it hurt.

The Caribana parade the next day provided further opportunity for wonder. Instead of driving, they all took the subway. In Brooklyn, most of the subways are not underground but elevated and called "trains." But the recently opened St Clair West station was like no train station the kids from Brooklyn had ever seen. It was spacious and positively glistening, and the artwork on the walls was not of the spray-can variety. The boys were sure they'd be thrown out "on their butts," that they had strayed into the lobby of some fancy hotel, the kind they'd seen successful, big-time drug dealers patronizing on TV's "Starsky and Hutch." A gleaming train—which Lesra and William assumed was brand new, as it had "not yet" been covered in graffiti—pulled in and they got on. Fellow passengers actually smiled at them.

Downtown, settling in a shady spot under some maples opposite Trinity College, they were able to join the cheerful crowd and get a clear view of the parade route around Queen's Park. Soon throngs of partying, dancing, singing wavers and shakers and jazz and steel bands on floats thundered by. Lesra and William were mesmerized.

Each "mas'" (masquerade) band had its own "King" and "Queen" arrayed in fabulous costumes that shimmered and bobbed and twirled. The drums had a Caribbean beat—reggae, calypso, Afro-Cuban—so irresistible that whether you were Canadian, American, West Indian or Martian, you could not *not* dance to the music. The ranks of each band were swelled by hundreds of revellers, young and old, black and white, who danced out into the street and followed the floats down the parade route, bridging the gulf between spectator and participant. The boys noticed that even the cops swayed to the rhythm.

More than the parade itself, the Canadians relished the mixture of awe and delight they saw on the boys' faces. Lesra and William were astounded that so many people could get together and genuinely enjoy themselves—without trouble. Nary a gunshot was to be heard. No one was fighting. No one was even arguing.

The end of the parade brought the *coup de grâce*. Scarcely had the last float passed when half a dozen men in jumpsuits appeared from out of nowhere. "Who dat?" asked Lesra, watching them perform a singular feat of magic. The crew made discarded pop cans, ice-cream wrappers and empty film packaging disappear. In less than a minute, the street-sweepers and litter-collectors had returned the avenue to pristine condition.

"Man, dey take trash serious here!" observed Lesra.

"Yes," laughed Sam. "Garbage is against the law here. In Canada, you can get busted for littering."

Although Lesra understood that this was intended as a humorous comment, a trip to the zoo the following day made him wonder whether his hosts hadn't been serious. They had just left a concession stand, and Lesra was munching away on a chocolate bar. When he finished it, his hand mechanically opened and let the wrapper drop as he walked on. Suddenly he felt a tap on his shoulder. He turned around, scared—on the streets of Brooklyn you never knew what could sneak up on you. And his fear grew when he saw behind him a disgruntled cop making strange hand motions. The cop was big and burly and his sign language unintelligible. He was pointing first down to the ground, then over toward the refreshment area.

After a moment, Lesra cupped his hand over his mouth. He realized the policeman was telling him to pick up the offending wrapper and throw it into the nearby garbage bin. "There's a good lad," said the constable, as Lesra nearly tripped over himself in his haste to pick up the litter and deposit it in the bin. Lesra hadn't meant to do anything wrong, and he certainly didn't want to be sent to prison.

If Lesra and William found some of Canada's customs puzzling, the Canadians, for their part, found the youths' lack of basic information incomprehensible, their "education" appalling. That trees and clean streets and friendly subways were unfamiliar to them was scandalous enough. And maybe it shouldn't have been surprising that the youths didn't know how many continents there were ("continent" was a word that they seemed never to have heard). But the Canadians were stupefied when they realized Lesra and William didn't know the name of the country they lived in. All they knew was they lived somewhere called "New Yawk"—was that a country?

Though they couldn't tell a country from a state or a city, they could recite verbatim the Pledge of Allegiance:

> *I pledge allegiance to the flag*
> *Of the United States of America,*
> *And to the republic for which it stands . . .*

Not that they had any idea what the words "pledge" and "allegiance" meant, never mind "republic." Being asked to explain the concept of "standing for" something likewise elicited shrugged shoulders and blank stares.

Yet Lesra was about to go into the eleventh grade and had stood third out of his Bushwick class of forty-four! What did that say for the forty-one others? How was it possible for such obviously bright, quick-witted, curious, observant fifteen-year-olds to be so uninformed? They hadn't dropped out—these kids were still going to school! How was it possible to be in high school—apparently doing well—and know nothing?

The Canadians reeled at the consequences of such a state of affairs. To generalize from the particular, this meant an entire generation of inner-city youth was receiving no education. Being born into the poverty of the ghetto and denied access to the opportunities that an education would bring was a life sentence to poverty and all its attendant suffering. No one deserved such a bleak prospect. What had happened to the concept contained in the last two lines of the Pledge of Allegiance recited daily by Lesra and William?

One nation under God, indivisible,
With liberty and justice for all.

Lesra wanted to be a lawyer when he grew up. He had no idea what that entailed, but he knew that lawyers got paid money when people were in trouble, and the people Lesra knew were always in trouble. His older brother had already been to prison. The Canadians figured Lesra's chances of *needing* a lawyer were a lot greater than his chances of becoming one.

That they might be able to do something to improve the odds, if only on a small scale, didn't occur to the Canadians until several weeks later. Further research on their project was required at the EPA lab. As a result, Michael, Lisa and Terry went back to Brooklyn and were able to spend some more time with Lesra and William. They took the opportunity to meet the boys' parents.

The Canadians had sensed a certain rivalry between the boys, and their suspicion that its source lay in the economic disparity between the families was confirmed when they visited the kids at home. When William had come to Toronto, he had brought twice as many pairs of jeans as Lesra, and all of better quality; whereas Lesra's pants were unhemmed, William's had been altered to fit. And William had complained that although Lesra had been to William's house several times, Lesra would never return the invitation.

The Fullers, William's family, were indeed better off. Both his parents worked, and he had only one younger brother at home. They owned a tiny, two-storey, semi-detached house in Bedford-Stuyvesant. With the assistance of a small amount of Housing and Urban Development money in the form of a low-interest mortgage, Mr Fuller had acquired the abandoned shell of the house from the city and renovated it himself, installing the plumbing, heating and electricity. William, being tall, had dreams of becoming a professional basketball player. By comparison to Lesra's circumstances, William's life was relatively prosperous and secure.

Lesra's family, the Martins, lived in a run-down railway flat on the fourth floor of a four-storey building that had long since been condemned but was still home to eight families. The door to their apartment—at the top of a narrow, tumbledown stairway that had no railings—had no knob and locked only on the inside. The flat had two windows: the one at the front overlooked the street; the second, with a view of nothing but debris at the rear, had years earlier been nailed shut to keep out intruders and remained unopened, even in summer's sweltering heat. Lesra dreamed that some day his family would qualify to live in the projects. He and his family aspired to get *into* the rat- and roach-infested, government-subsidized high-rise apartments that other families on welfare were trying to escape.

During the school year, Lesra would bring home the money he made packing grocery bags at the supermarket. He wanted to be helpful and make his parents proud of him. Neither of Lesra's parents was employed: his father, Earl, had off-loaded trucks until he permanently injured his back. His mother, Alma, looked after their eight children, two of whom arrived *after* she'd had a tubal ligation to prevent further pregnancies. Both parents had a drinking problem. Lesra's consolation was that, unlike most families he knew, at least *he* had his father at home.

When the three Canadians dropped by Lesra's place again, the neighbourhood was instantly aware of their presence. Countless people of all ages, shapes and sizes smiled and stared at them from stoops and doorways. As Lisa, Terry and Michael negotiated the narrow stairwell in Lesra's building, doors opened and people emerged wanting to meet and talk to the strangers who had given Lesra a trip to Canada. At the top of the steps, Lesra's father, a thin man who looked older than his forty-two years, graciously invited them in, simultaneously dispatching one of his sons to the store to fetch something for the company to drink, their protests notwithstanding. They sat down knee to knee in the cramped living room, where an ancient black-and-white TV was blaring away, its picture compressed into an inch-wide band across the centre of the tube. (In contrast, William's house had a new floor-model colour TV with a huge, clear picture.) Watching TV at the Martins was akin to watching the radio.

The Canadians were eager to tell Lesra's parents personally how much they had enjoyed Lesra's visit to Toronto, how well-behaved he had been, how proud they should be of him.

And proud they were! Like most parents in that neighbourhood, it was rare for Earl and Alma to hear a good word about their children. "We taught 'm manners," Mr Martin said. "We taught 'm how to act right."

Alma Martin, a petite, attractive woman, also beamed at the compliments. "We raised up all our boys to be gen'lemens," she added, in a voice that sounded like Billie Holiday's.

At lunch-time on one of their last days at the lab, towards the end of the summer, Lisa, Michael and Terry asked Lesra if he'd like to take a drive to a shopping mall in Queens. Lesra immediately said yes. He always jumped at a chance to ride in a car, and he loved being around the Canadians. They explained to him that they were going to buy a TV set to take back to Canada with them, because TVs were so much cheaper in the States.

In the home entertainment department at A&S, a large department store, the Canadians appeared to be overwhelmed by the great selection of TVs and asked Lesra for help. "Why don't you pick out one that you like," Terry said. Lesra examined them all very carefully and pointed out a sleek colour model. "Then that's the one we'll take." After conferring with a salesman, Terry told Lesra they were going to need an American name and address to put down on the bill of sale so that the warranty would be valid. "Can we use yours?"

"Awright by me," said Lesra, and his name and address were recorded on the bill of sale.

As they were loading the TV box into the trunk of the car, Terry said to Lesra, "You know, that's *your* TV. We tricked you into picking out the one you liked best. We wanted to surprise you."

Lesra looked Terry dead in the eye. "You lyin'!"

"No," said Lisa, "it's for you and your family."

"Sure. Right."

"It's really yours," joined in Michael. "It's your TV."

"Giddouddaheah!" retorted Lesra, and he wouldn't say another word.

On the drive back to the lab, Lesra remained silent. Lisa voiced the thoughts she figured must be running through his head.

"At first you were sure we were joking. But you're remembering the airline tickets, which you were sure weren't going to be there but were. Nobody was playing with you then. So now you're wondering, 'Is there a chance it's for real? What if it's true? . . . Naw!' "

"You got dat right!" was Lesra's only response.

After work, the Canadians called a cab. They gave the white driver Lesra's address and paid for the trip in advance. Not until Lesra got into the cab alone with the TV did he believe that it was his. As the taxi peeled off, he slung a stubby, proprietary arm around the mammoth box.

"So that's your TV?" asked the cabby, trying to strike up some friendly conversation.

"Yeah," answered Lesra guardedly, with the "What's it to you?" understood. Trust was not Lesra's strong suit at the best of times, and his suspicions were fuelled when the cabby took a different route than the only one Lesra knew, the one the Canadians had used when they had driven him home. Lesra cut his eyes at the driver, giving him his most ferocious "Don't even try, mister!" look, and he hugged the box harder. "Ain't nobody be messin' with my TV!" he told himself. Not until the cab turned onto Bushwick Avenue and Lesra recognized he was close to home did he begin to relax.

The cabby helped Lesra unload the box and carry it to the stoop of his building. "How's that?" the cabby asked. "You want to go in and get somebody to carry it in with you?"

"No way!" thought Lesra, shaking his head. "This dude must think I'm a fool. I ain't about to leave this box any more than he's about to leave that cab out here on the street."

The cabby left, and Lesra waited until his little brother Damon, who had been playing in the rubble outside, ran upstairs to get his father.

Earl, looking out the window, told his wife, "Alma, they done bought that boy a television!"

Lesra and his father carried the box upstairs, unpacked the TV and put it in the living room. They moved the old black-and-white one onto the floor. By this time, the whole family had gathered around. Everyone sat there watching the TV, admiring it, but nobody turned it on. After about fifteen minutes, Earl stood up, took the bull by the horns, plugged the TV in and turned the knob. To everyone's amazement, it worked. It actually worked.

"I'm'a register this set!" said Earl, and he took the bill of sale with Lesra's name on it and went down to the police station. There he registered the serial number. He wanted some insurance. He couldn't count on such a fine thing not getting stolen.

Back home, the Canadians realized that they had fallen in love with both Lesra and William. But it was Lesra who was the more responsive, perhaps because he was the more desperate. They thought of bringing him to Canada to educate him. They had the ability and the resources, and it didn't seem fair not to use them. Although they realized they couldn't put Lesra in a school with his peers because he was too far behind academically, they could teach him at home. As it happened, he was the same age as Marty, Lisa's son, the only child in the group, and they had been tutoring Marty at home for years.

As a child, Marty had had trouble learning to read. At the age of eight, he had been pronounced retarded by an ill-informed school board. Rejecting their assessment, Lisa had had him examined by experts in the nascent field of learning disabilities. He tested above average in intelligence but had a severe form of dyslexia. It would be a miracle, they'd said, if he made it to grade eight; vocational training was the best he could hope for. There were no special programs for dyslexics offered by the Toronto Board of Education at that time.

By this point, the group had started to come together and they decided they had to assume the responsibility of educating Marty themselves. It was clear that, for Marty, school meant only humiliation, anxiety and frustration at his inability to do what other children seemed to find easy. They pulled him out of school. And not only did Marty go on to learn to read, but he got to learn first-hand about foreign cultures and religions by living in the Far East while his "extended family" was there on business. He developed a passion for archaeology, went on a tour of Egypt on his own and was later selected as a guide, a *shawabti,* for the King Tutankhamun exhibit at the Art Gallery of Ontario. By 1979, at the age of sixteen, he had begun to reenter the academic mainstream, taking grade eleven courses both at night school and through correspondence.

After these experiences, the group were not complete novices at encountering and tackling unusual problems in education. If Marty's success was any indication, they thought they could provide an environment that would allow Lesra to flower too.

But there were other considerations with Lesra. After all, they thought, who were they to tell Earl and Alma Martin that their son had no future if he stayed in Brooklyn, that it would be better for him if he came to Canada? Weren't white people always telling black people what's best for them? Wasn't there something obscene about whites offering black people opportunities that whites denied blacks in the first place?

Nor did they overlook the fact that Earl and Alma loved their son, and depended on him. Lesra contributed a great deal to the welfare of his family, not only by working, but by taking care of his little brothers, running errands and just paying a little attention to his parents. How could Lesra's parents let their son go, even temporarily, in the hope that an education would pay off in the long run? Lesra had told the Canadians that he would love to come to Canada, but that it wasn't his decision to make.

The Canadians discussed their idea with James McRae, an African-American poet they had met at the EPA lab, whose day-job was to test New York cabs for nitrogen oxide emissions. They valued his opinion, and he was enthusiastic. He said he would broach the subject with Lesra's parents.

McRae's visit to the Martins' apartment was well received. It turned out that Mrs Martin was familiar with James's poetry and had read a couple of his books. (Her generation was much better educated than the next.) She was honoured by his presence and would seriously consider anything he had to say.

"It would be a shame," he said, "to pass up an opportunity like this. Nothing is more vital than access to a decent education." The Canadians, he told them, wanted to bring them up to Toronto, to show them where and how they lived, to meet Marty, and to talk about Lesra's education.

It was the end of summer when Mr Martin flew up to Toronto. Lesra's mother didn't make the trip; she said she'd go along with whatever her husband decided. Lesra waited on tenterhooks at home.

Terry and Kathy picked up Earl at the airport. He was wearing an outfit that fifteen years earlier would have been considered slick: a small-brimmed hat, bell-bottomed pants and a shiny, patterned shirt with a wide collar. They took a scenic route back to the house, and Earl was impressed with the cleanliness of the city. Painted lamp-posts and decorated protective hoarding around construction sites caught his attention, as did the silence, the source of which took a moment to sink in. "Don't hear no car horns!" he eventually exclaimed. He found the silence noisy.

He'd always wanted to come to Canada, he said, but never had the chance. Terry asked if that had been his first airplane flight.

"No," he answered. "I've flown lotta times before."

"Oh, really?"

"Been to Europe, Japan . . . lotta places."

"Was that when you were in the armed forces?" asked Kathy.

"Nope," replied Earl. There was a long pause. "When I was performing."

"Performing?"

"Uh huh."

"Lesra never mentioned that. . . . Performing, eh?"

"Yeah, I was in a singing group. Lesra don't know. Least he don't remember. Wasn't hardly born then."

"What was the name of your group?"

"You woulda never heard of us. Was a long time ago."

"Well, give it a shot. What were you called?"

"Del Vikings," he said quietly.

"The Del Vikings? Are you kidding?" Terry shouted incredulously, then started singing:

Love, love me, darlin'
Come and go with me . . .

Now it was Earl's turn to be surprised. "You know that song?" he asked.

"Sure! Everybody knows that song! It was a big hit! Early sixties. Do-wop."

Their unbridled enthusiasm woke up dormant memories that Earl, now feeling more comfortable, found sweet to recall. He was genuinely shy about his past and had been reluctant to "brag on it," even to his son; it was so many light-years away from his present circumstances. After some gentle prodding, he revealed that he had started as a back-up singer for the group, became the lead singer and was singing lead when they performed "Come Go With Me" on "The Ed Sullivan Show." The Del Vikings toured the United States, Europe, Japan, and got to know a whole lot of big-time entertainers; he mentioned Gladys Knight, Ike and Tina Turner, Mavis Staples.

At the house, after meeting Marty and the others, Earl continued to reminisce. They stayed up most of that night listening to his stories and playing old records. Earl especially liked their collection of rhythm-and-blues: Elmore James, Otis Spann, Little Walter, Wilson Pickett, Otis Redding. Earl sang along, and although there was a richness in his voice, it was a voice that was weak, unsure of itself, struggling behind years of alcohol and cigarettes. And amidst the sadness, they laughed a whole lot.

After Marty told Earl the story of his education, Sam, Lisa and Terry talked about Lesra's potential. Like Marty, they said, Lesra needed tutoring if he wanted to go on to university. They pointed out that Marty and Lesra seemed to get along. They assured Earl that if Lesra came to study in Canada, they would be sure he went home for holidays, and that they would speak regularly by phone—collect, they insisted. Earl listened to everything carefully, but non-committally.

Before Earl went home the next day, someone commented on Lesra's unusual name, wondering where it had originated.

"Lesra?" queried Earl, as if the answer was obvious. "You know—*Lesra*! Like in the Bible." Suddenly the Canadians noticed that when Earl spoke his son's name, he did so with a pronounced southern accent, so that it sounded like "Lazra."

"Oh, you mean *Lazarus*? The guy who rose from the dead?"

"That's right," said Earl. "He's the one. Had two chances at life."

Two days later, Earl Martin called Toronto from Brooklyn—Lesra could have his second chance.

2

Lesra was not the most perfect-looking kid in the world when he first came to live in Canada. He was short—too short for his age—and square. His body, tense and condensed, looked as if it had gone through a compactor, as if his neck had been forced down into his shoulders like a compressed spring. "I ain't got no neck!" Lesra used to say to explain his lack of height. The whites of his eyes were blood-shot and tinged yellow, his nose seemed to run constantly and he always had a headache. His front tooth was chipped so badly that you didn't notice anything else when he smiled. He was a mess, but it wasn't because he was naturally unattractive; it was just that his health care had been so poor, it showed.

Where Lesra came from, the only reason to see a doctor—and the only time you *get* to see one—is for life-threatening, dire emergencies. More attention is paid to a ghetto youth on his deathbed in a hospital emergency room than is ever paid to him in life. Inner city hospitals, where opportunities abound for stitching together all manner of knife and gunshot wounds, may be great training grounds for surgeons (army doctors are sent there for combat-type experience), but as far as providing basic health services to the community, these hospitals fail pitifully. When, after injuring his head at the EPA lab, Lesra was sent to the hospital for an examination, he waited there unattended for six hours and then left without getting X-rayed. When you're on welfare, the concept of having a routine medical examination is laughable. It just doesn't happen; it's not available; no one even thinks about it. You get used to living with whatever ails you: as long as you're still alive, you're doing a lot better than some.

Before the Canadians could begin schooling Lesra's mind, they had to attend to his health needs. The cause of Lesra's headaches, it turned out, was twofold: eyestrain and excessive sugar consumption. His eyesight was so bad he had to squint to see anything at a distance of more than a couple of feet. (That his vision needed correcting was news to Lesra until he remembered he had once been given prescription glasses in school; he had lost them, then couldn't afford to get them replaced.) And his habit of heaping sugar by the tablespoon onto everything he ate, including rice, peas and meat, kept him constantly buzzing. His headaches disappeared as soon as he started wearing glasses and cut out the extra sugar. Lesra's runny nose and unhealthy-looking eyes were the result of a chronic infection, which was easily cleared up with antibiotics. He was stunned at the intensity of the discomfort he had grown accustomed to ignoring. The relief he experienced was enormous.

As for his broken front tooth, a cap provided an instant solution. His height was a little more of a problem. The Canadians took him to a specialist, an endocrinologist, to see whether his short stature had some organic cause and whether it could be corrected through therapy. (Lesra loved all this attention and was always smiling, now whole and toothy.) After careful examination and tests, the doctor concluded that Lesra's growth had been stunted not from a lack of growth hormones but from malnutrition; with a good diet, it was still possible for him to grow several inches.

"Okay," the Canadians told Lesra, "let's start our first science project. Let's see what three meals a day can do." They began to chart his progress. At home, Terry had Lesra stand up tall against the wall where they'd been keeping track of Marty's growth. He marked the spot reached by the top of Lesra's head, noted Lesra's initial and the date. The first notation showed "L. 9/79" at five feet, one inch. Even if that was eight inches shorter than Marty, Lesra was proud to have made a mark on the same scale.

The growth specialist had also said that stressful living conditions could retard, and even stunt, growth. Turmoil had indeed informed every aspect of Lesra's life. Like millions of others in the ghetto, he had been constantly under stress. Nothing had been stable. The poverty of his environment was not only responsible for a lack of decent food and medical care, but also bred mind-numbing alcoholism, drug addiction and violence. Fear permeated even the simplest activity. Lesra never knew whether he or his brothers or sisters would be shot on the way to school, at school, where armed cops patrolled the halls, or coming home from school; he only knew that he always had to be ready to duck. Home, too, was a powder-keg: he had to be constantly vigilant, prepared to intervene if he could, before his parents' drinking and arguing reached the flashpoint and exploded into physical violence. Always on the edge. Not a moment's respite anywhere. The bombardment came from all sides. In that war zone, there was no R and R, only the front lines.

Thus it was no surprise that in his new home in Canada, at the first hint of quiet, at the briefest lull in a conversation, he would fall asleep. Even when the television was on, if no one in the room was speaking, he would fall asleep. He was a refugee in the truest sense of the word, who, experiencing for the first time in long memory a comparative security and safety, allowed himself the luxury of relaxing, of sinking into the kind of rejuvenating sleep that middle class North Americans take for granted. For Lesra, only a short while before, rest had simply not been possible.

Lesra's speech was a curious mix of street phrases, disagreeing subjects and verbs (when Lesra used verbs) and bizarre grammatical constructions like triple negatives. The Canadians thought he needed to expand his vocabulary (the number of words at his command could probably have been counted), and expected to give him a little work in grammar and some practice in enunciation. They had already noted a certain weakness in geography, which was a small enough matter, they thought, to correct. But they had no idea what was in store for them.

How could they have suspected, for example, that for all intents

and purposes Lesra could not read? That, as measly as they had feared
it was, they had wildly overestimated Lesra's level of literacy? On a
printed page all that he could make out were the few words he had
memorized; the others he just guessed at. He was unable to sound out
a single new word. He was almost sixteen years old, supposed to be
going into grade eleven, and he could not read. They were going to
have to start back at grade one!

It was a shattering revelation, and personally devastating to Lesra.
It served as grist for his mill of prejudices, for Lesra harboured the insidious idea that blacks were stupid. He and his black classmates
couldn't read after ten years of going to school—didn't that prove
something? Also, the darker you are, the dumber you are—he'd heard
that all his life. Now he had proof.

And not only are black people stupid, thought Lesra, they are violent. "Ain't it true only niggers fight?" Lesra asked the Canadians not
long after coming to live with them. The question brought tears to
their eyes, it was so pathetic. Lesra's self-image was abysmally low, his
lack of information total. In Bushwick, he only ever saw black people,
therefore it was only black people he ever saw fighting.

The Canadians soon realized that educating Lesra was going to be
more complicated than just brushing up on English and geography.
And it was going to involve a little more than learning the rudiments
of reading, as if that wasn't challenging enough. Before they could get
anywhere, a number of Lesra's misconceptions were going to have to
be addressed, misunderstandings that had serious psychological repercussions. There was fifteen years of negative conditioning to deal with.

They impressed upon Lesra the meaning and value of an education. An education would show him there were explanations for seemingly random, disconnected occurrences: why ghettos existed, why his
parents drank, why drugs were rampant in his community, why he
couldn't read. Studying history would help him to understand why the
world was the way it was, and to see that it hadn't always been that
way. He'd learn that it was natural for black people to get along, that
they had co-operated first as hunter-gatherers and later as builders of
great African civilizations, including outstanding universities and cen-
tres of learning. That African-Americans calling one another degrad-
ing terms like "nigger" was a sign of self-hatred resulting from

centuries of colonialism and slavery. That it suited those in power to "divide and conquer," to have blacks segregated, narcotized and fighting among themselves, so that whites could continue to thrive economically, continue to feel different and superior and absolved of historical responsibility. He was going to find out that, not long ago, there were two world wars, that it was white people who started these wars and whites who senselessly and viciously slaughtered millions of other whites (not to mention all the people of colour). No one ever spoke of it as "white-on-white" violence, but that's what it was.

"To be educated," the Canadians told him, "is to live in a comprehensible world, to be able to discriminate a fact from a fiction, to be hip enough to know when you are being misled." That appeal was not lost on Lesra. He did not like being conned.

One of Lesra's first assignments was to find out what, if anything, makes people of different colours different. Lesra learned about the one factor responsible for skin colour: melanin. The darker your skin, the more melanin you have; the lighter, the less. He learned that albinos are missing this important element, which is why their skins are so white, almost see-through, and why their eyes are so pale.

"Melanin protects a person from the sun's harmful rays," they told Lesra. "Having a lot of it, being dark, means that you've got greater protection."

"That it?" asked Lesra, expecting something more complex.

"It's as simple as that."

"Yeah, but lighter is better—smarter!" pronounced Lesra.

"Not true!" the Canadians countered. "There is no connection between skin colour and brain power. None whatsoever!"

Lesra wanted to believe his tutors, but all of his life he had heard otherwise. Not only was he black, he was dark; therefore, he wasn't supposed to be too bright.

Among African-Americans, the Canadians learned from Lesra, the slightest gradations in skin colour are meaningful distinctions. Lesra would say, for example, one of his sisters was "two shades" lighter than so-and-so, who was "one shade" darker than someone else. At first, the Canadians didn't have a clue what he was talking about. It seemed to them a cruel irony that, for blacks, being darker was undesirable, because, as they informed Lesra, white people—liberals and rednecks alike—don't notice variations in shades of colouring, except maybe if someone is *very* light or *very* dark. And if whites do happen to notice, it doesn't matter anyway—you're still black!

They told Lesra that, through most of human history, skin colour never appeared to be significant but that it became important during slavery, as an obvious sign distinguishing property (black slaves) from people (whites). And if lighter-coloured blacks in America were favoured as "house niggers" (domestics) and treated better than the "field niggers" (field hands), it was because the majority of them were the illegitimate children of a white master and an African slave woman.

"Hardly sumpin' to get uppity ovuh!" said Lesra. "All that fussin' 'bout the in-between shades and they don' mean nothin'!"

The subject of skin colour, Lesra soon realized, was indeed rife with contradiction. "If bein' white suppose-a-be so great," he said, "then bein' whitest should be the greatest. So why ain't the President a albino?" The Canadians couldn't argue with the logic of his brilliant argument, which reduced the proposition of white supremacy to its inherent absurdity. It struck Lesra as odd that whites, while discriminating against blacks, seem themselves to want to be darker: "Always sunbathin' and tannin' theyselves, gotto mean bein' blacker is more beautiful."

"Lez," his tutors told him, "you're beautiful. You are beautiful. You're really getting the hang of this education business."

Such discussions made Lesra feel kind of dizzy. He would experience an unusual tingling in his head, like an electrical buzz. It was unfamiliar, and he thought something was wrong. His tendency to hypochondria—a trait he did not have the luxury to indulge in Brooklyn—led him to wonder whether he had a brain tumour. He didn't know that the tingling was the product of stimulation. That it was the feeling of thinking. Though disconcerting to him at first, it ultimately became the pleasurable sensation he would associate with learning.

Lesra's education was the Canadians' education; in many ways, his ignorance was no greater than theirs. They soon discovered that his speech was not haphazard, as they had originally assumed, but followed definable patterns. He spoke Black English,* a language in its

---

*In the mid-1990s, Black English came to be known as "Ebonics."

own right, with its own rules of grammar and diction, and as distinct from Standard English as Yiddish is from German.

The Canadians decided to start from scratch and to teach Lesra Standard English as if he were learning a totally foreign language. They used a textbook for learning English as a second language. Designed for adults, at least it didn't contain "kindygawden stuff," as Lesra termed the juvenile "Fun with Dick and Jane" primers he was used to.

They started with conjugating the verb "to be." Lesra first had to learn what a verb was (they didn't dare tackle the word "conjugate"), then what the grammatical concept of "persons" was and, finally, what singular and plural meant. He was then ready to repeat out loud:

> *I am; you are; he (she, it) is;*
> *We are; you are; they are.*

Lesra found second person especially noteworthy because it was the same in the singular and in the plural, and he thought there was some kind of trick. His tutors assured him they weren't pulling his leg.

"Then how you tell," he asked incredulously, "if 'you are' one person or a whole lotta persons?"

"In Standard English," Sam said, "you don't know if 'you' refers to one or more than one, except from the context. Sometimes, however, you'll hear some people say 'youse' to denote the plural form, but that isn't considered proper. Sometimes, especially around our house, you'll hear 'You guys,' which is meant to include everybody and can be confusing if you think it refers only to males."

Lesra looked thoroughly perplexed.

Sam tried another approach. "Is there a plural form for 'you' in Black English?"

Lesra thought about it for a moment, then shook his head.

"Well, for example, how would you ask your family, how they were doing?"

"I dunno."

"Let's say you go home for Christmas and you walk into the apartment and you see your brothers and sisters. What would you say?"

"Merry Christmas!"

The Canadians laughed. "Go on, what else?"

"'S up?"

Everyone cracked up. Lesra's answers were not quite what they were looking for.

"How would you ask all your brothers and sisters together at once how they were doing?"

"I dunno. . . . I'd say, 'How y'all doin'?'"

"That's it!"

"What it?"

"Y'all! You all. Second person plural. Black English."

"Y'all? Yeah: *y'all*. Awright, y'all!"

"And what if there are a whole lot of Y'all's you're talking to, then what do you say?"

"All y'all!" shouted Lesra, grinning from ear to ear. Black English was so sophisticated it distinguished not only singular from plural in the second person, but had a super plural form as well! As far as Lesra could tell, Black English had Standard English beat by a mile. And he had thought it inferior!

The Canadians, too, gained an appreciation for Lesra's native tongue. Rapping had just been born on the streets of Brooklyn, and Lesra brought it to Canada with him. Not shy, Lesra would pick up the DJ's microphone at dances he and Marty went to, and in a driving rhythm, he'd belt out verses like the following:

Cause my name is Lesra Dee
And I rap quintessentially
Check it out and
You don't stop
And you don't stop
And you rock!

Me and Supe,
We had a fight,
So I hit 'im in dah head
Wid a kryptonite
I hit him so hard

Went through his brain
And now I'm bustin' out Lois Lane!

Ah, check it out, y'all
And you don't stop
And you don't stop
And you rock!

Lesra could go on and on, and it made him very popular.

Lesra tried to teach his tutors Black English, but met with only limited success.* Black English conveyed all sorts of subtleties not readily apparent to Standard English monolinguists—like nuances in the timing of actions, for example. As Lesra explained to the Canadians, in Black English the phrase "they be done gone" indicates they will have left. The sentence "They gone" means they aren't there now. And "They *been* gone," (pronounced "bin") means they've been gone for a good while now, or, to be more exact, they left long enough ago that "it's a fact, Jack!"

Lesra's students got to where they could *understand* Black English, even if they couldn't speak it well; they never did get those past tenses straight. They told Lesra they felt kind of stupid.

"It be's that way sometime!" said Lesra, consolingly. "Learnin' ain't always easy."

And learning to read was not easy for Lesra, but only because he assumed he already knew how and he didn't. His "reading" consisted of getting a vague sense of the shape and size of a word, how many "sticks" were above and below the line, and then matching that picture up with the memory of the picture of a word he had seen before, and hoping to hell it was the same one. He would glance down quickly at a word, then stare up at the ceiling and wait for the flash of recog-

---

*The similarity of Black English to Standard English, rather than making the language accessible, is a constant source of confusion. For example, a word like "raggedy" has a broader application in Black English, in which it is used to describe anything shabby, not just fabric. Additionally, words in the two languages, while retaining the same meaning, often vary by a single letter or sound. Lesra would say *foam* for "phone," *brought* for "bought," *every since* for "ever since," *Long Ranger* for "Lone Ranger," *credick* for "credit" and *hippmo* for "hippo."

nition. At school in Brooklyn that was the way he read, and he had read a great deal, he thought.

Words Lesra had not memorized he had no way of deciphering. He could have sworn the letter "b" sounded like *br* and the letters "br" were *b*; "beauty" he pronounced *bruty* and "brute" was *butte*. And everyone knew the letter "c" sounded like *cl*. His misapprehensions were staggering. Like many of his peers in Brooklyn, he would fall asleep in class at his desk, a relatively quiet spot by comparison to the chaos everywhere else. Every once in a while he would wake up and catch a few snippets of information from the teacher, which he would patch together in a crazy quilt riddled with holes. If Lesra's class *was* taught the concept that letters stood for sounds, the Canadians speculated, he must have woken up during the lesson on sounds of consonant combinations, but missed the original lesson on the sounds of consonants by themselves.

The Canadians marvelled that he could get away with this nonsense undetected. Not that he could be blamed; no one expected anything more from him. Lackadaisical, overburdened and fearful teachers; inadequate and shoddy facilities; the hyperactivity, malnutrition, and sleep deprivation of the children, and the constant fear they lived with—these elements conspired to make learning virtually impossible for Lesra and his classmates. And it didn't seem that anyone really wanted to know how bad the situation was. True-and-false and multiple-choice tests don't reveal much, and those, said Lesra, were the only kind of tests they ever had.

"But," asked the naive Canadians, "didn't you ever have to write anything? Like an essay?"

Lesra shook his head in bewilderment.

"How about a paragraph? Didn't you ever have to write a paragraph?"

"I don't do paragraphs," declared Lesra. And those four words seemed to say it all.

During his first year in Canada, Lesra had to confront the reality of his pitiful education. It was painful at his age to have to learn how to sound out words. Everything he thought he knew had to be discarded. He felt stupid. He lost all confidence. He went through a period in which he became almost despondent. There were times when reading even a cereal box he thought beyond his ability. Whatever he did read, he read a second time to himself, disbelieving he could understand anything on one go-through.

The irony was that reading and language skills were actually quite easy for him to master. His mind was quick and his comprehension excellent. The Canadians constantly reassured him, encouraged him, prodded him. But the emotional trauma was tremendous.

No one had ever demanded much from him intellectually, and he thought he was unequal to any task. Tackling a book on his own was too daunting. The Canadians would take turns reading aloud to him to allay his fears (and his loneliness); he particularly liked Claude Brown's *Manchild in the Promised Land*. After hours and hours and months on end of consistent work, he had come a long way. He just didn't know it.

The breakthrough came the day Lisa, Terry and Sam tried to get Lesra to read *My Bondage and My Freedom*. "We want you to read this," they said, handing him Frederick Douglass's moving account of his own life and times in and out of slavery. "It's time for you to try something substantial on your own."

Lesra froze. Sitting on the couch in the house library, he appeared suddenly tiny, a wall of books looming behind him. All he could see was the book's thickness. "Look like a *foam* book!" he said.

"It's not a phone book. It's about Frederick Douglass. His autobiography, how he grew up in the South as a slave, how he learned to read, how he escaped and became a persuasive speaker and writer in the forefront of the American abolitionist movement. We want you to read it," said Terry.

"No way I can read that!"

"Yes you can. Just give it a go."

"Uh, uh." He thought the Canadians had gone off the deep end. Didn't they understand what they were asking?

"Come on, Lez. You'll find this really interesting."

"Then you read it to me."

"No. It's time you read to us."

Still sceptical, Lesra opened the book to a well-thumbed page and, stumbling badly, tried to read the following out loud:

The frequent hearing of my mistress reading the bible—
for she often read aloud when her husband was absent—soon
awakened my curiosity in respect to this *mystery* of reading,
and roused in me the desire to learn. Having no fear of my
kind mistress before my eyes, (she had then given me no reason to fear,) I frankly asked her to teach me to read; and,
without hesitation, the dear woman began the task, and very
soon, by her assistance, I was master of the alphabet, and
could spell words of three or four letters. My mistress seemed
almost as proud of my progress, as if I had been her own
child; and, supposing that her husband would be as well
pleased, she made no secret of what she was doing for me. Indeed, she exultingly told him of the aptness of her pupil, of
her intention to persevere in teaching me, and of the duty
which she felt it to teach me, at least to read *the bible.* Here
arose the first cloud over my Baltimore prospects, the precursor of drenching rains and chilling blasts.

Master Hugh was amazed at the simplicity of his spouse,
and, probably for the first time, he unfolded to her the true philosophy of slavery, and the peculiar rules necessary to be observed by masters and mistresses, in the management of their
human chattels. Mr Auld promptly forbade the continuance
of her instruction; telling her, in the first place, that [teaching
slaves to read] was unlawful; that it was also unsafe, and could
only lead to mischief. To use his own words, further, he said,
"if you give a nigger an inch, he will take an ell;" "he should
know nothing but the will of his master, and learn to obey it."

Lesra looked up at his tormenters, simultaneously triumphant and
ready to concede defeat. Didn't he just prove he was right?

"I can't read this. I don't understand a fuckin' thing. What the hell
is a ell?" he asked, frustrated that even such a tiny word seemed beyond his grasp.

"More!" Sam said, his arms outstretched, indicating a measure-
ment of about three feet; and Lesra, not knowing whether Sam was
translating the word or ordering him to continue reading, read reluctantly on:

"Learning will spoil the best nigger in the world;" "if you teach that nigger—speaking of myself—how to read . . . , there will be no keeping him;" "it would forever unfit him for the duties of a slave;" and "as to himself, learning would do him no good, but probably, a great deal of harm—making him disconsolate and unhappy." "If you learn him now to read, he'll want to know how to write; and, this accomplished, he'll be running away with himself." Such was the tenor of Master Hugh's oracular exposition. . . .

Lesra slammed the book shut and dropped it onto the table. "I can't do it!" he sobbed. He insisted there was no way he could read a book that had so many commas and huge words, not to mention the little words and the sentences that rambled on for a whole page. "Period!"

"You're right. You're absolutely right." His torturers now appeared to agree with him. But they had made him miserable.

"With that attitude," Lisa said, "nothing is possible. Besides, what can a man like Frederick Douglass, who lived in slavery over a hundred years ago, tell you anyway? What could he possibly have in common with you?"

For a moment Lesra thought he had won a reprieve. But then Sam picked up the book and continued to read:

It was a new and special revelation, dispelling a painful mystery, against which my youthful understanding had struggled, and struggled in vain, to wit: the *white* man's power to perpetuate the enslavement of the *black* man. "Very well," thought I; "knowledge unfits a child to be a slave." I instinctively assented to the proposition; and from that moment I understood the direct pathway from slavery to freedom. This was just what I needed. . . .

Sam handed the book back to Lesra. "Read it!" And Lesra burst into tears because the book was just too hard and too big and he felt so stupid and why were they being so unfair?

His torturers cried too, but still they insisted he could do it.

"Don't worry about understanding specific words," said Lisa. "Get the overall sense of what Douglass is saying. You can hear him talking to you. Just listen to what he has to say and you'll hear it. You can do it."

Lesra felt his feelings of inadequacy were not getting the attention they deserved. Nobody was taking them seriously, giving them any credence. The Canadians kept him focused on the book. They were relentless.

Finally Lesra capitulated and picked up the book. Struggling bravely on, he surprised himself: he managed to comprehend what he was reading! The story of Douglass's life was so fascinating and his passion so powerful that they transcended whatever difficulties Lesra had with the author's florid, Victorian prose and carried him through to the end. He was amazed to find someone who actually spoke to him from the pages of a book written in 1855, someone he could relate to, someone inspiring.

The world opened up for Lesra, just as it had for Frederick Douglass when *he* first learned to read. Lesra felt suddenly powerful and capable; there was nothing now he couldn't do. Once he got his feelings of inferiority in check, he became "a learnin' fool," and his progress was phenomenal.

3

Everyone in the house participated in Lesra's education, and everything they studied together they connected to his own life. Geography, for example, was not a remote, abstract subject. It was a lesson on how to get around.

Worse off than a runaway slave who followed the north star to Canada, Lesra hadn't a clue where to find North. He had no concept of basic directions. And he couldn't read a map. So his tutors started with a map of Toronto. Fortunately for Lesra, Toronto is an orderly city. On the map, Lesra could see that most of its streets were laid out squarely on a grid, running either up and down or side to side; Lake Ontario was "the blue blob" at the bottom of the page.

"Lake Ontario borders the city on the south," Kathy explained. "And how do we know it's south? On this map, as on every map unless it indicates otherwise, North is up at the top, East is on the right, West the left and South down at the bottom."

"That's why we say, 'Down south' and 'Up north,' " added Sam.

After studying the map, Lesra went outside with Gus and looked around. They spotted the CN Tower. "The world's tallest free-standing structure," said Gus, parroting the slogan of its claim to fame.

"I know dat. That's down by the lake, right? It's where me and Marty go to the disco—'Sparkles.'"

"Right! And what direction is that, Lez?"

"Up."

"No . . . yes . . . of course, it's up. It's a hundred and fourteen storeys up. But use the directions you just learned."

"Oh, yeah. It's north. 'Sparkles' is up north of the bottom of the CN Tower."

"Uh, okay. And where is that tower in relation to our house?"

"What's the matter whichoo, Gus? Can't you see? It's over there . . ." Lesra enjoyed pulling Gus's leg.

Lesra eventually learned that if he were ever lost in Toronto, all he had to do was look for the CN Tower and the chances are that it would be south of him. Then, if he faced North, East would be on his right, West his left, South behind ("N-E-W-S" to Lesra). Becoming oriented made public transit accessible to him. He was able to read a subway map and know whether to take a north- or southbound train on Yonge Street, an east- or westbound train on the Bloor Street line.

With Marty, Lesra studied the globe. Marty showed him the Far East and Malaysia, and these places became real when Lesra found out that was where Marty and the group had lived. On the globe, Marty traced the airplane route he'd taken to get there, and he and Lesra talked about the people, their foods, their customs. Using an atlas, they recreated Lesra's flights home to New York, crossing over Lake Ontario and back. They did the same for Marty's trip across the Atlantic Ocean and the Mediterranean Sea to Egypt. And Marty told Lesra not only about the pyramids along the Nile River, but also about the black Nubians he had met in Egypt, the fishermen whose livelihoods had been ruined by the Aswan Dam, which had made the Nile where they used to fish too shallow. Watching the news on TV, they would always have the globe at hand. When a place was mentioned, they would immediately try to find it on the globe and this game would spark Lesra's interest so that, for the first time in his life, he would pay attention to the news.

Directions, atlases, the globe, current events—these were suddenly comprehensible to Lesra. The world was bigger than just three square

Bushwick blocks. And school was not just a nine-to-three affair; in this house, the learning went on all the time.

Lesra loved the freedom of travelling around the city by himself or with Marty, using the public transit system, the TTC. He had been used to the subway in New York where, at certain predictable stops, whites would get off and blacks would continue their ride into the heart of the ghetto. When he took the TTC, he'd wonder to himself whether anyone could predict what station *he* was going to exit at. He felt very self-conscious the first time he got off the streetcar at the stop closest to his new home, because he was the only black person getting off. He couldn't help thinking that the white people still on the street-car were staring at him and wondering what a black kid was doing in this neighbourhood of fine houses. But then he would have to remind himself that this was Toronto, not New York, and, while wealthy, pre-dominantly white areas and different ethnic neighbourhoods did exist, none was racially exclusionary. He had no reason to fear being out of place; there was no "place" to be out of. The only things out of place were his old fears. These psychological realizations were more mo-mentous to Lesra than his mastering of facts.

One day, as Lesra was going down the stairs to the subway, he no-ticed a middle-aged white woman beside him, struggling with a heavy package and trying to get to a train before it pulled out. He hesitated for a moment, then offered to carry the woman's package. The woman readily handed it to him, delighted to have some assistance. They ran down the stairs together. As Lesra jumped onto the train, the doors started to close. Using his knee, he held the doors pried open until the woman was able to get onto the train too.

"What a polite young man—a gentleman!" said the woman, as Lesra set the package down on a seat beside her "And they say young people don't have any manners today." She thanked him profusely.

Lesra felt proud, pleased with himself—indeed, he was positively euphoric. The experience had a profound effect upon him, but he didn't tell anyone about it until after he had begun to digest it, to sort out its ramifications.

"That woman trusted me!" he explained to the group later. "She actually trusted me!"

"That's wonderful," said Lisa, "but you deserve to be trusted! That was a thoughtful gesture on your part."

"Yeah, but you know, I coulda just let the train doors close and gotten away with her package without even tryin'! Not that I ever woulda done that, but I can't help thinkin' . . . of the difference. . . . You know, I can't help thinking that, in New York, I woulda never even offered to help that lady in the first place, because I know she wouldn'ta accepted. She woulda been sure it was some sorta scam, that I was goin' to rip her off or somethin'. Hmmph!" he snorted, pausing for a moment as he gathered his thoughts. "People can be people here! And not everyone's gonna be afraida you just because of your skin colour. She didn't care that I was black. It's what you do that really counts!"

Years later, Lesra was to remind the Canadians of this incident when a shooting in a New York subway was all over the news. A white man named Bernhard Goetz had pulled out his gun and shot four black teenagers because, when one of them approached him, he immediately assumed they were going to assault or rob him.

"A hell of a long way from that white woman's attitude to me on the subway here!" commented Lesra pointedly. "In New York, no one white expects anything but trouble from young black males. It's a goddamn shame!"

The Canadians saw to it that Lesra also became acquainted with the less noble aspects of his adopted country; the disgraceful treatment of native peoples, still ongoing, from outright land theft to physical and cultural genocide; the centuries of conflict and hatred between French and English Canadians; the shameful internment of Japanese Canadians during the Second World War; the discrimination experienced by blacks in Nova Scotia, East and West Indians in Toronto, Chinese in Vancouver.

Learning about other cultures—ways people manage, or don't manage, to live in harmony—was a major part of Lesra's curriculum. With the Canadians as guides, he walked through Farley Mowat's books, *The People of the Deer* and *Never Cry Wolf; The Heart of the Hunter* by Laurens Van Der Post; Peter Freuchen's *Book of the Eskimos; Lame Deer, Seeker of Visions* by John Fire / Lame Deer; *Seven*

Arrows by Hyemeyohsts Storm; and even *Siddhartha* by Hermann Hesse. He studied European history, both its accomplishments and its disgraces, from British monarchs (Lesra would frequently get lost in genealogical detail, and Gus invented a game called "Who's King now?" to liven things up) to colonialism in the Third World.

Much of what Lesra studied concerned African-American history. He read *From Slavery to Freedom* by historian John Hope Franklin and *Before The Mayflower* by Lerone Bennett, Jr. Lesra desperately needed black heroes. His tutors sought out biographies of great black Americans like George Washington Carver, Harriet Tubman, Nat Turner, Dr Daniel Drew and Robert Franklin Williams. Reading about the accomplishments of these people provided the necessary fertile ground in which Lesra's sense of self-worth could be nurtured and flourish. He gobbled up the most inspiring books concerning the realities of black life in America: *The Autobiography of Malcolm X;* Richard Wright's autobiographies *Black Boy* and *American Hunger,* his novels *Native Son* and *The Longest Dream; Coming of Age in Mississippi* by Anne Moody; *The Street* by Ann Petry; *Seize the Time* by Bobby Seale; *Confessions of a White Racist* by Larry L. King; Carter Woodson's essay *The Miseducation of the Negro;* the poetry and short stories of Langston Hughes. Lesra's appetite for books was insatiable.

One late summer day in 1980, about a year after Lesra arrived in Canada, there was a book sale held by the Metropolitan Toronto Public Libraries in a huge warehouse at Harbourfront. It wasn't a rock concert or major-league baseball game, but it proved to be a popular event. On sale were thousands of books from libraries across the city—discards too worn for further public use, others in near-perfect condition but dated or no longer popular, spanning a full range of subject matter. Hardcover books were going for a dollar, paperbacks a quarter. The library system's need for additional shelf space turned into a bonanza for hungry readers.

Lesra and the group showed up early. As they feared, the line-up was already long. A strategy had to be devised. Once inside, they split into smaller, more efficient, hunting-gathering units and dispersed among the crowds. Around the book-laden tables the competition was fierce, leaving little room for discrimination. Anything that at first glance looked remotely interesting they snapped up and tossed into a carton.

Two hours later, in a quiet corner of the building, Lesra's party reassembled. The fruits of the hunt were pooled and evaluated. They had got carried away and wound up with some ten boxes full of books. They sorted through these together, eliminating first all the duplicates. They winnowed the catch down to three cartons, holding onto the books that looked the most promising. One of these was a well-worn volume entitled *The Sixteenth Round: From Number 1 Contender to #45472* by Rubin "Hurricane" Carter.

You can't judge a book by its cover, but book titles, Lesra had been learning, can say a whole lot. They rejected a book called *Joe Louis: A Credit to His Race,* even though it was about the champion heavyweight prizefighter they all admired, because the title of this book turned them off. On the other hand, although none of them knew much about middleweight boxer "Hurricane" Carter, they decided to keep *The Sixteenth Round.* It appeared to strike on two themes they had been discussing: how sports is one forum in America (entertainment another) in which blacks are allowed to succeed; and second, why it is that strong black men, black heroes like Malcolm X, can be found in the nation's prisons. What makes a man go "From Number 1 Contender to #45472"? And what kind of fight lasts sixteen rounds when championship bouts (at that time) went fifteen?

Out of all the books they brought home from the sale, this was the book Lesra picked to read first. From its pages Rubin Carter spoke directly to him, with power and clarity and in a voice and language that Lesra well understood. Lesra was acutely aware that Carter's was a life that just as easily could have been his own—and almost certainly would have been, had he remained in Brooklyn. From ghetto streets you matriculated to prison cells.*

From the very first "round," as Carter named his chapters, Lesra was captivated. He was intrigued by the origin and significance of

---

*According to a recent NAACP study, in America, one of four black men in their twenties is either in jail or on probation or parole, compared with one in sixteen for whites. There are more young black men under the control of the criminal justice system than the number of black men of all ages enrolled in college.

Carter's triple-barrelled name. "Rubin," Carter's Christian name, like Lesra's, was from the Bible: As Carter wrote, "Other than both of us being black, that's about the only thing the Bible and I ever had in common." The name "Hurricane" was earned as a result of his prowess in the boxing ring; it accurately described "the destructive forces that rage within my soul." And "Carter," like "Martin," was "the slave name that was given to my forefathers who worked in the cotton fields" of the South, a "worthless" name that "was passed on to me."

Lesra was so affected by *The Sixteenth Round* that he had to read parts of it aloud to the others. "Check it out. Y'all won't believe this." He read them the passage from the Third Round, when Rubin was just eleven years old and living in Paterson, New Jersey, where he grew up. One fateful day, he and his friends were swimming near the Passaic Waterfalls when they noticed a white man nearby, pretending to be drunk. Flashing his gold watch, he enticed one of the boys to come closer. He then grabbed the youth and called him "darling." Young Rubin, who was afflicted with a crippling stutter, was unable to tell the man to leave his friend alone; instead, he threw a bottle at the man. Seeing that the man had been knocked over from the blow, all the boys fled, with Rubin at the rear. The man got up and, bleeding from the head where the bottle had struck, lunged at Rubin. The man caught him, lifted him up in the air, and threatened to throw the little "black bastard" over the cliff, which he now approached. Stammering and pleading as best he could, Rubin tried to get the man to let him go. But to no avail. Dangling near the precipice, Rubin reached into his pocket, pulled out his scout knife and stabbed the man in the head. Although the man shrieked and threw Rubin to the ground, he kept coming after the young boy, now trying to assault him sexually. Rubin stabbed him again, this time in the side.

"Good God!" exclaimed Sam. "Was the man still alive?"

"Yup, but Rubin didn't know it. He got the hell out of there, ran back home and hid in his bed, under the covers, scared to death," answered Lesra. "Rubin couldn't stop hisself from crying, and his mother didn't know what was wrong cause Rubin never cried."

"Didn't he tell his parents what happened?"

"Uh, uh. He was too scared. And, anyway, he couldn't talk. He started seeing things that wasn't there and they thought maybe he was going to die. His mother called a doctor and he had a hundred and six fever."

"Sounds like Rubin was delirious. He hurt himself as much as he hurt the man who attacked him," commented Terry.

"You don't know the half of it," harumphed Lesra. "The man recovered and *Rubin* was the one charged with assault! In court, the cops told the judge the man Rubin stabbed was a pillar of society. Rubin tried to tell them what happened, but his parents wouldn't believe that that white man would do such a thing. And the judge didn't either. He called Rubin a menace to society. He said he was an animal that should be locked away in a cage, and he sentenced Rubin to the Jamesburg State Home for Boys until he was twenty-one!"

"For ten years?" Sam queried incredulously.

"And you wanna know what the real kicker is?" Lesra asked his Canadian friends, who were rivetted to Carter's story. "The police *knew* that the man at the swimming hole liked little boys! The cops even joked about it outside the courtroom, how it was bound to catch up with him sooner or later. But that ain't what they told the judge."

"That's got to be the worst—the bottom of the barrel. . . ." said Kathy.

"No it ain't," interrupted Lesra. "You don't know about the rest of his life."

The Canadians were now hooked, and Lesra, over a period of several days, read Carter's autobiography out loud to them.

At Jamesburg State Home for Boys, the young Rubin underwent a hair-raising initiation into the juvenile justice system. What he encountered during his first day there was an ordeal of unrelenting horror that Lesra found impossible to forget. Rubin had to fend off attacks first by a bully, then by the bully's gang, then by a gang of blackjack-wielding guards. Then he had to witness the nightly ritual of sexual abuse of some of the younger, weaker boys, many of whom had gone to the authorities begging for help, only to be subjected to experimental shock treatments and have their brains burned out by "sadistic technicians" who "sent them right back . . . smoking." It didn't take long for Rubin to realize that he "was no longer a member of a sane society." Being a good fighter wasn't enough, and inevitably, to protect himself against the violence and degradation, he shut down emotionally. "The death of a young soul," is how Carter described it.

At the age of seventeen, Carter's warders reneged on a promise to release him from Jamesburg for good behaviour. He decided to make good their promise, so he escaped and ran off and joined the army. But the army was no refuge from injustice. The troop buses were segregated just as the "cottages" at Jamesburg had been, and blacks were treated as second class. The year was 1954. The United States Supreme Court had just decided in *Brown v. Board of Education* that segregation in the nation's public schools was unconstitutional. But integration was a long time in coming, and old attitudes were a longer time going.

Carter went through the rigorous training of a paratrooper and became one of the first African-Americans to be accepted in the Rangers, the "Screaming Eagles" of the 101st Airborne, considered the army's toughest and bravest fighting elite. He was stationed in Germany, and it was there that he met a man who was to have a profound influence on his life. His name was Ali Hasson Muhammad, an African from the Sudan, who Carter described as "about two shades darker than I," "fiercely proud," but also "soft-spoken and gentle." Hasson exhibited a "moral self-sufficiency" and "stamina of the soul that outweighed any of my [superior] physical attributes."

At every opportunity Hasson would speak to Carter about philosophy and religion, Africa and slavery. Carter listened but resisted Hasson's overtures of friendship. Carter didn't know how to trust. He couldn't communicate. He still couldn't speak without stuttering badly, so he kept silent.

It took some time but Hasson got through to the brash, obviously troubled young man. One night they were watching the army's boxing team sparring. Suddenly Carter stammered out: "Shit! I-I-I can beat all of these niggers." Hasson turned on him, saying it was clear now why Rubin seldom spoke: when he did, he would say the most ignorant things.

Carter was surprised at the vehemence of Hasson's disgust at his use of the word "nigger." Carter was even more surprised when Hasson then called him on his fighting boast and arranged for a match between him and the army's heavyweight champion. Then Carter proceeded to surprise himself by knocking out the champ in the first round. Carter joined the boxing team and ended up becoming the European light-welterweight champion two years in a row. And he got to know himself as well. With Hasson's help, he attended classes in Germany and became a voracious reader. Hasson inspired in Carter self-confidence, pride in his blackness and a thirst for knowledge, all of which helped him overcome his stutter. He learned to love to talk and, finally, could share with someone, with Hasson, "the million-and-one atrocities" in his life he had kept pent-up deep inside for so long.

Carter was invited to compete in the 1956 Olympic trials, but it would have required him to re-enlist. His two-year army term was up and he was anxious to go home. Carter returned from Europe to his parents' New Jersey home a new man. He had found dignity and self-respect. He was an "at-peace-with-himself Rubin."

But back in the U.S., things hadn't changed. Carter was considered the same "young hoodlum" who had escaped from the State Home for Boys two years before. It didn't matter what he had accomplished, that he wanted to settle down, that he had a job, found a girl-friend, bought a car. In the middle of the night, the cops storm-trooped into his house and arrested him for the Jamesburg escape. They deposited him in Annandale Reformatory.

Carter despaired at the injustice:

I felt that I had struggled, vainly, to become something. . . . Sitting in that cell, I realized the lunacy of even having tried.

Maybe it was this vacuum of personal helplessness, of my having taken it for granted that justice would be done, that all wrongs would be righted, and all that other storybook shit. But once thrown back in the penitentiary . . . I felt different.

I berated myself for believing the bullshit about justice in this fucked-up society.

This second stint behind bars had a profound and insidious effect on him. When he came out, he was angry and depressed. He had lost his job, his girlfriend, his car. He also lost his GI benefits, which he had counted on to pay for a college education; these were withdrawn when the authorities found out he had entered the army illegally.

It wasn't long before, mechanically and without knowing why, he snatched a woman's handbag and knocked down two men in the process. It was the most humiliating moment in his life, and he felt relieved when he was arrested. Pleading guilty to the charges, he was sentenced to serve three to nine years. He was twenty years old.

He was sent to Trenton State Prison, "a nasty, stinking, medieval cubbyhole" built in the first half of the nineteenth century. Once inside, he was assailed

> by an impalpable wall of unmitigated musk. The air was fouled by the rancid odor of stale feces and mildewed humans, and intensified by the rotten pungency of men sitting idle too long on shelves, like fetid cans of black caviar. Sitting there doing nothing, killing time, wasting away the years, and growing old, rotten, and stale against life, against people.

This and other of Carter's graphic descriptions of life in prison gave Lesra some sense of what it must have been like for his brother to have served time. Lesra now understood why his brother Fru, like virtually all prisoners, was close-mouthed about his prison experiences, no doubt because they were too humiliating and too frightening to share even with one's family.

"But I can't understand," said Lesra, "why, after telling us all those horror stories about prison—after scaring me half to death about Jamesburg and Annandale—how could Rubin do somethin' that would get himself sent right back there?" Lesra had put his finger on the thorny issue of recidivism.

"There've been books written on that subject," Lisa replied. "It doesn't appear to make sense on any rational level. It's like asking, why does a battered wife return to an abusive husband, if she ever leaves, that is? Maybe it has to do with being drawn to what's familiar, to what you know. And even if it's destructive, it's become normal for you, acceptable on some level, what you think you deserve, what you've grown to feel comfortable with, a kind of horribly defined security. Familiarity pulls you back like a magnet. When your self-esteem has been so assaulted it doesn't seem to matter much how bad your conditions are; they only match how bad you feel about yourself.

And when they get you that young and for that long, it's especially tough."

When Rubin Carter left Trenton State Prison in 1961, after four years inside, he "vowed upon everything holy never to come back alive." He had dreamed of becoming a professional prizefighter and despite the obstacles he was to encounter—lack of money, inadequate training facilities, unscrupulous managers—he persevered. His daily prison regimen, which included five thousand pushups at 4:00 A.M. while other inmates slept, had paid off. With a shaved head, a Fu Manchu moustache and a baleful stare, this fierce bundle of energy stormed into the ring and into the limelight. He won most of his bouts by quick knock-outs and thus the name "Hurricane." He was becoming so good that ranked fighters sought to avoid him; he had trouble even finding sparring partners. Within a short time, he had become the top middleweight contender, a high-profile and popular figure.

He was flamboyant, wore shark-skin suits and drove a block-long Cadillac with his name emblazoned in silver on the side (he thought gold would be overstated). He frequently fought at Madison Square Garden, where his televised fights could be seen by millions of fans in the United States and Canada. In 1963 he won acclaim for knocking out then-welterweight champion Emile Griffith in the first round. In 1964 he lost a controversial split decision for the middleweight title to then-champion Joey Giardello.

In addition to a successful career, he got married and had a daughter upon whom he doted.

This was the early sixties, the civil rights years, when black people in America were still disenfranchised, the years of marches and demonstrations and boycotts countered by gun-toting sheriffs, water cannons and police dogs. Carter was a vocal critic of injustice and the hypocrisy of a supposedly democratic country that had two classes of people, one white and one black. Carter participated in the Poor People's March on Washington in 1963, the largest civil rights demonstration in history. But when called later by Martin Luther King to take part in the voting rights march on Selma, Alabama, Carter declined. He never took kindly to the idea of being clubbed over the head by racist cops, and he made his opinions known. After the Harlem fruit riots, when innocent black children were brutalized by a mob of

white police officers, Carter questioned the wisdom of passive resistance; he believed black people had a right to defend themselves. *The
Saturday Evening Post* reported that Carter had joked to a friend:
"Let's get our guns and go up to [Harlem] and get us some of those
cops."

Such comments, even in jest, did not ingratiate Carter with the
powers that be. He became a target for deliberate harassment from the
New Jersey police and the FBI. Like many outspoken black figures of
the time, Carter was shadowed wherever he went, all over the country.
In his home state of New Jersey, the police constantly pulled him in on
trumped-up petty charges. In Carter's words, "The *Law* was out to pin
the Hurricane's black ass to the wall!"

Nineteen sixty-six was the year following the assassination of
Carter's friend Malcolm X. It was the year Martin Luther King was
stoned in a Chicago march, the year racial violence was recorded in
forty-three American cities, the year Stokely Carmichael launched the
Black Power movement. June 16, 1966 began as a day of no particular consequence to Carter, but it proved to be one that would change
his life totally and forever. That night, he and a nineteen-year-old
youth named John Artis, who was riding in Carter's car, were brought
in to the Paterson, New Jersey police station for questioning. Carter
thought it was just another in a long series of harassments. He and Artis didn't know anything about white people being shot in some bar in
Paterson. The police interrogated them separately for seventeen hours
including a trip to the scene of the crime and to the hospital, where
they were shown to one of the victims. Then the police let them go.
And Carter thought that would be the end of it. His being brought in
for questioning was noted in the press; the prosecutor's office "emphasized that the twenty-nine-year-old fighter was never a suspect" in
the Lafayette Bar murders.

Carter went to South America for a bout with Rocky Rivero, and
when he returned to Paterson, he began to negotiate with middleweight champion Dick Tiger for a title fight. It was a fight that was
never to be.

In the fall of 1966, Carter and Artis were arrested and charged
with the Lafayette Bar triple murder. They were put on trial in 1967,
the year Muhammad Ali was stripped of his heavyweight boxing

crown and sentenced to five years in prison for refusing induction into the armed services, the same year rioting gutted Newark and the year before Martin Luther King was assassinated. The State of New Jersey sought the death penalty—the electric chair.

The case against Carter and Artis rested on the word of two white career criminals, Alfred Bello and Arthur Dexter Bradley, the only "eye-witnesses" to place the defendants at the scene. Bello and Bradley testified they had been committing a break-and-enter near the Lafayette Bar that night. Bello said that as he approached the bar to buy some cigarettes, he heard shots coming from inside. He continued to walk toward the bar. He claimed he then saw Carter and Artis coming around the corner outside the bar with weapons. "They were laughing and talking loud." The gunmen, he said, chased him into an alley, jumped into a white car and drove off. Bello then entered the bar. Ignoring the dead and the pleas of the dying, he couldn't resist the sight of the open cash-register. He waded through the carnage and helped himself to what was left in the till. He said he was just looking for a dime to call the police, but he ran out and gave the money he had stolen to his cohort, Bradley.

Carter and Artis were convicted by an all-white jury. The jury recommended mercy, indicating their serious doubts as to the certainty of their verdict. The defendants were sentenced to triple life prison terms.

Carter makes a convincing case for his innocence. On the night of the shootings, he and Artis passed lie-detector tests. The victim who survived the shooting said they were not the gunmen. All original eye-witness descriptions of the assailants (including Bello's and Bradley's) were consistent—two tall, thin, light-skinned Negroes, no beards, both wearing dark suits—and didn't come close to matching the defendants: Carter was dark-skinned, very stocky, had a thick, prominent goatee, was five foot eight and wearing a white jacket; Artis was clean-shaven and wearing a light-blue pullover with his initials, "JAA," written in three-inch-high letters across the pocket. No one mentioned Carter's trademark bald head; as a famous fighter and hometown celebrity, he would have been recognized instantly. It wasn't until Bello and Bradley were brought in for questioning about their own crimes that they "identified" Carter, and they themselves were never charged with the crimes they committed that night. Fred Hogan, an Irish former policeman, then an investigator for the New Jersey public defender's office, uncovered evidence that secret deals, involving bribery and coercion, had been made with Bello and Bradley in exchange for their testimony. Carter also shows that his alibi witnesses had been intimidated by the police and that racism pervaded the entire trial.

Nevertheless, Carter's legal appeals were rejected by the New Jersey state courts. Carter ends *The Sixteenth Round* with this powerful appeal to the reader:

> This book is my life's blood spilled out on the fifteen rounds of these pages. The sixteenth round is still being fought, and there's much more at stake here than a mere boxing title, or a big fat juicy purse.
>
> This fight isn't sanctioned by the World Boxing Association, nor is it governed by the Marquess of Queensberry's fair rules. The weapons are not padded boxing gloves, left hooks, or knockout punches. . . . There won't be any glaring lights, cheering crowds, or well-wishers awaiting me at end of this final round, if I lose it; only steel bars, stone walls, mind-bending games, mental anguish, and near insanity. . . .
>
> I come to you in the only manner left open to me. . . . Now the only chance I have is in appealing directly to you, the people, and showing you the wrongs that have yet to be righted. . . . For the first time in my entire existence I'm saying that I need some help. Otherwise, there will be no more tomorrow for me: . . . no more Rubin—no more Carter. Only the Hurricane.

The book deeply moved Lesra and everyone in the house. They were fully aware this was not the first time in American history that a black man had been railroaded into prison. Nor was it the first time in New Jersey history that a man the police had to know was innocent had been convicted of murder. They were reminded of Richard Hauptmann, who was executed in the infamous Lindbergh case.

"Where do you think the Hurricane is now?" asked Lesra. No one had any idea.

"Did he write an epilogue or some kind of 'Note to the Reader'?" Sam asked.

Turning to the acknowledgments section at the front of the book, they saw that it was dated September 1, 1973, Rahway State Prison, New Jersey.

"But that's seven years ago!" said Lesra. "What's happened since? He can't still be in Rahway, can he? He musta gotten out!"

"Lez, you still want to be a lawyer?" asked Terry.

"Uh-huh," Lesra answered, wary of what was to come.

"Then you have to know how to do research. And now's as good a time as any to learn."

As Lesra stood by, Terry called *The Toronto Star* and asked whether they had any recent articles about Rubin "Hurricane" Carter on file. He found out that the *Star* had carried a Reuters' item on February 10, 1977 and that on December 20, 1977, *The Globe and Mail* had reprinted a *New York Times* article. Copies, he was told, could be obtained from microfilm at the Metropolitan Toronto Reference Library.

"C'mon, Lez!"

"Hey, wait up!" shouted Kathy and then Sam, as they grabbed their coats. Terry and Lesra had already disappeared out the door.

4

"Look at this headline," Lesra said. " 'Boxer gets life for murder.' "

"Life for murder? That can't be 1977," said Terry. "It must be 1967, the year of Rubin's trial. We got the wrong decade."

Lesra checked the date of the newspaper displayed on the screen of the microfilm reader; it was February 10, 1977. The article was what they were looking for, but not what they had hoped to find:

> PATERSON, New Jersey (Reuters)—Former world boxing contender Rubin (Hurricane) Carter yesterday was sentenced to three life terms for the 1966 shotgun murders of three people in a bar.
>
> Carter, and his sparring partner [sic], John Artis, were retried in December after Bob Dylan, Joan Baez, Muhammad Ali and Coretta King, widow of civil rights leader Rev. Martin Luther King, had campaigned for a new trial.
>
> The two men were given essentially the same sentences they received nine years ago: Two consecutive and one concurrent life terms for Carter and two concurrent and one consecutive terms for Artis.

With credit for nine years already served, Carter will be eligible for parole in about 20 years and Artis in about five.

"Say what?" exclaimed Lesra.

"Carter and Artis got a new trial . . ."

" . . . and were convicted *again*?"

"Impossible!"

"Can't be real!" snorted Lesra. "How could that have happened?"

"Muhammad Ali! Coretta Scott King! And Bob Dylan! They all came out for him."

The Canadians had been Dylan fans in the sixties. In fact, they had even named their fabric/fashion import business Five Believers' Batiks, after a little-known song of his, "Obviously, Five Believers." Terry vaguely remembered that in the mid-seventies Dylan had written a song called "Hurricane."

More digging in the reference library was necessary. They looked up Rubin Carter's name in *The New York Times Index* and, starting from 1974, they found an incredible number of articles listed, including several front page stories. These they retrieved and pored through, piecing together the following sequence of events.

Just weeks before *The Sixteenth Round* was published in the fall of 1974, both Alfred Bello and Arthur Dexter Bradley, the State's key witnesses, stated that they had lied when they identified Carter and Artis at the trial. They admitted first to investigator Fred Hogan, then to reporter Selwyn Raab of *The New York Times* that the Paterson police had pressured them into committing perjury with promises of reward money and lenient treatment for their own crimes.

"I was twenty-three years old and facing eighty to ninety years in jail," Bradley told Raab. "I just bought my way out. . . . There's no doubt Carter was framed. . . . I lied to save myself."

Bello told Raab he "had never been able to identify Carter and Artis." The detectives, calling Carter and Artis "niggers, Muslims, animals," told Bello he'd be performing a "public service" by "getting them off the streets." Without Bello's identification, "there was no evidence in the case," and he was threatened that if he didn't help the prosecutors by incriminating Carter and Artis, then he might become a suspect in the murders himself. The police, Bello added, "promised they'd take care of me if I got jammed up [arrested] again. . . . The cops told me I'd be doing justice for the families of the white victims— it would be an eye for an eye. . . . They told me help your own people, and I went for it."

The combination of the publication of *The Sixteenth Round* and the front-page exposés in *The New York Times* incensed the public. The *Times* stories confirmed the corruption and deceit Rubin had alleged in his autobiography. The police and the prosecution, of course, denied the charges. "Nonsense," declared Detective Lieutenant Vincent DeSimone of the Passaic County prosecutor's office, "we don't manufacture witnesses."

Carter's lawyers immediately sought a new trial based on Bello's and Bradley's confessions. A hearing was held to see whether a second trial would be granted.

"You'd think," said Terry to the others, "that a new trial would be automatic."

After hearing sworn testimony, Judge Samuel Larner, the same judge who had presided over the original trial, concluded that the "ring of truth" was "totally absent" in the recantations. In his opinion:

> [Bello's] extensive criminal record hardly adds to his trustworthiness as a witness. . . . The criminal minds of Bello and Bradley are so devious and amoral that it is impossible for a court to analyze their motivations and mental gyrations in order to arrive at a reason for their conduct.

The judge denied the defence motion for a new trial.

"That ain't right!" exclaimed Lesra. "How come Bello and Bradley are believable when they testify against Carter and Artis, but they're bullshit liars when they testify against the cops?"

"Look," said Sam, pointing to another article on the screen. "That's exactly the question everybody was asking back then." According to press reports, the public's outrage had been stoked.

Thanks to a massive publicity campaign to help "Free Carter and

Artis" organized by New York advertising executive George Lois, the state of justice in the State of New Jersey was not looking too good. This was the era of the Watergate scandal, when illegal abuse of power by those sworn to uphold the law was less tolerated. Governor Brendan Byrne was under pressure to grant clemency to Carter and Artis. He refused.*

During this period, Carter sent Bob Dylan a copy of *The Sixteenth Round.* The Hurricane had by now been moved to Trenton State Prison, and Dylan was moved to go there and talk to him in person. They felt an instant kinship of spirit. As Carter stated at a prison press conference, "When he [Dylan] walked in the door—this white brother—he knew and I knew that neither one of us had any choice. . . . Two men can always meet." The result of this meeting was "Hurricane," the pull-no-punches song that Dylan wrote with lyricist Jacques Levy about Carter, the injustice and racism that fired his case.† The song was released first as a single, then as a cut on the album *Desire,* and was broadcast over the airwaves almost incessantly through the fall of 1975 and into 1976. "Hurricane" was also a main feature of Dylan's repertoire on his "Rolling Thunder Revue" tour. Dylan staged benefit concerts for Carter at Madison Square Garden (which sold out in five hours) and the Houston Astrodome ("The Night of the Hurricane" I and II), as well as a show for the inmates at the Clinton Correctional Facility, where Carter was incarcerated for a short time. Roberta Flack came to the prison to perform, as did Joan Baez, Ramblin' Jack Elliott, Ronee Blakely, Paterson poet Allen Ginsberg and Canadians Joni Mitchell and Robbie Robertson.

Indeed, dozens of celebrities gave their support to freeing the Hurricane: Ellen Burstyn, Dyan Cannon, Muhammad Ali, Coretta Scott King—all participated in rallies and marches; The Who, Richie Havens, Stevie Wonder, Johnny Cash, Stephen Stills, Isaac Hayes, Ringo Starr and many others performed at the concerts for free. Nov-

---

*Few outsiders could appreciate the Byzantine nature of New Jersey politics. Byrne himself had played a role in the case when he was a county prosecutor, having personally approached certain judges requesting lenient treatment for Bradley as a result of his co-operation in the Carter case.

†The lyrics to "Hurricane" are reproduced in Appendix A on pages 331–34.

elist Nelson Algren became obsessed with the case, which held more than a passing interest to fellow writers Norman Mailer, Claude Brown, Gay Talese and George Plimpton, and columnists Jimmy Breslin, Dave Anderson and Pete Hamill. Politicians who added to the effort were Edward I. Koch (in his earlier incarnation as a liberal congressman), former U.S. Attorney General Ramsey Clark, U.N. Ambassador Andrew Young, Jesse Jackson, Julian Bond and NAACP Executive Director Benjamin Hooks. Entertainers Dick Gregory, Harry Belafonte, Melba Moore and Cleavon Little took the Hurricane's side along with broadcasters Pat Collins and Geraldo Rivera and athletes Hank Aaron, Walt "Clyde" Frazier and Earl "the Pearl" Monroe. In addition, lawyers, athletes, university professors, ministers, film and TV directors and producers, corporate executives and book and magazine publishers also participated on the many committees formed on Carter's behalf.

At the library, Lesra and the others learned that the war was fought on two fronts: in the media, in rallies and demonstrations, on bumper stickers that read "THERE IS ONLY *ONE* INNOCENT HURRICANE!"; and in the New Jersey Supreme Court, where Carter's New York attorneys were appealing Judge Larner's decision. Eventually, in March of 1976, the New Jersey Supreme Court issued its unanimous decision. The Court ruled that the prosecution had suppressed important evidence favourable to the defence. Among other things, there was a secret tape-recording providing concrete proof that, contrary to their denials at trial, promises and inducements had indeed been given by Lieutenant DeSimone to the State's key witnesses, Bello and Bradley, in exchange for their identification testimony. "I will go to the top people in the State of New Jersey," DeSimone had vowed to Bello, to help him out with his problems with the law. "I promise you this."

The Supreme Court threw out the convictions and ordered a new trial.

Carter and Artis were released on bail pending retrial. Picked up at the prison in a limousine by Muhammad Ali, they were whisked off to a suite at the New York Hilton for a victory celebration.

But the prosecution was also busy.

At the 1976 retrial, the prosecution painted a classic us-versus-them scenario, which was well-received by the local jury: it was the outsiders, the slick New York shysters and the stars of Hollywood, versus the decent, honest, law-abiding citizens of New Jersey. Bello recanted his recantation and once again testified against Carter and Artis. Bradley, who was sticking to his recantation, fled to the Boston area and refused to testify for the State. But neither could he give evidence for the defence: the authorities arrested him on a rape charge and kept him in jail until the retrial was over, then dropped the charges on the day Carter and Artis were resentenced. The prosecution vilified everyone who had been a party to Bello's recantation, including *New York Times* reporter Selwyn Raab, calling them "perverters of justice [who were] trying to sell a phoney recantation." "Yes," the prosecutor admitted to the jury in summation, Bello was "a conniver, thief, repulsive, disgusting," but nevertheless you could believe him. He had been manipulated away from the truth and had now seen the error of his ways.

"I get ya!" popped in Lesra, sarcastically. "Bello got himself on the right side again."

But, as the news reports showed, the factor that appeared decisive at trial was the prosecutor's blatant appeal to racial prejudice and stereotyping. Although no motive for the murders was offered at the first trial in 1967, nine years later the prosecution was allowed to argue that the motive was "racial revenge." In the mid-sixties, said the prosecutor to the jurors, there was a lot of racial unrest around the country and, unfortunately, not everyone was a Martin Luther King. The State claimed, in effect, that on June 17, 1966, Carter and Artis had appointed themselves avengers for the black race and indiscriminately slaughtered three whites in a Paterson bar because a black man they did not know had been killed by a white man they had never heard of in another Paterson bar earlier that night! The prosecutor said that the police had eliminated robbery as a motive, so "What other reason could it have happened for?" The jury couldn't think of one. Given Rubin's dark, menacing appearance, given the fact that he was a boxer and boxing is violent and brutal, and given the prosecutor's inflammatory arguments, it apparently took little imagination and no evidence of personal involvement to convict Rubin Carter again.

"He was reconvicted even after that public exposé!" uttered Sam incredulously.

"Maybe it was because of it," said Kathy.

By the time Lesra and the Canadians had finished reading about the retrial, they were overwhelmed by the details of the case and numbed into silence at the magnitude of the injustice. They were all wondering the same things. After the indignities that Rubin Carter had suffered on account of his race, now *he* was supposed to be the one who was racist? Talk about blaming the victim! How was Rubin handling all of this? To have gone through one trial, been convicted and had that guilty verdict overturned nine years later, having all along proclaimed and demonstrated his innocence, was terrible enough. But to have had a second trial and again been convicted, after being free for a scant nine months, seemed too much.

"So, what 'Hurricane' doin' now?" asked Lesra, slipping into no-nonsense Black English. "And where he at?"

The December 20, 1977 article they found in *The Globe and Mail* provided some answers. At least it gave them an inkling of where Rubin was and what his attitude had been three years earlier. Over a photo of a bald, bearded man wearing wire-rimmed granny glasses, Lesra read the words: "Cause célèbre fights alone." Leaning over the microfilm reader, all four read silently on:

> NEW YORK—Rubin (Hurricane) Carter spends his days alone in a tiny, 19th-century prison cell, rarely speaking with any other inmate or any guard.
>
> Eighty miles away, John Artis works and studies in an atmosphere of fertile country fields at a prison farm without bars or walls.
>
> Today, the once celebrated New Jersey murder case that sent Carter and Artis to such contrasting prisons is all but forgotten. But almost a year after they were convicted for a second time and sentenced again to life terms, their tangled case is heading for a new round of court battles.
>
> Defence lawyers said that an appeal would be filed soon to overturn a guilty verdict that was handed down in Pater-

son, NJ., on Dec. 21, 1976. The legal move, the lawyers said, was delayed for a year by their inability to get free transcripts of the six-week trial involving a triple slaying. . . .

Carter confined in dimly lighted cell
[The 40-year old] Carter, who was once a leading middleweight boxer, is confined in a dimly lighted, maximum-security cell at Trenton State Prison. It is five feet wide and seven feet long in a cellblock that was built in 1850.

"Holy shit!" blurted out Lesra, forgetting he was in a public library. "He's back in that Trenton hell-hole!"

. . . Carter has isolated himself from 900 other inmates inside the grimy, red-brick prison walls. He declined to participate in any work or educational programs or even to eat prison food.

Still asserting his innocence, Carter, in an interview at the prison, declared that conforming to normal prison life would be equivalent "to admitting I'm guilty and that the state has a right to take away my freedom and keep me here."

Carter said that most of his time was spent reading—including legal texts—and writing. In 1974, his autobiography, entitled *The Sixteenth Round,* was published.

To feed himself, Carter has a friend, Thom [Kidrin], a song writer, bring him a 25-pound supply of food, mostly canned soups and vegetables, every month. With an electric coil, Carter heats and eats the food in his cell.

Except for [Kidrin], who is 25 years old, there are few visitors for Carter, who for three years was a national legal *cause célèbre.*

In the last year, Carter has become estranged from his wife, who is the mother of his two children, and she no longer visits him. None of the politicians, business executives or sports and show business personalities who formerly rallied to his cause have met or communicated with him since the last conviction, he said. . . .

No comment on planned appeal

The chief defence lawyers [are] Myron Beldock and Lewis Steel. . . . The legal defence fund of the National Association for the Advancement of Colored People is known to be considering . . . join[ing] in the appeal.

Burrell I. Humphreys, the Passaic County prosecutor, has declined to comment on the planned appeal. But, alluding to the vigorous campaign by the defunct Carter Defence Fund for a second trial, he said the 1976 verdict was important because "it proved that a contest between an American jury and Madison Avenue hucksters is no contest."

Because of the alleged racial bias and the defence charges that the prosecutor's office concealed evidence and intimidated witnesses, Steel said, the Carter-Artis case "is going to be seen as a major criminal-legal struggle in American jurisprudence. This case will never be forgotten no matter how it is ultimately decided," he added.

"This is too fucking much!"

"He doesn't see his wife, kids . . ."

"Damn!" was all that Lesra could say.

They left the library, hoping against hope that, in the three years since that article was published, maybe something else had happened and Rubin was freed.

Someone suggested they call the prison.

"You can do that?" asked Lesra.

"Yes, *you* can do that!"

When they got home (with photocopies of the articles for the others) they showed Lesra how to call long-distance information in Trenton, New Jersey, and get the prison phone number. Lesra called Trenton State Prison and asked if Rubin Carter was being held prisoner there. His call was transferred to someone in the mailroom.

"What's his number?" the curt voice barked.

"What ya mean 'number'?"

"*Number!* Prison number. Every inmate got a number!"

Lesra looked down at the cover of *The Sixteenth Round,* which was sitting on the desk in front of him. "It *was* #45472 . . ."

The sound of files flicking. "Carter? Rubin Carter? Sure, he's here. Locks in 2-Left."

Lesra's heart sank. He slowly put down the receiver and turned to the others. "He's still there. In goddamn Trenton."

PART TWO
RECALLED TO LIFE

He lowered the window, and looked out at the rising sun. There was a ridge of ploughed land, with a plough upon it where it had been left last night when the horses were unyoked; beyond, a quiet coppice-wood, in which many leaves of burning red and golden yellow still remained upon the trees. Though the earth was cold and wet, the sky was clear, and the sun rose bright, placid, and beautiful.

"Eighteen years!" said the passenger, looking at the sun. "Gracious Creator of day! To be buried alive for eighteen years!"

—Charles Dickens
A TALE OF TWO CITIES

5

The decision to correspond with Rubin Carter was not made without some reflection. Although Lesra and the Canadians couldn't help wondering what Carter's state of mind would be, curiosity alone was not a good enough reason to write. They were aware that getting involved with people in prison—where situations are so complicated and needs so desperate—was not something to be done lightly. But they had listened to Carter and heard him; it was not a matter of choice. At minimum they had to say, "Hello, you're not alone."

Terry called the prison to find out whether Rubin Carter was allowed to receive mail and whether it was necessary to be on a special mailing list in order to write. After repeating his questions three times to a distracted guard in the mailroom, Terry was told he could write to anyone he wanted to, without prior approval, that there was no such thing as a mailing list at Trenton. The next question was the real stumper: "What's the address?"

"Hey, Rocky," shouted the voice on the phone, "what's the address here?"

"You mean the street address?" answered another voice in the background.

"Yeah."

"Third and Federal. I dunno the number. Whaddya wanna know for?"

"Somebody wants to write a letter."

"Shit, man, you want the mailing address, not the street address!"

"Look, you're so fuckin' smart, answer the phone yergoddamnself!"

There followed a lot of bangs and crashes, as if the receiver had been dropped and let smash against a wall several times before it finally came to rest. Then Terry heard a voice that sounded a lot like Rocky's, but more distinct now.

"Put the inmate's name and number on the envelope, Drawer 'N', Trenton, New Jersey, 08625. It'll get here." And the line went dead.

Just the possibility of writing to Rubin excited Lesra. He didn't believe that someone who wrote books—by his definition, someone great—could actually be a real, living person! Furnished with Rubin "Hurricane" Carter's address, coupled with a lesson on how to write the "friendly letter," Lesra's ability to correspond with a hero soon became a reality. Numerous drafts and corrections later, his letter to Rubin Carter, his first to anyone, was finally completed. It was dated September 20, 1980. In it, he told Rubin a bit about his background and explained what he, a Brooklyn native, was doing in Canada. He also said:

> The thought of writing to you scared me, but not because of your reputation—I know you wouldn't hurt a flea (unless it bit you). I feel frightened and vulnerable because I have to see you now not just as an author, but as a human being. It is hard at the best of times for black people to open up with each other because where we come from, you learn to be tough when you learn to walk.
>
> . . . My eldest brother did time up state in New York. Before I read your book, *The Sixteenth Round,* I really thought he was cold and crazy, a lot like people thought you were. But now, since I read your book, I can understand him and his problems a whole lot better. You were not only asking someone to help you through your book, you were also helping others.

All through your book I was wondering if it would have been easier to die or take the shit you did. But now, when I think of your book, I say if you were dead then you would not have been able to give what you did through your book. To imagine me not being able to write you this letter or thinking that they could beat you into giving up, man, that would be too much. We need more like you to set examples of what courage is all about!

Hey Brother, I'm going to let it go here. Please write back. It will mean a lot.

Your friend,
Lesra Martin

The Canadians wrote Rubin Carter a letter too and echoed Lesra's sentiments. They thanked him for the openness and sincerity of his book and for standing unapologetically by his principles. In a society that was "moral and just," they said, he would be "an honoured member" and they would be writing to him at a different address. Regardless, it was a privilege.

Along with the two letters they included a money order, so that not having the money for stamps (which is often the case in prison) wouldn't be a reason for not replying. They told him that if he thought not writing back to them wouldn't matter, he'd be wrong, because "Friendship always matters!"

Lesra's interest in the mail escalated dramatically. He always managed to be in the vestibule (he called it the "vestiview") the moment the mail dropped through the front door slot. This was usually around 11:00 A.M. But invariably he found nothing. With waxing scepticism and waning enthusiasm, he would return to his studies.

Although he didn't think this particular Wednesday in mid-October would be any different, Lesra assumed his station. Being disappointed had become a weekday morning ritual. He heard the footsteps of the mailman coming up the walk toward the house. He saw the brass flap lifting, the mail tumbling in. A quick look now at what was spread on the floor, then he would go back upstairs and hit the books. One envelope this time caught his eye; he picked it up. There was no Queen in its corner but two fifteen-cent stamps brandishing the Stars and Stripes.

"It's here!" he shouted. "It's here!" He didn't have to read the stamps' capitalized caption, "THE HOME OF THE BRAVE—THE LAND OF THE FREE," to know who the letter was from. This was it, no question.

Lesra called up the stairs and toward the back of the house. "Hey, y'all! All y'all! He wrote us back! Can you stand it? He wrote us back! I can't believe it! Rubin *Hurricane* Carter wrote us back! . . . 'Course I knew he would." And everyone in the house quickly gathered.

Carter's letter, dated October 7, was addressed to all of them. It was one page, typewritten and punctuated with a lot of underlining and exclamation marks. Rubin began by apologizing for taking so long to respond. He had needed stamps and had had to wait to get them. In a tone more philosophical than apologetic, he quoted one of his favorite aphorisms: "But he who bemoans the lack of opportunity, forgets that small doors often open up into large rooms." He thanked Lesra and the group effusively for their kind thoughts and good wishes. Their humanity, he said, was palpable on the page, and reading their words had filled him with "immense joy." The man knew how to gush.

Lesra and the Canadians were elated. It seemed that a small door had indeed been opened.

Many exchanges of letters followed, through October, November and into December. They asked Rubin all kinds of questions—about *The Sixteenth Round,* whether he was working on a sequel, who was handling his appeal and how it was going, whether he was still getting a twenty-five-pound supply of food every month, what he thought Ronald Reagan's election as president would mean for the direction of the country. Rubin was very warm but also reticent. Although he appeared eager to correspond, and was responsive to how the Canadians lived together as a group and what they'd been doing with Lesra, he avoided answering their questions. He seemed to have retreated from the world in the sense that he wasn't interested in discussing politics, the day-to-day particulars of his life or even his case. He was extremely well-read. Esoteric philosophy had occupied his attention, sustained him. He was interested, he said, not in transitory facts but in eternal truths, in communing with Buddha, Socrates, Jesus, Krishna-murti—not Reagan, Nixon or Ford. No one could argue with his choice of companions, nor with his focus on getting beyond illusion; it was just a question of approach. They wondered whether his separating himself from the day-to-day things could wind up separating him from everything.

The Canadians were gratified that Lesra had taken such an active interest in Rubin Carter. They felt it their responsibility to ensure that Lesra never forgot where he came from. If he became alienated from (or, worse, felt superior to) his roots in any way, then they had failed miserably in an education they had hoped would promote understanding and care, not divisiveness and shame.

It was thus important that Lesra not only maintain but strengthen his relationship with his family, and his father's phone calls every Sunday helped tremendously in that regard. Unfortunately, the news from home was seldom good. After these calls, Lesra would often be thinking and worrying about his family; and while his concerns frequently interfered with his ability to concentrate on "school work," he would share them and discuss them with everyone in the house. This was all a vital part of his schooling, as were his twice-yearly trips "back home."

These trips were especially difficult for Lesra to come to terms with. Emotionally, he would be in Brooklyn days and even weeks before he actually arrived and would remain there weeks after he had physically left, until the experiences were sorted out. He felt guilty about being the only one in his family to have been lucky enough to come to Canada. He didn't deserve it, he thought. It wasn't fair. He couldn't help feeling that he had abandoned everyone, particularly his brother Elston, who was a year younger and was now left with the responsibility of looking after the two youngest boys as well as fending for himself on the streets.

It was painful for Lesra to be reminded of how the rest of his family had to live, to have to face not just the material contrasts but, more importantly, the psychological ones: the instability, the constant and oppressive fear, the lack of self-esteem, the helplessness, versus his own growing sense of security, confidence, promise. But his family and friends were quick to let him know that his success, his getting out of there, was as meaningful to them as it was to him. By being in Canada and being educated, they would tell Lesra (and he would constantly have to remind himself), he was not being selfish: he was giving everyone hope.

Christmas time was approaching, and Lesra was going back to the States once again to spend the holidays with his family. The Canadians thought it might be a good idea for him to use this trip as an opportunity to go to New Jersey, to visit Rubin; that is, if Rubin was allowed visits and would agree to one.

Terry called his "old pal" Rocky at the prison mailroom to find out what the rules were for visiting. Many phone calls and much incomprehensible prison jargon later, he managed to find out about the ninety-minute "contact visits," where you could actually touch, as opposed to the thirty-minute "window visits," where you were separated by thick, bullet-proof glass and had to speak through telephone receivers. Contact visits were held only on weekends and during rigidly prescribed times, commencing every two hours from 8:00 A.M. to 2:00 P.M., and you had to be there hours early to ensure that you'd get in.

The whole idea of going to Trenton terrified Lesra at first, and he didn't think he could do it. His anxiety eased somewhat when they discussed the logistics of the trip and how exciting it would be to meet Rubin in person. They reminded Lesra that he was an experienced traveller: he'd already made trips to New York and back on his own. From his parents' place in Brooklyn, he could take the subway to Penn Station, on the west side of Manhattan. From there, he could catch a train down to Trenton, which was about an hour away. And from that point to the prison, it would be simple enough for him to take a cab. They reassured him that he was capable of handling it, that, if anything, it was the emotional aspects of the trip, not the physical getting from one place to another, that would be difficult. Lesra had to agree—but he was still scared.

Lesra wrote to Rubin and asked him whether it would be possible to see him in person, to have a contact visit, on the Saturday or Sunday between Christmas and New Year's. In the same letter, the Canadians asked Rubin if he had received their latest letters, because he hadn't addressed any of the questions they'd been asking.

Rubin's reply did not arrive until mid-December. It seemed that they had touched a nerve—that Rubin wanted a visit and didn't want a visit, that he wanted to be touched and didn't want to be touched and was wary of being touched. So he was laying back and was going to, in the famous words of former Canadian Prime Minister Pierre Trudeau, let "the universe unfold as it should."

That clinched it for Lesra. He was now determined to go see Rubin. Nobody should have to spend Christmas alone.

The group gave Lesra some Christmas cards and a letter to deliver in person. They had already mailed Rubin a Christmas package of clothes, including a snuggly, velour jogging suit in dark earth tones that would appeal to a Taurus (his birthdate, they had noticed in his autobiography, was May 6, 1937—the same day the *Hindenburg* exploded, also in New Jersey). They had enclosed, as well, a hand-drawn card with a sketch of what they thought he'd look like in the jogging suit. The card's caption read "Keep on Keepin' On."

The Canadians worried constantly about Lesra when he was back in the States. Not that they were being paranoid. Statistics showed then, and still show today, that the number-one cause of death of black males in America between the ages of fifteen and twenty-five is murder (at a rate ten times that of white males the same age). The streets of Bushwick and Bedford-Stuyvesant were treacherous even if you'd grown up there. Teenagers lucky or enterprising enough to own a then-fashionable sheepskin coat, in trying to keep it from being stolen, often had to pay with their lives. Drugs were rampant, weapons everywhere. With Lesra taking all the care in the world not to get involved in anything that might lead to trouble, it was not unreasonable for them to fear that he could be hit by a stray bullet. The danger was real.

They urged Lesra to call every day if he could. The Martins still didn't have a phone, so Lesra would call collect from the pay phone at the store on the corner of Broadway, the same phone his father used to call Canada. But talking on that phone wasn't easy. There was an elevated subway line within a few feet of the store, and every couple of minutes a train would screech by. The roar was so loud and intense that the building shook, the receiver trembled and all conversation ceased. Not the best conditions for a fluid exchange! Nevertheless, the sound of Lesra's voice (which, in Bushwick, was harder-edged) and the

fragments of information conveyed in these calls, were greatly antici-
pated and appreciated.

Laden with Christmas presents, Lesra was the prodigal son returning home. His father met him at LaGuardia airport and hugged him.

"I'm glad you're up there, boy."

That was an unusual greeting, thought Lesra. He looked around
to see if anyone else was there.

"Everything all right, Pop? How come you came alone?"

"Everybody waitin' on you at home. Lemme look at you." Earl
surveyed his son and liked what he saw.

"How's Mommy and everybody?"

"Oh, she fine. They fine."

"Where Elston at? How come he's not with you, Pop?"

Earl Martin shook his head and helped Lesra with his bags. They
went to find a bus. It was a long trek back to Brooklyn.

Lesra was coming to understand his father. Something was bothering
Earl but he wasn't ready to talk about it—just yet. He waited until they
were on the last of the three trains they had to take to reach Bushwick.

"I worry 'bout that boy."

"Elston, Pop?"

"Uh-huh. You know what I'm talkin' 'bout."

"What, Pop? Tell me."

"Your brother don' listen to nobody."

"Did somethin' happen, Pop?"

"Tol' that boy not to go where he don' belong . . ."

"What happened, Pop?"

" . . . Crossin' over that Myrtle Avenue like he do . . ."

"To the white section?"

"Almost got hisself shot."

"Damn!"

"But he awright."

"Damn! Aw, Pop . . . I'll talk to him, Pop."

"Somebody's gotta talk some sense into that boy. Lord knows I
tried." Earl suddenly stood up. "Get up, boy! We talkin' so much, we
like to of missed our stop!"

Lesra was mobbed as he approached his family's place on Linden
Street. He was suddenly very popular. Only Elston was laid back,

standing off to one side, talking to a girl, pretending not to notice Lesra's arrival. Several girls from around the corner were sitting on the stoop, there to catch a glimpse of Lesra as he walked up the street and into the building. To get hooked up with him could mean a ticket out. Even if he dressed kind of weird, at least he looked like those rich white kids on TV—"preppy" they called it. Two shopping bags bulging with wrapped Christmas gifts only enhanced the image.

Waiting for Lesra at the top of the four flights of stairs were his mother, sisters and other brothers. There was still no railing on the stairs, no knob on the apartment door. The surroundings hadn't changed. Nothing had changed. Until he was overwhelmed with hugs and kisses, he wondered whether he had ever left.

He had not been home for more than a few minutes, however, when Damon, who was six, suddenly burst into tears.

"What's wrong, Day-day?" asked Lesra.

"Where Lesra at? I wan' Lesra!"

"I'm Lesra, fool. Now get over here, little brother, and give me a hug!"

As Lesra reached for his brother, Damon shrank back and started crying even louder. "You look like Lesra but you talk funny! You not Lesra! Where Lesra at?"

"Shut up, Day-day!" shouted Fru. "That's Lez, awright. Now, give 'im a hug!"

"He don' soun' like Lesra," sobbed Damon.

"Course tha's 'im!" retorted Fru. "He jus' talk proper now, thassall—and you would too, if you could!"

"I can speak like that!" chimed in Nonie, Lesra's older sister. "Tha's how we talk in school, and I always get 'A's in English."

Nonie then challenged Lesra to a grammar contest, and soon everyone was arguing about the "correct" way to say this or that. Lesra tried telling them that it wasn't a question of right or wrong; there were two different languages: Standard English and Black English.

"Aw, go on!" said Nonie.

"Honest, I ain't lyin'!" said Lesra, now conscious of his choice of words.

Later that day, Lesra took advantage of a quiet moment and had a talk with his mother. She was in the kitchen fixing some black-eyed peas and rice. It was Lesra's favourite dish and he hadn't had it in ages. Nobody in Canada could make it like his mother. And he told her so, as he hugged her from behind. He remembered how much he loved watching his mother cook, how comforting it was, and also how rare it was.

Lesra mentioned that since he'd been home, Elston had been avoiding him.

"He'll come round," said Alma, not too concerned. "He had some words with your father. Now he just hangin' out."

"I know. When I came from the airport, I saw him outside, talking to Shirley. You know Shirley, ma. Miz Brown's daughter."

"Miz Brown what?" asked Alma.

"Daughter. You know—her daughter!"

"Her what?"

"Daughter!" shouted Lesra.

"Dotter? What're you talkin' about, boy? What Miz Brown doin' with a dotter?"

"You know, ma," said Lesra, surprised and frustrated at the unexpected difficulties he was having communicating. "When a woman has a baby girl—that her daughter."

"Oh!" exclaimed Alma, exasperated. She stopped stirring, put the lid back down on the pot, put her hands on her hips and looked at her son as if he had lost his senses. Enunciating carefully in her broad Brooklyn accent, she continued, "You mean *doe-aw-duh*?"

"Yeah, that's right, ma," said Lesra, embarrassed, realizing how foreign he must sound. "What I meant to say was 'Shirley is Miz Brown *doe-aw-duh*.'"

"Then why didn't you say so in the first place? Don't they be teachin' you nothin' up in Canada? . . . 'Course I know Shirley."

With a mixture of pride and dismay, Lesra related this story during one of his phone calls to the Canadians. He wanted to let them know that their efforts at teaching him were not in vain. He now had proof that he was losing his accent* and speaking Standard English.

*They had worked on modifying Lesra's pronounced Brooklyn accent. In speech patterns similar to those of the Archie Bunkers (his television neighbours from Queens), Lesra used to say *earl* for "oil" and *oil* for "earl"; *here* for "hair" and *hair* for "here"; and, of course, *woe-aw-duh* for "water."

He was not too thrilled, however, about sounding "white" in his home surroundings. The Canadians assured him that when he became more comfortable with Standard English, which was still relatively new to him, that he would be able to switch back and forth between the languages with ease. "Then, when in Rome, you can do as the Romans do."

"Maybe," said Lesra, "but I don't want to think about messin' with Italian yet!"

The Christmas presents from Lesra to his family were a big hit. He had saved money from working during the summer in Toronto, cutting lawns in the neighbourhood. In the fall, he raked leaves, and he and Marty, in the winter, had their own snow-shovelling business and a dozen regular monthly contracts of driveways to clear. He was working hard and he wanted everyone to share in his good fortune. There was nothing extravagant, but everyone's present was well thought out. For example, Damon and eight-year-old Leland each got a hand-held electronic football game that was then the rage. Earl and Alma received watches that Lesra had bought at an antique store and had refurbished.

Lesra had just about finished playing Santa Claus when Elston came home. "El," said Lesra, handing his fifteen-year-old sibling a well-wrapped gift in a large box. "Here, bro'. Hope you like it."

Elston remained aloof. Hesitantly he accepted the present. Unlike his little brothers, who had almost shredded the wrapping paper on theirs, he took his time and carefully unwrapped his. As he lifted a black leather cowboy hat from the box, he got excited. He immediately put it on and ran over to the mirror in the apartment's only bathroom, off the living room. Through the open door, his whole family could see him primping and smiling.

"Damn, Lez! That is one bad sky!" marvelled Elston, cocking it just so.

"Oooh, that's a fine lookin' chile!" exclaimed Alma.

Elston slowly turned and strutted over to Lesra and gave him "five," then another five, then a whole series of handshakes they used to do.

"Chill out, bro'! Don't be breakin' on me now!" mocked Lesra.

"C'mon, Lez. Let's get outta here. Let's go find Slick. He been askin' after you."

It was still light out when Lesra and Elston took to the streets. Elston was very cocky, sporting his new hat. They strolled along, waving and nodding at people they knew.

"Put me down on what's up, El."

"Ain't nothin' happenin'."

"You still mad at me?"

For a minute, Elston didn't reply. He continued to swagger down the street. He loved his new hat, but not more than he loved being with his bigger brother.

"Why you up there?" he blurted.

"C'mon, man. You know."

"You should be here, backin' me up!"

Just then a cop car with two white cops slowed down alongside them.

"Hey, you with the hat!"

Lesra and Elston froze. The cop in the passenger seat signalled to Elston to come over.

Elston walked up to the side of the car, while Lesra stood alert just behind him. He didn't know what was about to "jump off."

"Some hat you got there, boy. Where'd ya steal it?"

Elston said nothing.

"I said where'd ya steal it, boy?"

Again, Elston said nothing.

"I bought it and gave it to him," said Lesra. "For Christmas." The cop pretended he didn't hear.

Elston rearranged the hat imperceptibly on his head.

"You think it looks good?" continued the cop to Elston. "He thinks it looks good," he said, nodding to his partner. The cop drew out his gun and motioned with it to Elston to step closer. Cautiously, Elston inched forward.

"How'd it look if I shoot a few holes through it?" said the cop, taking aim. Neither of the kids moved a muscle. The cops burst into sardonic laughter. The driver stepped on the gas and the patrol car peeled away, burning rubber.

Lesra shook his head.

"How it look if I shoot a few holes through your dick?" shouted Elston, the cops disappearing into the distance and the fear slowly subsiding. Lesra turned to Elston. The two brothers started laughing and gave each other five.

6

Lesra's father accompanied him on the subway ride from Brooklyn to Penn Station, and Lesra was glad; they had to change trains at Grand Central, and Lesra didn't think he could have figured it out by himself. But it was on his own that he headed across the Hudson River and into New Jersey—past Newark, past Rahway, down toward Trenton, the Christmas cards and letter for Rubin Carter clutched tightly in his hand. Lesra had business to attend to. Earl Martin knew what Lesra was up to, and he was proud of his son. Nothing surprised him any more about Lesra. Earl expected only great things from him. It seemed fitting that his boy should be visiting Rubin "Hurricane" Carter. Sure, he knew about the Hurricane, had followed his career, and Earl sent along his best.

Lesra had been sitting alone on the train for about forty minutes, staring out the window, when a pleasant-looking older black woman sat down beside him. It took her a moment to get settled. She was carrying a cardboard box, its top covered in aluminum foil. Something inside the box started Lesra sniffing, and the woman smiled at him. They drifted naturally into conversation and the minutes and miles passed easily. The train skirted that bastion of the Ivy League, Princeton, then its training ground, Lawrenceville, home of the exclusive prep school.

The woman told Lesra that she was from New Brunswick. Lesra said he had come from Canada too.

"Canada?"

"Uh-huh."

"Who's talkin' 'bout Canada? We in New Jersey."

"I know but . . . New Brunswick—that's in the Maritimes."

"New Brunswick? That was two stops back where I got on. Whatchootalkinbout Mary Times?"

"Jus' sumpin' I learnt in school. Musta got it mixed up."

"Ain't hard these days. Don't nothin' make no sense!"

"Oooh!" said Lesra, pointing to her package. "Now that's sumpin' I know. Sweet-potato pie, right? Sure smell good!"

"Uh-huh. It's for my boy, Eric. In Trenton. I cooked it special."

"Ain't he the lucky one!" said Lesra. But his smile changed abruptly into a look of fear. "I'm going to Trenton too."

"The whole worl' be down in Trenton."

"But I'm goin' to the prison. State prison."

"That's what I'm talkin' 'bout, boy. Trenton State Prison. That's where they got my son at. He 'bout your age—what is it, sixteen, seventeen? He seventeen. Visit him every month. You goin' to see your brother or your pop?"

"Trenton!" trumpeted the conductor over the loudspeaker, his voice only slightly more audible than the squeal of brakes, as the train pulled into the station.

"Don't you worry 'bout a thing," the woman told Lesra. "You just stick with Miz Flemmings. That's me."

There was one cab waiting outside the station. Lesra and Mrs Flemmings jammed into the back seat, sharing it with two women who also were heading for the prison, going to visit their husbands. It was a ten-minute ride. The fare was two dollars each.

The penitentiary looked to Lesra as horrible as he had pictured it from Rubin's descriptions in *The Sixteenth Round,* which he tried not to think about. He tried not to look up at the gun towers, tried not to see the barbed wire that was being replaced by loops of deadlier "razor ribbon" (on account of a recent escape). Lesra followed the women down a hellishly long walk that ran alongside one of the prison's sooty, stone walls, past a mammoth pair of knobless steel doors, past more stone walls and up metal steps to another solid steel door. There, one of the women pushed a buzzer. A fat, black guard opened the door, and they walked up to what Lesra described as a "raggedy" plywood table that had another clipboard tied to it. Lesra had to sign in, giving his name and the name and number of the inmate he wanted to visit. He was then given a tiny slip of paper with the number twenty-nine scrawled on it in thick, black marker. Then he had to go through another locked door, which was operated from somewhere else by an electric buzzer.

Lesra walked into a waiting area full of tired-looking people standing about or sitting in uncomfortable, dilapidated metal chairs. There were a lot of families with kids. In one area, there were vending machines that sold soda pop, cigarettes and candy, and these were doing a brisk business. The woman from the train had told Lesra that they didn't allow you to take anything into the visiting area, so, when he saw a pass-through counter with a sign over it that said "Mail-room," he thought he'd better leave Rubin's mail there. Lesra went over and stood at the end of a line full of women lugging boxes. Mrs Flemmings, with her son's sweet-potato pie, was ahead of him.

When it was Lesra's turn up at the counter, he told the mailroom guard that he wanted to leave a letter and some cards for Mr Carter, number 45472. He placed them on the counter.

"No way!" said the guard, as if Lesra were really trying to pull a fast one. "Next!"

"Say what?"

"Next!"

"B-b-b-but . . . this is Christmas . . . cards . . . mail!" stammered Lesra, checking the sign again to make sure he had read it right.

"Against prison rules. Mail's got to come through the mail. Ya can leave a food package in the mailroom, but everything else's got to come through the U.S. mail. No exceptions. Next!"

Lesra was speechless. He was afraid that he had blown it some-how. But Mrs Flemmings, who had been waiting for him, told him not to worry about it. "Don't pay 'em no never-mind—they give *everybody* a hard time. Besides," she said, hearing a sudden flurry of activity in the adjacent room, "it's time to register." Lesra, puzzled, thought he'd already done that. He followed the woman anyway.

Standing behind a counter in the next room were two guards. One guard called for those people with numbers one to twenty to line up. Lesra didn't know what these numbers referred to, until he remembered the twenty-nine he was given when he first entered the prison and signed in. As each visitor, or group of visitors, approached the counter after their numbers were called, they had to show their identification and again give the name and number of the prisoner they wanted to visit. One guard would check their ID while the second thumbed through a carton of large, dog-eared yellow cards, one for each prisoner. The relevant yellow card was pulled, and if the visitor's ID was okay, a visit by that person was duly noted on the card, along with the date and time. If the visitor did not know the prisoner's number, that would really annoy the guard and lead to a long delay, and if the visitor did not have acceptable identification (what was acceptable was totally arbitrary), he would be summarily turned away, regardless of how much hardship or how many hours it had taken to get there.

Luckily, Lesra's identification passed muster and he knew Rubin's number. Once registered, he had to extend his right hand and the back of it was stamped with invisible ink. All the chairs were full, so he leaned against a wall and waited. And so did Mrs Flemmings. The hubbub was overwhelming.

After about an hour, one of the guards stood up in the centre of the room. "Y'all listen up, now!" he bellowed. Except for the clang and hiss of radiators, the din obediently ceased. "Visits for . . . Dickens, Gadsen, Holmes, Sigler, Leslie, Carter, Carlos . . ." He read the names from a clipboard. "Line up here!"

Lesra lined up with the others. There seemed to be close to a hundred people on this visit: a few whites, a few men, but mostly black women and children. Lesra looked around for the woman on the train. He saw her approach the guard.

"You didn't call my boy's name—Flemmings," she said. "Eric Flemmings. Sixty-five, six, sixty."

The guard checked his list. "Flemmings? Uh-uh. No visit for Flemmings today. He's in lock-up."

Lesra noticed his line had left and scurried to catch up with the rest of the visitors being herded outside. Looking back, he caught a glimpse of Mrs Flemmings, her head down, crying.

Once outside, the visitors had to walk halfway down the same long walk they had entered by, where the two enormous, solid-steel doors were set into the rock walls. There they lined up and waited again, and that final Sunday in December was cold. Eventually a signal was given by a guard on a tower perched on the wall. "Key up!" he shouted, and another guard on the inside opened one of the massive steel doors. As they passed through, one by one, each visitor had his right hand checked for the appropriate stamp by a guard with a portable ultraviolet light.

They then found themselves locked in a courtyard that, although within the prison walls, was still exposed to the elements and separate from the rest of the prison. In one corner were battered, grey metal lockers, where the women, who brought their own locks, locked up their purses.

The rituals were elaborate. Everyone now had to line up—females in one line, males in another—empty their pockets and display the contents in their hands. Then, as each person stepped forward, he or she would be frisked by one guard and scanned by another with a hand-held metal detector. Lesra pulled Rubin's undelivered mail out of his pocket and was promptly told that it was "contraband" and to leave it outside on top of one of the lockers.

Shivering from the cold, the visitors had to stand and wait some more. The guards seemed to be moving through their routines at less than a snail's pace. The minutes ticked away, reducing the length of actual visiting time by a corresponding amount. Eventually, the guards unlocked a steel-grille door as well as the solid metal door that was behind it, and the visitors filed into a small, dark, windowless room, where they were told to leave their coats and hats on a rack; of course, there were too few hangers. Then the visitors were locked in, packed shoulder to shoulder in that small space, the air stifling hot. Lesra, feeling as if he'd been sealed in a tomb, tried not to panic.

A short, heavy, black female guard emerged from the crowd. "Hey, Brenda! How ya doin' today?" several people mumbled. She nodded and, by rote, hollered out a list of rules, only a few of which Lesra could make out: ". . . No weapons! No money! No keys! No candy! One diaper only! Both feet on the floor at all times . . ." She then elbowed her way over to a steel door near the back of the room and banged against it with a ring of keys held in a tightly clenched fist. The echo was tremendous. "Ready on the outside!" she shouted.

A slot in the door, like a peephole, slid open and, after a few more minutes, a male guard hollered back, "Ready on the inside!"

"Okay, move 'em in!" shouted the guard as if on a "Rawhide" cattle roundup, and the door was cracked open just enough to let them file in one at a time. Prisoners waited eagerly on the other side.

Lesra walked through the door and into a corridor lined with benches along one side and a series of cells down the other. Among the prisoners, he saw a tall, muscular, bearded, bald black man. That must be Rubin, he thought—until he saw the man embrace a woman and three small children, and the family disappeared into one of the cells. Then Lesra started walking toward another black man with a goatee, but he too had visitors and settled onto a bench in the corridor. Finally there was no one left standing in the aisle but Lesra and a short, dark-skinned man with a bushy afro, a thick moustache and a great big smile on his face.

"You must be Lesra."

"Mr. Carter? That you? . . . Rubin 'Hurricane' Carter? . . . You got hair! You don't look like the pictures. I thought you'd be bigger!"

"Nope! I'm a little guy, just like you. But don't tell anyone, cause the guy they wanted for the Lafayette murders is supposed to be six-feet tall and light-skinned, and I don't want anyone getting upset thinking they got the wrong man!"

They both laughed and embraced. Rubin put his arm around Lesra and took him into one of the cells, where Rubin's plastic identification tag (with a bald-headed picture) and a pack of Pall Mall filterless cigarettes had reserved two chairs. They sat down, facing each other, knees touching. Rubin was animated and bubbling over with warmth. But Lesra was tense. He didn't know what to think.

"Lesra," said Rubin, looking at him intently, "I am mightily impressed you had the courage to come down here all on your own. Especially since I sent you that less than inviting letter. You're really brave, you know that?"

"I dunno. A lady helped me—came with me from the train. They wouldn't take the mail, and we waited on line for hours. Then those bastards said she couldn't see her son. And then I thought maybe I'd never get in to see you, too, and they made me leave your Christmas cards outside . . ."

"They don't make it easy."

"Yeah," said Lesra, looking around, absorbing the starkness of the environment and the plethora of menacing-looking prisoners and meaner-looking guards. "This is some place!"

"No," said Rubin, closely watching and interpreting Lesra's reactions. "No, it's not. This is no place. Not for human beings. No, don't you ever get used to a place like this!"

"Mr Carter, when they locked us up in that little room, I wished I was someplace else. I was scared, Mr Carter—didn't know what . . ."

"You with me now, and you call me Rubin, or better still, Rube." Rube slapped Lesra on the knee. "Ain't nobody gonna touch you in here—'cept me!" And he burst out laughing as he slapped Lesra on the knee again. Rubin had a wry sense of humour that escaped Lesra at the time, but his energy and charisma made Lesra gradually feel easy.

Rubin asked Lesra about his visit home to Brooklyn and how his parents were doing. Rubin readily understood how they must feel, Lesra's father having once been a star, having had the world in his hands and seen it disappear through his fingers. They talked about what it was like living in Canada.

Just before the visit ended, Rubin called over a prisoner who had been wandering around with a Polaroid camera.

"You like me to take a picture of you and your son, Mr Carter?"

Rubin chuckled and did not correct the picture-taker's assumption. "What do you say, Lez?"

"A picture of you and me together? All right!"

They posed, standing beside each other, both grinning happily, Rubin with his arm around Lesra's shoulder.

As they stood waiting for the photo to develop, a voice bellowed, "Visit up!" Lesra and Rubin had to say a hurried goodbye. Before Lesra knew it, the guards had separated the prisoners from the visitors. Lesra was swept along in the tide of people and hustled back into the coatroom. In the confusion, he didn't get the photo.

Locked again into the coatroom, Lesra and the other visitors had to wait until a count of the prisoners had "cleared." Then the visitors were counted and their hand stamps checked under ultraviolet light before they were allowed out to the open air in the courtyard. There, Lesra retrieved from on top of the lockers Rubin's cards and letter. He'd take them back to Brooklyn, he thought, and post them there. Then he would call the Canadians from the store on the corner. In the spaces between the passing trains, he would tell them about his visit. He would say that he was crazy about Rubin.

When Rubin left the visiting area, he was carrying the colour photo. But, unlike in the photo, he was no longer smiling. A guard told him, along with all the other prisoners from the visit, to strip naked. The guard then ran his fingers through Rubin's hair.

"Open your mouth," ordered the guard, stepping close to Rubin's face and examining the inside of his mouth. "Roll your tongue over," he ordered. "Lift your arms, turn around, lift your feet. Lemme see the soles! . . . Okay, bend over and spread 'em!" Rubin then had to drop his arms, grab his buttocks and bend over while the guard looked up his rectum. This kind of search for contraband was mandatory after every contact visit. That was just one of the reasons Rubin never went on contact visits.

Back in his wing, 2-Left, in his cell, number 194 on the fourth tier, Rubin lay down on his bed. He stared at the picture of himself and Lesra. Lesra had recently turned seventeen. Rubin remembered seventeen. That's how old he'd been when he escaped from the Jamesburg State Home for Boys.

7

Unlike other prisoners at Trenton, who had their names and numbers posted on their cell doors as the rules specified, Rubin, in defiance, had a sign on his. "If your name is: Lola Falana, or Jayne Kennedy, or Sarah Dash," it said, "*You* can *wake* me *up*! But if it's *Not*: Then hit the road, Jack—and don't cha come back no more, no more no more no more! Hit the road, Jack!"

A new young guard, who evidently couldn't read too well, had been assigned to 2-Left. On the morning this guard did his first count, he came upon Rubin lying asleep in his cell with his feet facing toward the bars,* the Polaroid photo from the previous day's visit with Lesra lying on his chest. The guard reached in and tapped Carter on the ankle. With the snap of a sprung mousetrap, the Hurricane was on his feet and face to face with the guard before the rookie knew what was happening. In the commotion, the picture wound up in the toilet.

"You touched me! You put your hands on me!" shouted Rubin. He called the guard every creative epithet he'd heard in his years in

---

*Every old-time prisoner sleeps feet, rather than head, toward the bars; otherwise his head would be vulnerable to anyone passing by. Such a precaution usually means having to sleep head next to the toilet bowl, and a prison toilet bowl has no seat and no lid.

prison and then invented some more. He ended on a menacing note: "In here, motherfucker, if you want to keep breathing, you keep your hands to yourself."

Other prisoners heard the ruckus. Rubin's voice could be heard all over the wing—a rare occurrence—and everyone was alerted that he was unhappy. Everyone knew, "Carter don't play."

"You messed with the Hurricane? Boy, is you crazy?" someone called out.

As the guard backed away from Carter's cell, he was accosted by the prisoner locking next door, who reached out and offered his ankle. At the next cell he encountered another prisoner, and then another one, and it wasn't long before the whole wing of a hundred and ten men had picked up the chant:

"I got something for you to grab, sweetie! Come on over here!"

"Come here, baby! Into my house, honey!"

"You wanna touch sumpin'? I got sumpin' special for ya!"

The rookie was still on the fourth tier, his emotions swinging from surprise to fear and finally to fury. In total frustration, he stopped and screamed back at Rubin: "Well at least I'm not a murderer!"

It was a comment that did not go over well. The men now let loose their worst jailhouse jeers.

A veteran guard had been watching the scene from below. When the young guard, scared witless, finally reached the ground floor (the "flats"), the old-timer, shaking his head in disbelief, looked at him and said simply, "You bothered the Hurricane." And in the way he said it, the "What did you expect?" was understood.

The rookie guard never returned to 2-Left.

It wasn't until the middle of January that Rubin received his well-travelled Christmas mail. It was then he wrote to the "Fightin' Canadians" about Lesra's visit. He explained why he had been reluctant to have Lesra come see him. It was not because he had feared human contact, it was because of where that human contact had been designated to take place by the ever-gracious (if mind-bogglingly sadistic) authorities: in the death house, the very place he had described in *The Sixteenth Round,* the place of horror that housed "that death-dealing, electric monster," the electric chair, where 256 people had been executed, murdered by the State under the colour of law and whose tortured presence could still be felt in the limbo of those confined quarters. Bringing Lesra down there to be subjected to that kind of degradation when every iota of Rubin's energy was focussed on getting up and out of there, just did not seem right.

But it does get lonely, wrote Rubin, and he was glad Lesra had come. Calling Lesra a "handsome rascal," he praised the young man's neat appearance and mannerly demeanour, on which he couldn't help but see the love and care of the Canadians writ large. For Rubin, Lesra was like Hope itself, radiant like the sun, its rays penetrating where the sun don't shine, where the frigid recesses of hopelessness and despair are condemned to remain untouched by light and by warmth. Other than meetings with attorneys, this was the first visit Rubin had had in almost five years. In spite of himself, he was welcoming the warmth that had been kindled in his heart.

At the prison, Lesra had expected to meet the bald-headed, goateed "Hurricane," and, judging from the drawing on their card, Rubin could see that the Canadians expected him to look like that as well. He had hoped to send the Canadians the picture of Lesra and himself as he now looked, but it had been damaged by water. So he was sending along an old picture of himself with Don King, because that was the only picture he had and he wanted to thank them for the Christmas presents, for the sweatsuit, for everything. He signed off with a line from an old popular song, "Open The Door, Richard":

"Open the door . . . because, baby, it's cold out here."

It took Lesra a while to come down from his trip to the States. He had been bombarded with inputs. Meeting Rubin had thrilled him, and the visit had reinforced his enthusiasm for learning. Reading had led him to experiences he would never otherwise have had. He could see that. He had been concerned that his friends in Brooklyn would think him an egghead, call him "Brainiac." But they hadn't. They still thought he was cool.

Back in Toronto, Lesra's plate was full, what with schoolwork, snow-shovelling and adding his thoughts to the letters being sent to Rube. Lesra was now taking correspondence courses through the Ontario Ministry of Education—English, mathematics, world history, chemistry, geography—and he continued to "bust these out," receiving consistently high marks. The ultimate reward came when Sam, his main tutor, told Lesra he was ready to take an English course at night school. It was a major step, a promotion, and Lesra was both excited and scared. He was about to go public, a debut of sorts, reintegrating into the mainstream. He enrolled in grade twelve English at North Toronto Collegiate for one three-hour class every Tuesday night.

Lesra was not too busy, though, to get together some photographs to send to Trenton. Recognizing the importance to a prisoner of being able to feast his eyes on something other than the starkness of a sense-deadening penitentiary environment, Lesra and the group selected some pictures of their garden to send to Rubin. These were evocative, springtime shots: the pagoda overlooking an amphitheatre of rock gardens, Japanese maples, Colorado blue spruce; the oriental-pruned pink-flowering honeysuckles, vibrant-coloured azaleas, French-hybrid lilacs, all in full bloom and offset by neatly-trimmed areas of grass; the meandering pathways and low stone walls softened by cascading perennials. The pictures showed a profusion of colour and texture naturally and artfully intermingled. It was a pity they had no scent, and no people.

Rubin had hinted that he wanted a picture of everybody. Being a camera hog, Lesra was more than eager to oblige. He coaxed the Canadians into sitting for a group shot on the centre hall stairs. Then Gus took a picture of Lesra lounging on the library couch, reading Rubin's book. Lesra loved the way the photograph came out: he imagined Rube looking at him looking at *The Sixteenth Round,* with Rubin's picture on the cover staring right back at him.

The volume of mail between Trenton and Toronto escalated rapidly. Lesra and the Canadians had made contact with an incredible energy force that was being contained (if only barely) behind the walls of Trenton State Prison. Rubin "Hurricane" Carter, for whatever reason, was ready for a change. He had already recently begun to shed his image by allowing his hair to grow. He had been responsive to their letters. Then, despite his valid objections to receiving contact visits under horrifying and repugnant conditions, he had not only accepted Lesra's visit, but also responded to him with great sensitivity. In Rubin's words, he had "tuned in" to Lesra, to the turmoil and fear that he could see washing over him. Rubin told them how he had helped to smooth Lesra out, to relax him, enabling him to become more open and vulnerable.

The Canadians sensed that Rubin was also describing himself, that he himself was smoothing out, opening up, becoming more vulnerable. This was a long way from the polished persona in the picture he had sent them, taken at a dinner in 1976: a gleamingly bald, goateed, bespectacled, tuxedo-with-brown-velvet-lapels-and-matching-bow-tie-wearing "Hurricane" Carter standing in front of a podium, next to the electric-coiffed Don King. "Do you always dress in such a simple, understated manner when you open your mouth to speak?" Lisa teased Rubin.

However much Rubin enjoyed their letters, cards and pictures, he balked at accepting material luxuries. As far as he was concerned, he already had everything he needed in his cell.

"That's too bad," replied the Canadians. "Maybe the prison is not such a bad place after all, if they can give you all you need."

The Canadians, Rubin thought, had a way of saying things that were at first jolting, then irritating. They poked and prodded; they were tenacious; they never let anything go. They were a lot like him. He wasn't sure whether they were very smart or incredibly stupid.

The Canadians offered to send him a TV set but he said he had to refuse. Becoming comfortable in there, he patiently explained to them, was not exactly a top priority. He didn't belong there; it was not his home. He said he never wanted any niceties, any amenities to distract him from fighting for the only thing that really mattered—his freedom.

He prided himself on his ability to withstand anything that the prison authorities could do to him, give to him or take away from him, anything that could possibly make him capitulate to a system that had kept him confined despite his innocence. Over the more than fourteen years he had spent unjustly incarcerated, he had refused to participate in prison programs, to work at prison jobs, to wear prison uniforms, to shave his beard and moustache when beards and moustaches were against prison rules. He had become immune to their threats and their punishments: months in solitary confinement in the "hole" or loss of the customary "good time" deductions from his sentence made no difference to him, did not cause him to change his behaviour. He wouldn't even go to parole board hearings because he knew he would never be granted parole as long as he continued to insist that he was innocent; besides, he was looking for exoneration, not parole.

The Canadians wrote back that they appreciated his unbending moral resolve and his unflagging resistance to the institution—that was what had attracted them to him in the first place. But they had to ask him whether he was so good at doing without, so used to having everything snatched away from him, that he was even better at it than the prison system itself. Was he denying himself material comforts before the authorities had the chance even to threaten to take them away, in a sort of pre-emptive strike? If that was his attitude, then the authorities were in control, they were still calling the shots. The Canadians said that as long as he knew there was nothing that was more important to him than his freedom, then if they threatened to take away a television set, he'd have no trouble relinquishing it.

"You know what you won't do to keep something that isn't important," they wrote. "There is nothing that can make you compromise yourself. Even if you get only one day's pleasure of watching TV and then have it taken away, that's okay. At least you will have allowed yourself the right to enjoy something, been kind to yourself. There's too much harshness and brutality in there without your adding to it. You've been mistreated enough."

In the spirit of warmth and softness, they sent the Hurricane a pair of fluffy, sheepskin slippers and a dark-brown velvet robe, which Michael and Mary designed, cut and sewed themselves. They made the robe with a hood, prizefighter style; they lined it in chocolate-brown silk and edged it in gold thread. Lesra, now almost the same size as Rube, was the model. Against his dark skin, the robe looked rich, draping and shimmering as he made like a boxer and bobbed and weaved. The robe looked magnificent, although it was hard to take Lesra too seriously padding around in those fleecy slippers.

Rubin's letter in response was so full of energy and honest observation that what he was accusing the Canadians of doing—literally overwhelming him—he did to them in this "short note" that ran for several pages and culminated with his acceptance of their offer of a TV. He accused them of tenderizing him, softening him up, with a barrage of letters and gifts and threats of gifts coming at him so fast and furious, he didn't know how to fight it. It embarrassed him to think that maybe the Hurricane was "nothing but a gentle breeze."

Yes, he admitted, he was frightened by what he called "the emotional genocide" that he witnessed daily in the penitentiary. But being frightened, Rubin explained, was an intelligent response to the brutality and inhumanity that surrounded him. You had to be tough not to be affected by it, although it was debatable whether that much toughness really existed. Still, he had tried. His confinement in prison was like "riding on the back of a man-eating monster" where dismounting could cost you your life. That was how he was used to doing time, and it seemed that the Canadians were interfering with that. What if he were to dismount: Where would that leave him?

Yes, being a Taurus, he loved luxury. But he feared it would weaken him in that environment. Nevertheless, he realized he needed to learn to relax, to be flexible and he thanked the Canadians for the opportunity. He told them they were "a *bad* influence" on him, they were letting him "get loose." And that, he decided, might just be a good thing. Perhaps he was now ready to handle it. What did they think?

A thirteen-inch portable colour TV, the maximum size allowed in the penitentiary, was delivered to Mr Mobutu, a seventy-nine-year-old friend of Rubin's, who locked on the same tier. Rubin had told the Canadians to send the TV to Mr Mobutu because it was unlikely that anyone in the mailroom would bother tampering with an old man's stuff.

Rubin had let Mobutu know it was coming and told him he could try it out. When it arrived, Mobutu unplugged his old black-and-white set, put it aside and plugged in the new one. He was glued to the television when Rubin was let out of his cell later and came to get it.

"Okay, Pop, it came, huh?"

"Damn, Rube! Now that's a real TV! Look at them colours! Look how clear it is! They got the right kind, eh Rube? Gits good reception even with all them bars aroun' here!"

It really tickled Rubin to see the old man getting such pleasure. They watched the news together for a while. Then Rubin unobtrusively reached down, picked up Mobutu's "raggedy" black-and-white set and silently left the old man's cell.

8

"I think Holden Caulfield didn't really want to grow up. It was too painful for him."

"What makes you say that—Lesra, is it?"

All eyes in the classroom were upon him as he nodded and stood up beside his desk. He was surprised that everyone seemed to want to know what he thought. They were all listening, waiting, as if he had something important to say. The interest, the vitality of the class, could hardly have been more different from his Brooklyn school experience.

"Well, it's like Holden's dream—like the title of the book—to be *The Catcher in the Rye*. He wants to protect his little sister and all the little kids from falling over the edge, from growing up, that is. They should be able to just play in the field forever."

"But that's impossible," said an older student. "Things change. How can you stop time?"

"Yeah, that's it," Lesra replied. "He wanted to stop time. But he couldn't. Not for his little sister and not for hisself—himself. He was feeling shut out like the ducks on the pond in Central Park when it freezes over in the winter. He didn't know his place any more."

"So, Lesra, you don't see any hope for him?"

"Hope? There's hope 'cause he's talking about it. And if he's talking about it, then maybe he can handle it. He's torn up, that's all—in different directions. He wants to move but he's scared. It's not familiar."

Rubin, too, was starting to talk about what was going on inside him. Although acknowledging feelings, let alone sharing them, was foreign to him, in his letters to Lesra and the Canadians, Rubin slowly opened up. It was difficult at first. Many things weighed heavily on him, and he had been used to bearing the burden himself.

For one, he felt guilty about John Artis, who was sent to prison only because he happened to be with Rubin when the police came down on Rubin. He felt responsible for John, even though there was nothing he could have done to prevent John's getting ensnared. In June of 1966, John was nineteen years old and was planning to go to college on a track-and-field scholarship. Although not a boxing fan, he was familiar with Rubin as a popular sports figure from his hometown of Paterson, New Jersey, and had met him a couple of times before.

On the evening of June 16 they met by chance, and Rubin gave John a lift home. That's why he was in Rubin's car when it was stopped by the police after the incident at the Lafayette Bar. A classic case of being in the wrong place at the wrong time. An innocuous ride home marked the beginning of an inescapable legal nightmare. John had never before been in trouble with the law. Now, fourteen years later, along with Rubin, he was still in prison.

But the police had never been particularly interested in John Artis. It was "Hurricane" Carter they were after, the loudmouth, the troublemaker, the shit-disturber. At any point, John could have saved himself by simply "rolling over" on Rubin, fingering him as the gunman. Indeed, he was under considerable pressure by the police to do so, especially in early December 1975 at the height of the "Free Carter and Artis" campaign, after Bello's and Bradley's recantations and the Bob Dylan song, when public outrage was most intense and the freeing of Carter and Artis appeared unavoidable. One afternoon, John was inexplicably removed from the prison and taken to his family's home in Paterson. While sitting in the living room with his mother, he was promised he would be back home in time for Christmas if he just admitted he was with Carter at the Lafayette Bar at the time of the shooting and that Carter had done it. But John wouldn't and couldn't. No matter what deals were offered—and they were offered repeatedly—he would not veer from the truth.

The truth, however, was no guarantee of justice.

Rubin couldn't say enough about John's strength and extraordinary courage for not caving in to what should have been irresistible pressure. Over the years, Rubin had kept his eye on Artis, making sure that he was safe in a system that devoured young men like him. But, Rubin lamented, it was impossible, in Dylan's words, "to give him back the time he's done." Prison had also stolen John's health. His circulatory system permanently damaged, he had lost portions of his fingers and toes to amputation. All this, Rubin said, because he had asked for a ride home one night.

Rubin's father had died just three weeks before Lesra came to visit. Rubin mentioned this in one of his letters, but only in passing. The Canadians encouraged him to write about it. How powerless he must have felt! And how alone. They asked when he had last seen his father. Had they reached any kind of understanding? Had he ever forgiven his father for not protecting him when he was a child?

Rubin answered their questions at some length and in a characteristically roundabout African way: he wrote in the same way he spoke. You wondered sometimes whether he had missed the point, but like a slow spiral inwards, his answers never failed to hit the target. Yes, he did see his father the day before he succumbed to cancer. His father was no longer able to speak, but he was able to see, and what he saw was his son, handcuffed and shackled and escorted by armed guards into the hospital room. (Rubin's brother had had to pay the state $500 for the privilege.) It was not a happy picture Rubin's father took to the grave with him, and Rubin wondered whether at some deep level he had wanted to hurt his father, to get some payback for his not being able to protect Rubin.

In his letter to the Canadians, Rubin reminisced about his childhood summers picking tobacco, peanuts, and cotton in the fields of Cochran, Georgia, where his family was from. He, his siblings and cousins, would work "from can't-see-in-the-morning until can't-see-at-night" so they could earn some money to buy clothing for school back in Jersey. Every Sunday, a white man, "a cracker," would station his ice cream wagon just outside the church where he knew all the "Pickaninnies" would be, their pockets itching with their week's earnings, and to whom they gladly gave their money. Rubin recalled the time his father caught him standing next to the white man. The father grabbed the son by the scruff of the neck, hauled him off and, despite Rubin's protests of innocence, beat him mercilessly. He was trying to teach the boy a lesson (Stay away from white folks cause they'll hurt you bad!), and instilling the fear of a good whooping was the only way he knew how. But instead of making Rubin hate the white man, the beating made him hate his father: he had done to Rubin what the white man had not done (at least, not yet). It was a long time, Rubin wrote, before he was able to forgive his father, to see that this was his way of being a father and protecting his son as best he could.

A point was soon reached where communicating only by letter was inadequate. The nuances and immediacy so vital to communication were missing on paper. The wait for responses seemed interminable; mail between the countries, even by Special Delivery, just took too long. When the Canadians found out that it was possible for inmates to call out from the prison collect, they gave Rubin their phone number and asked him to call whenever he could.

A couple of weeks later the telephone rang and a long-distance operator asked if they'd accept a collect call from Rubin Carter. The house buzzed with electricity. They had hooked up a system by which everyone was able to listen, though not talk. Rubin's voice sounded tight, higher than they had expected, but as they spoke, it became deep and rich and resonant.

He called several times over the next few weeks. The noise coming from the prison in the background—like the noise from the elevated trains in Brooklyn when Lesra's father called—constantly interrupted their conversations. Their talks were aborted, too, when Rubin would suddenly, and without warning, say "Got to boogie, y'all. Bye for now!" It seemed they were always calling for "counts" in the prison, and for these, prisoners couldn't stay out on the tier or on the flats where the phones were located, but had to be locked in their cells. Thus, even direct communication by telephone was difficult and frustrating.

It would be more satisfying, they figured, if they could speak face to face. Rubin said he realized it was his turn to come up to Canada to visit, since Lesra had already come down to the States to see him, but he was temporarily "inconvenienced" and wondered whether perhaps they could meet "somewhere in New Jersey."

Lesra was ecstatic about the idea, and so were the rest of the group. But contact visits were limited to a maximum of four people. Being an experienced guide, Lesra of course had to go; the other three, it was decided, would be Lisa, Terry and Sam.

It was late February 1981 when the four flew down to Philadelphia, rented a car and drove the forty minutes northeast to Trenton.

"There it is!" shouted Lesra when they turned a corner. Just beyond the railroad tracks up ahead was Trenton State Prison. Situated smack in the middle of a working-class, aluminum-sided, residential neighbourhood, it looked as though it had materialized in the wrong century through some time-warp. Studded with guard towers, it looked more like a medieval fortress than a "house of correction." Soot-encrusted stone walls, three-feet thick and twenty-feet high, barricaded an area equal to several city blocks. Nail-making had been the chief productive industry on that site in the years leading up to the War of 1812. It was, in all respects, a hard and hideous anachronism.

Sam parked the car on the street in front of a tiny house with a chain-link fence, a barking dog and a Negro jockey lawn ornament. They were silent as they crossed the street and walked down the length of the prison wall, under the guard towers, past the great steel doors. Lisa gagged, then almost threw up. They all felt physically ill.

They walked up the set of metal steps, and Lesra pressed the buzzer. He continued to shepherd the Canadians through the rest of the procedure: the registering, the hand-stamping, the lining-up; the going back outside and down the walkway to the steel doors, the lining-up; the checking of hand-stamps, the inner courtyard, the lining-up; the emptying of pockets, the frisking, the metal detectors, the locking-in.

The execution chamber, where they left their coats, was the ultimate horror. Lesra's terror at being locked in that tiny airless room now gripped Lisa, Terry and Sam too. They couldn't even talk about it. The marks on the floor where the electric-chair used to be bolted made them cringe. And worse, they could still sense the 256 human beings that Rubin wrote about, the ones who had met their untimely deaths there. They thought about Richard Hauptmann, the man wrongfully convicted for the Lindbergh baby kidnapping and murder. He was executed in that very place forty-five years earlier. They were about to visit another innocent man, someone who had only narrowly escaped the electric-chair himself. The atrocities, the outrage, the phenomenal injustice—nothing had changed.

"Lesra, didn't I tell you not to be getting used to this place?" Rubin hugged Lesra heartily and then Terry, Sam and Lisa. "I'm so glad you could come," said their perfect host, a big smile masking his reticence.

They had expected to meet a giant, and they did, but as Lesra had forewarned them, he did not look like one. In fact he looked almost fragile. The contrast between this little guy and the man with the awesome reputation was striking. He was thin, weighing no more than 135 pounds (his fighting weight was 156), and his hands, though large, moved with delicacy.

"You look more like a writer than a prizefighter," said Lisa, holding both his hands. "These hands wield pens, not boxing gloves."

"Girl, you got to be crazy," said Rubin, embarrassed. "You really think so?"

"You're blushing!" said Terry.

"Aw, go on! You know us coloured folks don't blush!"

"Yeah," said Sam, "we used to think so, until Lesra blew your cover."

"Why you rascal," said Rubin, grabbing Lesra around the shoulders, "you're always up to no good." Lesra lit up "like a bub." He was proud to have brought everyone together.

They sat down, chairs in a circle in a cell that Rubin had reserved for them with his photo-identification tag. Rubin made sure his back was to the wall, so that he faced out to the corridor and could see what was going on.

Rubin was wearing a black, long-sleeved shirt, buttoned to the neck, and a pair of blue jeans that were impeccably clean and well-pressed ("sharper than a mosquiter's peter," as Rube was wont to say). He carried himself with unmistakable dignity and class. But his shirt was so old that the material had frayed at the cuffs and become shiny from years of use. The age of his leather boots, while polished to the nth-degree, also could not be concealed. And this was the man who used to wear shark-skin suits and drive Cadillacs.

In contrast to Lesra's first visit, Rubin was now the one with the cautious reserve. And he was the one whose knee was playfully slapped. His visitors didn't treat him like a celebrity, and they teased him unmercifully about being a "tough guy." It was a clever ruse, they told him, but they didn't believe it for a second.

What surprised Rubin most about the Canadians, he told them later, was their lack of fear of the Hurricane. Everybody had always been afraid of him, he said. "Should we be?" Terry asked him, rhetorically. "Are you?" added Lisa.

Unlike most prisoners, who are careful to avoid lengthy eye-contact so that they don't offend anyone, Rubin would deliberately prolong eye-contact so that everyone, guards and prisoners alike, would know "not to fuck with him." His "baleful stare" had become famous in his boxing days.

At the visit, the Canadians noticed something about Rubin's eyes. They looked slightly different from each other. Rubin told them why. His right eye, he said, saw inwardly, while his left eye looked out. Not long after he had been railroaded into prison in the sixties, he started having trouble with his right eye. He was told by the prison doctor that the retina in that eye was in danger of becoming detached, and he needed an operation to save it. The authorities refused to let him get treatment in a hospital outside the prison, even though a specialist had offered to perform the operation free of charge. Rubin had no choice but to let a prison doctor do the operation in the penitentiary. The stitches weren't removed as they should have been, and his eye became infected. Then the administration withheld the medication he needed (a not-uncommon prison occurrence). He went blind in that eye shortly afterwards.

More devastating than the blindness itself was its repercussions. Rubin had to bury his dreams. He knew that even if his name were cleared and he was released, the loss of his eye meant the loss forever of his professional boxing career. He could never be champion of the world. By law, boxers are forbidden to fight without full vision. But that was all academic anyway—ancient history. He was too old now and there were steel bars still barring him from the ring.

Before they knew it, a guard hollered, "Visit up!" Reluctantly, the five of them got up and walked slowly toward the death-chamber door. Prisoners were congregated there, saying goodbye to their loved ones.

There was an excitement in the air when Rubin approached the door. The prisoners who recognized him under his new growth of hair were happy to see him, after they got over their initial shock at finding him in the visiting area in the first place; *everyone* knew that the Hurricane never took visits.

For Lesra and the Canadians, saying goodbye to Rubin, knowing he had no more reason to be locked up than they did, was heart-wrenching. As they were leaving, they looked back. The prisoners had formed a kind of reception line, and Rubin was walking down it, shaking everyone's hand. "Hey, brother!" they heard him say.

"Mr Carter, we ain't seen you in years, Mr Carter!"

"Rube, I told that dummy you was in here that other time. He said, 'That ain't him!' "

"Was that your son, Mr Carter? A 'splittin' ' image!"

"Hurricane, man, good to see you, man! You makin' a comeback?"

When the four returned to Canada, Rubin was very much on their minds. They worried about him—and with good reason. After their trip to Trenton, Rubin didn't call for days. When he finally did, he told them that he hadn't been able to get to a phone until then: the prison had been shut down because three prisoners had been stabbed, one to death, in the mess hall. Whenever violence erupted, which was often, the administration called a state of emergency, a "lock-down," and everything stopped, including phone calls, until the administration decided that the tension had subsided.

Aside from the physical constraints, there was another reason Rubin hadn't called. Contact with Lesra and the Canadians reminded him that he could feel, a realization that he seemed to fear as much as welcome. He didn't particularly relish remembering how good it was to feel. He had been doing all right on his own.

Rubin realized he was resenting the overtures of the Canadians, their intrusion into his life. He was resisting opening up. At least, though, his reticence was a phenomenon he was willing to examine and discuss. He could see that it was based on mechanical patterns and old fears, harkening back to his time in Jamesburg when he first became hardened and had closed off a part of himself from the brutal realities of life behind bars. Having feelings made him vulnerable. It meant acknowledging and living with not only his own pain but the pain of others. If he didn't feel something, then it didn't exist; and if it didn't exist, then he could keep on keepin' on. And the Canadians couldn't argue with that. This mechanism had obviously enabled him to survive in prison where the stakes are so high that being vulnerable or soft could mean losing your life. But it was survival at what cost?

Rubin reminded the Canadians that being in prison was like "riding on the back of a man-eating monster," that he "dared not dismount." But, they asked, if he continued to deny his feelings, ("frailties," he called them) so that he could survive, then wasn't this monster relentlessly carrying him to where *it* wanted to go, and on *its* terms? While mounted, wasn't he still a prisoner? Perhaps in dismounting lay the possibility of freedom.

And there were more phone calls in which they talked about being responsive and fluid, not rigid; about being open, not closed. They talked about discarding old patterns that had outlived their usefulness. These were not new concepts for Rubin. But was it possible, or even desirable, to actualize such philosophically attractive principles in a penitentiary? Could this man-eating monster be safely dismounted?

The Canadians were aware of the danger they were asking Rubin to expose himself to, and they questioned the wisdom of disturbing his mode of survival. What right did a group of outsiders have to second-guess one of the most powerful and experienced men in the prison system? Rubin was the one who had everything to lose. But with his courage as a guide, together they forged ahead. The old rules were no longer satisfactory. They had no choice but to examine new possibilities.

This dialogue continued through many letters, phone calls and another personal visit to the penitentiary. It culminated in a poignant letter from Rubin to the Canadians shortly after their return home. Dated "Forever" and addressed to his "Dear Beautiful Friends," it was the most moving and heartfelt missive they had ever received. Rube lovingly related the new buoyancy he was feeling as a result of their presence. They had come down "like a Hurricane" and left him reeling with a miraculous sense of rebirth, of being born again into the flow of life, of being able to walk on equal footing with all that is Good and True. Their persistence in hammering away at his resistance had enabled him to realize that the many defences he had constructed were limiting, no longer necessary and could now, finally, be let go. He could not thank them enough for this epiphany, for this gift, for their love. He feared it might all be a dream and had to remind himself that it wasn't. Most incredible for him was the realization that, for once in his life, he trusted somebody, trusted somebody absolutely and unconditionally: he trusted them!

9

Rubin's forty-fourth birthday was coming up, and along with over-sized greeting cards containing funny messages, Lesra and the Canadians sent him some clothes they'd noticed he needed. As far as they were concerned, the Hurricane deserved only the best. They pored over colours, fabrics and styles to get just the right thing, even though what was allowed in the prison was very limited. They paid attention not only to selecting the gifts and making sure they would fit, but also to wrapping them in elegant paper with lush ribbons and fancy bows to inundate Rubin's deprived senses. Until the prison authorities invented a rule against it, the wrapping managed to get through the mailroom (albeit crumpled) and into Rubin's appreciative hands. He saved and savoured everything.

They asked Rubin whether his friend Thom Kidrin* was still sending him the twenty-five-pound box of food every month, as they had read in the papers. Yes, the food was still coming, he told them. They remarked that that wasn't much to keep a man going a whole

---

*Rubin spoke glowingly about Thom, a dependable, decent human being, whose heart was in the right place. He was Executive Director of the International Committee Against Injustice and had worked tirelessly on Rubin's behalf.

month. Rubin said that was all anyone was allowed to get. Besides, other prisoners, like Mr Mobutu, would sometimes help supplement his diet.

Mr Mobutu, who used to be a chef in the merchant marine, loved to cook. Although he himself received no food packages from the outside, he worked in the officers' mess and occasionally managed to sneak back to his cell the odd egg and onion, and sometimes bacon. Using an electric coil called a "stinger," Mobutu would whip up tantalizing dishes that he shared with his young friend, Rubin.

After the Canadians found out what foods were allowed, what containers were allowed and what (allowed) foods Rubin particularly liked, Mr Mobutu began receiving monthly deliveries from United Parcel Service. "Look, Rube!" he would say. "Salmon, tuna, nuts, chocolate cake. Now we can really 'greaze' [eat]. I'm gonna put some meat on your bones yet!"

The Canadians knew that Rubin's lawyers had launched an appeal of his 1976 conviction, and were eager to know how it was progressing. Time and again they questioned Rubin, but he didn't like to talk about it. The case was so rotten and the legalities so convoluted that he didn't want to waste precious phone calls or visits getting into complicated explanations.

"Well," the Canadians would ask, trying to bottom-line it, "surely you're going to be freed by the courts? It must be just a matter of time—how soon would that be?"

Rubin answered, "I've been screwed by the courts so many times, how can I possibly expect justice or fairness from them?"

Yet they sensed that he did. But he wouldn't even attempt to pinpoint a possible release date. That was *not* how you did time in prison, he'd tell them.

"You take it day by day. You can't think in normal terms of time. It's what—March now? That makes six months since the New Jersey Supreme Court heard oral arguments in our appeal. And they haven't reached a decision yet."

"What exactly are 'oral arguments'?" asked Terry.

Rubin sighed. He could see there was no way around starting from square one.

"When you appeal a conviction to a higher court—an appellate court—you first file written submissions, 'briefs,' explaining why your conviction was unfair and illegal. The State, which usually means the county prosecutor . . ."

"That'd be like a Crown attorney up here."

"Yeah, that's right—Canada follows the British system. Once the briefs from both sides are filed, the appellate court usually calls for the two sides to present their arguments in person, giving the judges the opportunity to ask them questions. So that's what's meant by 'oral arguments.' After that, the court considers what to do—in legalese 'takes the matter under advisement'—and some time later comes down with a decision."

"So how did the orals go?"

In answer, Rubin sent the Canadians a September 1980 article from a local newspaper, *The Trenton Times,* which described what had happened at that State Supreme Court hearing. Under a large, bold headline, "Wilentz hits race motive in Carter case," ran the following:

> New Jersey Chief Justice Robert Wilentz yesterday accused the attorneys who prosecuted former boxer Rubin "Hurricane" Carter and John Artis of assuming that all blacks think and act alike.
>
> "Isn't there something about that idea that is revolting?" Wilentz asked Passaic County Assistant Prosecutor John Goceljak during a hearing before the Supreme Court.
>
> Carter and Artis [are seeking] to overturn their convictions for the supposedly racially motivated murders of three whites in a Paterson bar in 1966.
>
> Wilentz asked Goceljak what he thought the motive for the killings was.
>
> Goceljak replied that there was racial unrest in Paterson and that on the night of the shooting a white man had killed a black man at the Waltz Inn (a local bar).
>
> Wilentz asked what that had to do with the defendants.
>
> Goceljak replied that Carter and Artis were members of the black community.
>
> Wilentz pressed on, getting Goceljak to admit that there

was no evidence that the two defendants had any malice towards whites.

Wilentz said he found "invidious and intolerable" that prosecutors had thought it fair to assume that Carter and Artis would have been angry enough to kill simply because they are black.

This rationale for the conviction of the two men was a theme to which Supreme Court justices returned repeatedly in five hours of questioning prosecutors and defense attorneys yesterday. The questioning by other justices generally paralleled Wilentz's approach. . . .

"We read the article," Sam said when he, Lisa and Terry were on the phone to Rubin about a week later. "At least somebody's thinking straight—that's promising. Wasn't it the New Jersey Supreme Court, Rube, that threw out your first trial conviction in 1976?"

"Yeah, that's true," he enthused. His tone then changed abruptly. "On the other hand, I can't help wondering whether that wasn't just a set-up for a second trial and a bigger fall. I mean, why didn't they declare Bello an incompetent witness? They knew he was a habitual liar—a perjuror. He kept changing his sworn testimony. And they knew his original testimony had been paid for by the prosecution—he admitted it. The Supreme Court should have ended it then and there. They should have declared him unfit, but they didn't. Without that punk, the case would have died."

"Well, Rube, maybe it will die now. The Supreme Court seems to have cut through to the heart of the issue, the racism. Wilentz's questions . . ."

"Robert Wilentz," interrupted Lisa, "the Chief Justice—is he any relation to David Wilentz, the prosecutor who it's been said engineered Richard Hauptmann's conviction in the Lindbergh case?"

"Aha! Now you're getting the hang of Jersey Justice! That's his daddy."

"Oh, no!"

"But," pointed out Rubin, "we gotta remember that the son is the one who called the prosecutor on that racial revenge bullshit at orals. So there's hope."

"I'm beginning to see why you're ambivalent about your chances, Rube," said Terry. "It's like being a yo-yo—up with hope one minute and down with despair the next."

"Now," exclaimed Rubin, "you're getting the hang of serving time."

Rubin told them he'd just received some mixed news from the Supreme Court. Before the Court could render its final decision on the appeal, it needed more information about one of the issues and had ordered an "evidentiary" or "fact-finding" hearing to take place in the trial court. Once again, the testimony of Alfred Bello, the supposed eyewitness, was going to be the subject.

Prior to the retrial in 1976, before deciding whether or not to proceed with Bello as a witness, the prosecutors had given Bello a lie-detector test. They wanted to see whether his 1967 trial story was true. The prosecution later informed the defence and the judge that they were putting Bello on the stand again to repeat his first trial story because he had passed the lie-detector test. After the retrial, the defence discovered that Bello had actually failed the test, and the prosecutors had known it all along. Now, in the spring of 1981, the Supreme Court wanted a fuller record of the circumstances surrounding these events. That was the good news.

The bad news was that Bruno Leopizzi, the Passaic County judge who had presided over Carter's retrial and who had demonstrated over and over again his pro-prosecution bias in the case, was going to conduct the hearing, to be the "fact-finder." Rubin's lawyers filed a motion (for the umpteenth time) to have the judge disqualified. Incredibly, it was up to judge Leopizzi himself to decide whether or not he was biased and should be removed and, in his opinion, he wasn't and shouldn't.

The hearing, beginning on Monday May 18, 1981, was to be held where the trial had taken place, in the Passaic County Courthouse in Paterson. Rubin was to be transported and housed in the county jail so that he could attend. Monday arrived, and Rubin called Toronto late in the afternoon.

"How's it feel to be back in Paterson?" Terry queried.

"Who's in Paterson? I've been shaved, dressed and ready to go since the crack of dawn, and nothing's happened. I'm still in Trenton!"

"What do you think's going on?"

"I can't tell yet. Could just be typical prison bumbling, or maybe it's something else. Why don't you call Thom? He was supposed to be at the hearing today. He'll be able to fill you in on what's happened. There's a count. I got to get off the phone."

Terry called, and Thom was very excited. "It was a shame Rubin wasn't in court," he said. Rubin's lawyer had asked Judge Leopizzi why his client wasn't there, when his presence had been assured. Leopizzi said he couldn't understand it; he had filled out the necessary writ in plenty of time to have Carter transferred. The hearing started without him. (John Artis wasn't present because he was in the hospital.)

Thom told Terry that Bello was the first witness to take the stand. Terry wondered whether the reason Rubin hadn't been brought to court that day was that the prosecution was protecting Bello from having to come face to face with the man he had framed.

"Probably so," Thom replied, " 'cause Bello looked up anxiously every time someone came into the courtroom. But you gotta hear what he said. Rubin won't believe it."

"I gather it won't be the first time," said Terry.

"Bello said he was *in the bar* when the shootings took place—not out on the street! Can you believe it? In the bar! He's going with the in-the-bar story!" That didn't mean much to the Canadians at the time, but it was clear Thom thought it was great news for Rubin.

On Rubin's next call, Terry and Sam passed this information on. Like Thom, Rubin was excited to hear Bello was switching stories again.

"Serves those motherfuckers right! They should have read the warning tattooed on his arm: 'Born to Raise Hell!' "

"After all that's been said and done," asked Terry, "how can anyone believe *anything* that Bello has to say?"

"Beats me. But let me tell you what this is all about. If it seems muddled, that's just 'cause we're dealing with Bello.

"On the night the crime occurred, Bello did not identify anyone. Like all the witnesses, he said he saw two coloured males, both five-foot eleven, both slight build. But he had a different story at the trial in 1967. He told the jury that on the night of June 17 he had been acting as a lookout—'playing chickie,' he called it—for his buddy,

Bradley, who was breaking into a factory near the Lafayette Bar. After a while, Bello said he started walking down Lafayette Street towards the bar . . ."

"Yeah, we read about it in your book. He was going to buy some cigarettes! Right in the middle of a B and E—left his post, left his partner—he's gonna go into a bar so he can be seen and recognized as being in the vicinity when a robbery that he's involved in takes place? That doesn't make any sense!"

"I never believed that shit about the B and E!" said Rubin. "But Bello needed an explanation for being at the bar that night. And it's strange—at trial, because he was confessing to a crime, it made his whole story, including his identification of John and me, believable to the jury. Because testifying meant incriminating himself, the jury figured he must be telling the truth about everything."

"Yeah, I remember Bello's story," said Sam. "He's supposedly walking up the street to the bar, hears loud noises coming from the bar, thinks it's a band playing. He continues to walk toward the bar, hears what he then knows are gunshots. Just outside the bar, he comes face to face with two gunmen, one tall, the other short and stocky . . ."

"Right," continued Rubin, "coming around the corner, swinging their guns and laughing. He said he got a good look at them and claimed they were John and me. Now check this picture out. John and I are supposed to have seen him and we have guns. We're supposed to have just shot everyone in the bar but we don't shoot Bello—a witness. We chase him, he says, and we can't catch him. Bello is this short, fat punk, he's overweight, he's been drinking, he's wearing high-heeled platform shoes. Now John's a track star and I'm a boxer whose strong suit is running. We can't catch him and we don't shoot him. PLEASE!! Then he says we get in a car and, as we pull away, he sees distinctive 'butterfly' tail-lights light up across the back. That's his *on-the-street* story.

"In 1974, Bello recants this testimony—first to investigator Fred Hogan, then to *New York Times* reporter Selwyn Raab and then under oath to the first trial judge. He stated that he had not seen John and me on the night of the crime and that the police had invented the story he told at trial. During the next two years, he came forward with a number of different versions. These had a common nucleus: Bello himself was present *in the bar* before and at the time of the shooting, and he didn't see us in the bar. He said that a black woman entered the bar and bought a bottle from the bartender shortly before the shooting. Then when the shooting went down, Bello used Hazel Tanis, one of the victims, as a shield, thus avoiding getting shot himself."

"Mighty, dare I say, white of him—a sterling character," commented Sam.

"But in 1976, on the eve of the second trial, Bello reverted to his first trial version of events," continued Rubin.

"Convenient, wasn't it?" Terry remarked.

"Oh, they had an explanation for it. The prosecutors explained to the judge and the defence that the reason Bello was switching back to his on-the-street testimony was because they had given him a lie-detector test which 'proved' that version was the truth. They had the polygrapher's report. But the prosecutors knew that the polygrapher had actually concluded that Bello's on-the-street trial testimony was a lie and that his in-the-bar story was the truth."

"That's incredible! How did you find that out?"

"My lawyer, Myron Beldock—it was a flash of intuition. After the trial, Myron just felt there was something wrong with that lie-detector test, something he couldn't put his finger on. After restudying the documents provided by the prosecution, he picked up the phone and called the polygrapher himself. Beldock almost fell off his chair when the polygrapher told him that he had found Bello's in-the-bar story to have been true. Beldock asked him why his written report said that Bello's testimony at the 1967 trial was true. And the polygrapher answered: 'Because in 1967 Bello testified to the in-the-bar story.' And Beldock said, 'No, he didn't. You got it backwards. His testimony in 1967 was that he was on the street.'

"That's what this hearing is about. The prosecution is in the hot-seat now, and they're going to have to work hard to cover their asses."

The Canadians could see why Rubin had been reluctant to get into the specifics of his case. Their eyes glazed over at the welter of confusing details, but they could smell the stink "loud and clear."

Rubin was transported to Paterson the next day. But if the prosecution had hoped to keep Rubin away from Bello, they had mistimed the moment: Rubin was brought into the courtroom before Bello had finished testifying. Hearing the courtroom door open, then the sound of shackles and chains, Bello kept his eyes trained on the floor in front of him. Not that he would have recognized Rubin had he glanced up; Rubin looked completely different from the last time the two had met at trial five years before. No one recognized Carter at first, not even his lawyers.

Rubin was led to the defence table where the three lawyers embraced him warmly. Myron Beldock, the head of the team, had represented Rubin since 1974, the time of Bello's recantation. Initially, Beldock had refused to get involved in Rubin's case. When he was first approached, he had just finished representing George Whitmore, another black man who had been wrongfully imprisoned.* It had taken five years to clear Whitmore's name, and Beldock was emotionally and physically exhausted. It was only after visiting Rubin in Trenton and being overwhelmed by his powerful personality, intellect and knowledge of his case that Beldock agreed to join the struggle to free him. Beldock figured Carter's conviction was so legally and factually flawed that Rubin would be free within the year. Now, seven years and another trial later, Rubin was still in prison, but Beldock's commitment held fast.

Next to Beldock sat Professor Leon Friedman, a distinguished academic at Hofstra University Law School and co-author of a five-volume definitive history of the justices of the United States Supreme Court. An expert on federal and constitutional law, Professor Friedman, since 1978, had been guiding the Carter-Artis appeal. "The Carter case," he would say, "stands with Sacco and Vanzetti, the Scottsboro Boys case and the Tom Mooney case as one of the most significant cases of American injustice in this century, except that it did not happen in the remote past or in the remote South, but in New Jersey in our own time."

The professor found the machinations of the state court system hard to believe. On the first day of this latest hearing, for example,

---

*Whitmore, having been falsely accused of three sensational New York City rape-murders, was convicted of an attempted rape. An investigation by Beldock and reporter Selwyn Raab resulted in Whitmore's total exoneration and became the basis for the pilot to the popular television series *Kojak*.

Friedman had had to smile when Judge Leopizzi had expressed concern and sympathy for Bello. "I just don't want to impose on Mr Bello any more," the judge had said, as if Bello were the victim and not the author of this absurd miscarriage of justice. Professor Friedman was then castigated by the judge for smiling in the courtroom, for conducting himself "as a clown" rather than a professional.

Next to Friedman sat Lewis Steel, the tough-talking, ardent advocate for John Artis since 1974. Judge Leopizzi found him, of all the defence lawyers, the most trying and abrasive. At the 1976 trial, Steel, ever quick on his feet, had accused the judge of "turning the trial into a racial nightmare" by permitting the prosecution to submit its racial revenge motive theory to the jury without factual basis. Leopizzi, characterizing Steel's remarks as "idiotic," slapped Steel with contempt of court charges. Neither did Beldock escape the judge's scorn; Leopizzi at this hearing was to call him "an absolute liar."

Beldock, Steel and Friedman, all prominent New York attorneys, had dedicated themselves to working on the Carter-Artis case *pro bono*, without a fee. Thousands of unbilled hours later, they were still at it.

The lawyers quickly briefed Rubin on what he'd missed the day before. Bello's testimony had been revealing: "I remember there was an in-the-bar and out-of-the-bar, and I have told . . . a few different things," he had said. He admitted, upon questioning by Beldock, that he had difficulty with his memory. "I had a serious drinking problem. . . . I don't have . . . remember vaguely anything about this case or what transpired in different court appearances. I've been in many of them. It expanded [sic] a period of sixteen years, and it's very hard for me to recall." But he did remember how he'd "co-operated" with the prosecution: "And someone asks you to do this and someone asks you to do that. That's exactly what it boiled down to. And I did what different individuals asked me to."

Under Steel's questioning, Bello had said that his best recollection was that he had given the in-the-bar story at the second trial. Bello had got it wrong again. Here Judge Leopizzi had intervened and asked Bello to step out of the courtroom. The judge conferred with the lawyers. Leopizzi suggested that Bello be given the opportunity to refresh his memory about what he had said at the trial. Reviewing the transcripts overnight would enable Bello to distinguish the on-the-street story he'd given at both trials from the in-the-bar story of his re-cantation period (1974-76). Beldock and Steel strenuously objected, arguing that Bello's memory was hopeless and "unrefreshable as a matter of law." Even Bello, when he came back into the courtroom, was hardly more optimistic, doubting whether reading the documents would enable him to remember anything more than what he could momentarily retain from reading the documents. At this point, Judge Leopizzi asked Bello: "Did you ever see or witness the actual shoot-ing?" Bello answered: "I'm not sure. I don't know. I can't recollect." Protestations notwithstanding, the judge had insisted that Bello read the transcripts.

So now Bello was back in court for a second day. Rubin watched and listened carefully. As was his habit during the innumerable trials and hearings in his case, he took extensive notes, recording pertinent testimony and observations on yellow legal pads.

Rubin was now able to hear Bello's "refreshed" answers in per-son. These alternated between "may have" and "don't recall." Bello couldn't remember what he had read the night before. He managed to outdo himself, nevertheless, and swore that both versions under dis-cussion—never mind that they were mutually exclusive—were "true." It was obvious to everyone that Bello's testimony, the centrepiece of the State's case, was utterly useless.

Rubin sat listening, finding it hard to be angry with someone so pitiful. He would have been amused were he not the one paying the price for Bello's nonsense. Even the prosecutors were relieved when Bello finally left the stand.

The next witness was Leonard Harrelson, the polygrapher hired by the prosecution to test Bello prior to the 1976 retrial. Harrelson tes-tified that the Passaic County prosecutor had told him in the summer of 1976 that, because of all the adverse publicity about the Carter case, the prosecution was under tremendous pressure not to continue with a second trial. They wanted to test Bello to settle the question of where he was at the time of the shooting; without him, they had a weak case. "In conducting your investigation," the prosecutor had in-structed the polygrapher, "please bear in mind, as I know you will, that this office has absolutely no interest or bias in the outcome of these tests or this case other than to see that the truth is revealed, justice is done and the chips fall where they may."

Immediately after testing Bello, Harrelson conferred with Vincent DeSimone, the (acting) Chief of County Detectives, who had been the officer in charge of the original Lafayette Bar murder investigation and who continued to play a key role in the case. Harrelson told Chief DeSimone his unequivocal conclusion: Bello was *inside* the bar before and at the time of the shooting. Bello couldn't have been in the bar, insisted DeSimone. If he were, he could not have made the identification of Carter and Artis that was the crux of his testimony at the first trial and which they desperately needed "confirmed" in order to proceed with the second trial. Aware that his case had just collapsed, the Chief of Detectives was adamant that the polygrapher's conclusion was impossible. But Harrelson stuck to his guns. Nothing would make him change his mind, he said. His opinion was not tentative and would not alter upon further review; it was what the graphs showed.

So, Harrelson was now asked, why did he submit a written report that said just the opposite? What made him state in writing that it was his opinion that Bello's "testimony at the [1967] trial was true" when that testimony was the on-the-street story? Harrelson explained that this apparent about-face was unintentional. He claimed he had mistakenly "assumed" Bello's trial testimony was the in-the-bar story.

The hearing revealed that Harrelson had operated under other erroneous assumptions. At the time he tested Bello, Harrelson was told that Carter and Artis had failed lie-detector tests on the night of the Lafayette shooting.

"I remember discussing about them taking a test," recalled Harrelson, under Steel's questioning. "I believe that probably originated when I pointed out, tried to point out how simple the whole thing would be—just let me test Carter."

"Were you told anything about a black polygrapher?"

"I was told that—I was told that—again, I don't recall who told me. I was told that Carter would not take a test from me and the person telling me quoted Carter as saying that was because my skin was white. I was told that they [Carter and Artis] took a test and they—I was told that the person that conducted the test on them in 1966 was black."

"Who told you all that?"

"Someone in the prosecutor's office."

"Well, do you have any idea for what purpose they told you all that information?"

"I don't know why they told me."

"And you don't know who it was that told you. . . . Could it have been DeSimone?"

"It could have been."

Rubin was dumbfounded when he first heard this in court, and he was dumbfounded again when he read his notes later over the phone to the Canadians. He had never refused to be tested by Harrelson. The fact was (as even DeSimone had testified at the original grand jury) Carter and Artis had *passed* their polygraph tests in 1966, and the polygrapher was *white*.*

Nevertheless, the prosecution was successful with these few well-placed lies. At the hearing that day, Harrelson bristled at being grilled by Steel and Beldock and at the implication that he had colluded with the prosecution in any way. Harrelson was "convinced" that the defendants were guilty, and Judge Leopizzi permitted him to freely express for the record his belief that "Carter and Artis were the perpetrators of the annihilation."

Rubin's attorneys leapt to their feet and vociferously objected to this outrage. The polygrapher, they argued, had no licence to pronounce on objective truths. As a polygrapher, the most Harrelson was qualified to say was whether or not Bello was intentionally lying. Besides, prosecutorial misconduct was the issue. The point was that the prosecutors had used what they knew were erroneous test results to get Bello to switch his story from the in-the-bar to the on-the-street version that they needed for the second trial, and then hid the matter from the defence.

---

*When Harrelson had asked the prosecutors in the summer of 1976 to let him examine the original charts of that test, he was told they were "unavailable" because there was "some water in the basement" and they had got wet. But Harrelson testified that when he looked at the manilla folders that the allegedly missing charts had been stored in, he saw no signs of the folders having been wet.

On his yellow pad, Rubin, noting that he was the only African present in the court room, remarked at how painful it was having to listen to everyone try "to protect this thing," having to watch "this poisonous system" infect everyone it touched.

The conditions in the county jail in Paterson were much looser than what Rubin had been accustomed to at Trenton State Prison. The access to phones was virtually unlimited, whereas in the penitentiary prisoners were allowed only ten minutes and the phone lines were cut off, unfinished sentences and all, by a central switchboard at 9:30 every night. In Paterson, Rubin and the Canadians stayed on the phone until close to midnight; their calls lasted for four or five uninterrupted hours.

This extended time together was invaluable. It gave them a chance to talk about how Rubin felt being in that courtroom, handcuffed, defenceless, being repeatedly vilified as a murderer, all the while knowing he was innocent. The Canadians said they wouldn't be able to take it. They'd find the degradation appalling. Their point of view surprised Rube and enabled him to re-examine his experiences with fresh eyes. The situation in court was something that he was almost inured to. It was so familiar.

He *had* to be there, he said, it was his "responsibility." He had to know what was going on, so that he could continue his fight. But did he? they asked. Maybe being responsible meant something different. Maybe it meant that he didn't have to sit there and have abuse heaped upon him yet one more time. Maybe there was another way that he could protect himself. Was this an old groove, dug deeper each time it was replayed—the line of least resistance? Wasn't this tantamount to staying on the back of the man-eating monster? Was there some other way to handle the situation, something not quite so personally brutal? In the spirit of being kind to himself, was it possible to avoid this abuse?

Rubin thought that for him not to be there at the hearing would be equivalent to running away. Yes, they agreed, it would be running away—from degradation and humiliation. Being repeatedly called a murderer, regardless of the falseness of the accusation, has its effect, takes its toll; having to listen to it over and over again is debilitating, self-negating. Couldn't he, they asked, find out exactly what happened at the hearing by reading the transcripts of the proceedings? Did he really need to hear the denigration of his character in person?

Rubin said he'd have to think about it, and then think about it some more. It was certainly a different perspective.

Everything in Rubin's life was not only being re-examined, it was being turned upside-down. When he was placed in the "bullpen" with other prisoners at the county jail, nobody noticed him. No one knew who he was. Ordinarily, conversation would cease when the fearsome Rubin "Hurricane" Carter appeared. Everyone would feel self-conscious. No one would even attempt to compete with the man whose reputation throughout New Jersey's prisons was legendary. But here the prisoners continued as usual, taking little regard of the unimposing stranger in their midst. They bragged about themselves and told exaggerated stories about how "bad" they were. It had been a long time since Rubin had been privy to such loose jive talk, and he was enjoying it. Now that he had shed his trademark exterior, the trappings of his persona, doors were opening to him. His anonymity was giving him a measure of freedom.

Rubin slogged it out in court another day, but when he called Toronto that evening, he told the Canadians he'd had enough. He was tired of sitting in that courtroom and taking notes about Carter being "the perpetrator of the annihilation," as though they were talking about some rabid dog. He'd had enough of this bullshit to last a lifetime. He told them he'd requested to be transferred back to Trenton the next morning.

In the meantime, they had all evening to talk. The Canadians were happy for Rubin; even if he was still in prison, the freedom he was now enjoying could not be denied. They were impressed that he had the audacity to try something new, to be flexible.

Rubin asked to speak to Lesra and Marty. He hadn't had a chance to comment on the essays they'd sent to him in Trenton. Marty's was on racism and Lesra's was on *The Catcher in the Rye*.

"I want you to know they were excellent," Rubin said to them. "Smart. Informative. And very sophisticated. If you guys don't mind I'm gonna pass these papers around to some of the young fellows at Trenton and do a bit of bragging—if that's all right with you."

He didn't need to ask.

"Look," continued Rubin. "You keep up the good work, you hear? And keep on driving—don't give up your licences and don't let anyone take them from you. You understand what I'm sayin'?"

They did.

"And always be thankful that you have loving friends who refuse to give up and out on you. That's power and that's beautiful. And so are you."

10

A contingent of Canadians—Kathy, Sam and Terry—left Toronto in the small hours of the morning so that they could get to Trenton in time for a visit the next day. Rubin was dismounting the monster and they wanted to be there with their enthusiasm and support when he returned from Paterson.

On the way to the prison, they turned on the car radio and heard the impassioned and eloquent voice of an expert on the criminal justice system: "There are more black men in America's prisons than in its universities. There are more native North Americans being incarcerated than matriculated. Notwithstanding the issues of social justice, these statistics make no sense on the most basic economic level: it is more expensive to keep someone in prison than it is to send him or her to the best university on the continent. But prisons are accessible, universities are not. What does that say about our priorities?"

They thought of Lesra in Toronto, college-bound, while his brothers were in Brooklyn, prison-bound. More money would be spent on them, more attention would be lavished on them to put them behind bars than to stimulate their minds. Any way you looked at it, it didn't make sense.

At the prison, the Canadians were greeted by "trusties," who were sweeping or picking up garbage outside the wall. They smiled and nodded and asked the Canadians how they were doing. Inside, when the Canadians tried to register at the mailroom window for a visit with Carter, number 45472, they were told they couldn't because he wasn't there. Terry, knowing that Rubin had called Toronto the minute he returned, said yes he was. The guard behind the counter said he was up at the Passaic County jail. Terry insisted that he wasn't; he'd come back that morning. The guard flatly disagreed and dismissed them. Two minutes later, looking up and seeing that they hadn't budged, the guard picked up the phone and called up to Rubin's wing, certain that he was about to prove them wrong. He asked the officer on wing duty to "verify the absence of Carter's presence." After a moment's silence, and without a shred of embarrassment or apology, he registered their visit and handed over a telephone receiver. As Terry reached for the receiver, he read the guard's name tag—"Rocky."

The window visits were held just off the waiting area, in a long, narrow, filthy room that was more like a corridor or an alleyway than a room. Summer or winter, the place was stuffy and swelteringly hot. Glaring yellow enamel paint, chipped, peeled and gouged, lay in thick coats on everything and only intensified the overheated atmosphere. About half the ancient linoleum tiles on the floor had lifted, never to be replaced, and underneath, the inkblot patterns of gungy black glue had hardened into dirt-encrusted permanence. There was nothing that didn't look old and grotty.

One wall was divided into a dozen sections, each with its own window, although "window" is a bit of a misnomer; "window" usually means something you can see through. This was thick, bulletproof glass, about eighteen inches square, scratched and filthy, and had the effect of darkening the light and obstructing rather than facilitating views. Canny, seasoned visitors would wipe the glass clean with a dampened Kleenex. This remedy, however, was lost when a diamond-patterned, heavy steel grille was welded over the window so that the glass was now inaccessible. If visitors were lucky, they could make out tiny diamond-shaped fragments of a prisoner's face, but as the months of grime built up, even the geometric segments became blotched and obscured. The lighting was such that the only thing visitors could see clearly was a metal stretcher suspended ominously against the wall behind the row of visiting prisoners, like some prop from a 1940s melodrama set in a mental institution.

Each window area had its own yellow-painted, beat-up steel stool, the hardness of which was calculated, no doubt, to lessen any danger of comfort. Beside each window was a telephone jack where you plugged in your receiver when the person you were visiting appeared on the other side, usually more than an hour after you had registered. As often as not, you would then discover that the receiver you were given didn't work and you had to go back to the mailroom, line up again, explain to a surly guard that you weren't trying to make his life difficult but you needed a new phone—all of which took precious minutes off your allotted visiting time. Even when your phone worked, the connection tended to be full of static, crackly. As for the broken phones, they were never repaired, just recycled and handed out to the next unsuspecting visitor. Prisoners had about the same luck with their phones on the other side.

During the week, window visits lasted an hour; weekends and holidays they were only thirty minutes, allegedly to accommodate more visitors during those days, although visits were cut short and the phones disconnected whether anybody was waiting or not.

Weekends were bedlam. The phone room was used as an auxiliary waiting room for the scores of people waiting to go on contact visits. Babies cried, kids ran around and guards hollered. To make matters worse the only way to get to the restrooms was through the phone room, so that conversations were continually interrupted by the slamming of doors, the flushing of toilets and the frenzy of visitors trying to stash contraband in some obscure place on their bodies before they were called in for contact visits. And then there was the competing noise from the other window visitors who were trying to make themselves heard above the general din, or through those faulty receivers. (Such settings for prison visits, hardly conducive to sane communication, never seem to be portrayed realistically in movies, where prison windows are usually large and sparkling clean, and it's so quiet you can hear a thought drop.)

Rubin's delight in the presence of the Canadians made the adversities of the visiting environment vanish in an instant, such was the force of his energy, even through bullet-proof glass. His charisma was infectious. He literally shone, intense and vibrating, eager for the next word, the next exchange, which would only make him glow more. Everyone felt wonderful, inspired.

The Canadians' trips to Trenton gradually expanded from a weekend with one contact visit on Saturday and one on Sunday to include a couple of weekdays for window visits.

For several years after his second trial, Rubin had lived an almost monastic life, finding company primarily in books. He participated in no prison activities. His social interaction had been limited to his one close friend, Moko, who he enjoyed talking to. Moko could always make Rubin laugh and see the funny side of things; Rubin loved him for that. In fact, everybody inside loved Moko; his cheerful disposition made him incredibly popular.

When Moko's time was about up and he was scheduled for release, he was concerned that Rubin would have nobody to talk to, that he would retreat totally and get too cut off from people. So before Moko left, he introduced Rubin to his "homeboy," a hometown friend called Sam, who had just come into the penitentiary. He had a quick and stimulating mind and a great sense of humour. Moko hoped that Sam and Rubin would be good for each other, and they were. They hit it off quickly, and after meeting out in the yard a few times, Sam introduced Rubin to "Zig," and the three of them used to walk and talk in the yard regularly.

Sam and Zig were a little younger than Rubin and untutored in using their minds for anything but hustling. As a basis for their discussions in the yard, Rubin gave them books on philosophy to read. Up until then, Sam had been practically illiterate. With Rubin's encouragement, he was learning not only how to read and write, but how to communicate ideas, of which he had many. Because his handwriting was illegible, he was also learning to type. By contrast, Zig had beautiful, dainty penmanship; his letters were beautifully drawn and neat to a fault. Zig had the form down pat; what he needed, Rubin told him, was to concentrate more on substance. "Perhaps a little more thinking and a little less weight-lifting."

By the time Lesra and the Canadians entered the picture, Sam and

Zig were taking great strides. Their earnestness at learning was coupled with a desire to please their teacher, who they both revered.

The two had been following Rubin's growing involvement with the group from Canada, first with concern because the interlopers were monopolizing so much of Rubin's attention, and then with fascination at the discernible, if puzzling, changes they sensed in him.

They finally met the Canadians one day on a contact visit. Sam, whose formal name was Ulysses Leslie (the Canadians called him "Sam South" to distinguish him from their own Sam, "Sam North"), had light skin, and eyes that tended to slant. He was African-American but his face looked Mongolian. He was slim, with the lanky physique of a baseball player, and had been a major-league pitching prospect until an untimely knee injury derailed his career. Robert Sigler, "Zig," on the other hand, was dark-skinned and huge. He sported a beard, and the Canadians commented that he looked uncannily like pictures they had seen of Frederick Douglass. Zig didn't know who Douglass was, but he was intrigued that he looked like somebody famous.

Although prisoners seldom ask one another what they are in for, the Canadians, who didn't know the rules, always did. They found out that Sam, whose case was under appeal, had been convicted of homicide; Zig had been convicted of armed robbery. Zig and Sam had met each other as they were being brought into the penitentiary in 1979, each with a thirty-year sentence. That year, the sequential, five-digit numbers that the New Jersey Department of Corrections was handing out were in the mid-sixty-four-thousands. There was only a handful of men left in the prison with numbers under fifty thousand; Rubin was one of them. His number, 45472, indicated to everyone that he was an old-timer. Subtracting from Sam's number, the Canadians calculated that Rubin had entered the system 19,146 prisoners earlier.

For neither Zig nor Sam was this the first time in the joint; actually, it had been a kind of home-coming. Neither of them had anything on the outside: Zig had come from West Virginia, where his father had been a coal-miner; Sam was from Asbury Park, New Jersey, and had essentially raised himself.

The Canadians talked about how revolting they found the prison, how abhorrent they found it that human beings could be treated so atrociously. Zig and Sam paid lip-service to these sentiments but found it difficult to comprehend the extent of the visitors' revulsion. The Canadians, they felt, were exaggerating. To them, as with most of the prisoners, life on the streets was at least as miserable and equally fraught with peril.

Sam and Zig slowly became responsive to the Canadians. In addition to the occasional visits, they began corresponding by mail. Rubin acted as a sort of Postmaster-General, the hub of the wheel, all correspondence being relayed through him so that he was always abreast of what was going on and could tailor his yard discussions accordingly. Having first felt excluded, now Sam and Zig revelled in being part of the circle. They called the Toronto group "the Family." After all, wasn't a family a group of people who cared for each other?

Sam, especially, thrived on the attention and the stimulation. The Canadians sent him books. He got a real kick out of the difficult-to-read but rewarding classic *The Robber Barons,* by Matthew Josephson, describing the skulduggery of the first captains of American industry. "They're just like the hustlers I know on the street, except these cats ran a big-g-g-g scam!"

Sam started to write poetry and share his creations with Rubin and "the Family." In one poem, which he titled "The Rose Finds Friends," he compared himself to a "thorny thing" hidden in a "god-forsaken garden" that, with a little care and nurturing, blossomed into a rose. From then on, he signed all of his correspondence "The Rose."

One day, Terry answered a disturbing call from Rubin.

"Listen, I only got a minute now. I didn't mention this to you before, cause I thought it was nothin' but a rumour. And if you hear something once in jail, that's what it is—a rumour. But when you hear it twice, it's a fact. And I heard it twice now. Something happened to Moko. You know, it's been some time since he's been outta here. Last I heard he was goin' out west. Word is he was arrested in the midwest somewhere and. . . . Find out for me, will you?"

In the background a loudspeaker boomed, "Yard out!"

"Got to go now. Moko's name is Riley, Lester Riley."

It took a few phone calls for the Canadians to track down the information. They got the story from Associated Press, and they weren't looking forward to breaking the news to Rubin.

"This isn't good," said Terry when Rubin had the opportunity to call back.

"We're so sorry, Rube," said Lisa, picking up an extension.

"Just read me what it says."

" 'A man who served eighteen years in a New Jersey prison and was about to be extradited for a parole violation, Lester Irving Riley, committed suicide by tying his socks together and hanging himself from a curtain rod. He arrived Sunday in Rawlins, Wyoming. He was arrested and accused of stealing $120 from a woman. A witness said he saw Riley putting the money in his socks. Six twenty-dollar bills were found in his socks. They found a ticket indicating he was en route to California. The sheriff said Riley had signed a waiver of extradition and showed every sign of being co-operative. "I love you always and kids" was written in toothpaste on a mirror.' "

"That's it, Rube," said Lisa. "How terrible! We know how you felt about him."

"S-s-s-sideways? He went out s-sideways?" stammered Rubin incredulously, using prison argot for suicide.

"So they claim," said Terry.

Rubin was completely silent. The talking on the phone ceased. All that could be heard were sounds coming from the background in the prison. Then came the outburst.

"Cut off that fuckin' tap!" Rubin shouted to a prisoner mopping the floor not far from him. "Can't you see it's dripping?" The Canadians had never heard that tone in Rubin's voice. He always spoke to other prisoners respectfully. But he was shouting at himself, they realized. It was his own pain he was trying to cut off.

11

In the summer of 1981, Lesra enrolled in a couple of summer-school courses in Toronto. The class he was most excited about was Introductory Spanish. To get into the University of Toronto, which he was determined to do, a foreign language was required. He liked the idea of studying Spanish because there were so many Puerto Ricans he could talk to back home. When he was young, he had pretended he was "Rican"; it was considered classier than being "just a nigger."

Because he was busy with schoolwork, he had little time to spend with his family that summer. On Lesra's first day back in Brooklyn, Starlene, his oldest sister, and Nonie, his only sister still living at home, had prepared Lesra's favourite dinner. Nonie was nineteen, a year and a half older than Lesra. Since he'd left she had started cooking, taking care of the two youngest boys, shopping when the food stamps came in and cleaning. To cook she used a hot-plate. They had a stove, but the gas had been cut off. Over the winter they had had to rely on the oven for heat and eventually the bill had got too high. In their building, no other source of heat was available.*

---

*According to New York's latest welfare rules, landlords were guaranteed their rents and welfare tenants were not allowed to move for a period of two years, regardless of the condition of the building. In effect, landlords had no obligation to provide "amenities" like heat and hot water, and tenants had no recourse if they didn't.

Lesra sat on the couch with his brothers. Damon and Leland, each with a heaping plate of food on his knees. Nonie and Starlene watched with delight, their faces glowing, as Lesra dug into the beans and rice, thoroughly enjoying himself.

"Y'all sure can burn! Where d'you learn to cook like that? Haven't had some of this in a long time!"

Nonie and Starlene were elated.

Lesra continued to eat with relish, until he bit into a rib. He spat it out on his plate.

"This goddamn meat's rotten!"

"Can't be, Lez," protested Nonie. "Starlene bought it fresh today."

Lesra sniffed it, then got up, went into the kitchen, rummaged through the garbage and came back with a bag. He scooped the ribs off his little brothers' plates and into the bag.

"Lesra, what ya doin'?" they asked.

"Y'all can't eat this shit!"

By this time, Starlene was beside herself. "I spoiled the dinner," she sobbed, tears streaming down her face. "I wanted you to like it. Now everything's ruint!"

"It's not your fault, Star. Don't blame yourself! Where you buy this at? That store down on the corner?"

Starlene, still sobbing, nodded. "You know, Lez, every place else too far! Don't have no car. Ain't no bus . . ."

Lesra took her by the hand. "Come on," he said, and they were out the door.

Lesra strode down the street, Starlene half running to keep up. They entered the meat store at a furious clip. Starlene, embarrassed, hung back as Lesra approached the white man standing behind the counter. Lesra plopped down the bag of ribs.

"My sister bought this here this morning. You sold her rotten meat!"

The butcher nonchalantly opened the bag and looked in. "Listen, don't get excited. Why don't I give you some good ones?"

Starlene started to smile.

"How you gonna do that, mister?" said Lesra, loudly so the other customers would hear. "There ain't never no fresh meat in here. My sister wants her money back."

The butcher was surprised at the directness and vehemence of Lesra's response. So was Starlene. She thought for a moment her brother had gone crazy. But the butcher wanted to get them out of his store fast. He looked at the price scrawled on the side of the bag, reached into the register and handed Lesra the cash. Lesra checked it, spun on his heels, stuffed the money into his stunned sister's hand, grabbed her by the elbow and left the store.

"The reason Pop let me go to Canada was to learn. And I learned we don't have to accept garbage."

Starlene, bursting with pride, stood up on her tiptoes and kissed her little brother.

Rubin's fact-finding hearing in Paterson had lasted three weeks, and when Rubin read the fourteen volumes of transcripts, he was sure he had made the right decision in leaving the hearing early. It was all there on paper, and he hadn't had to subject himself to further abuse. His lawyers had managed to uncover all kinds of shenanigans and the prosecution was hard-pressed to invent plausible tales to cover its misdeeds.

The Canadians wondered what the hearing was supposed to have accomplished and why all this mattered when the point was that the State had incarcerated two innocent men. Although the Canadians had learned that in U.S. criminal appeals guilt or innocence was not the issue, they still found it hard to fathom why it wasn't. And they were still confused about the Bello lie-detector test.

"There's no point in talking about the specific details," Rubin told them. "The details keep changing—it's nothing but sleight-of-hand, the same old tricks."

"What tricks?"

"It's called prosecutorial misconduct. The prosecution comes up with a theory, and if the facts don't fit the theory, they suppress the facts and make up new ones. To find out what really happened, you have to cut through all the bullshit. You have to go back to the beginning. That's what I tried to do in *The Sixteenth Round*. But we didn't have anything near the amount of information then that we now have—the exonerating evidence they tried to keep hidden."

"But how did they get away with it?"

"In 1966, 'discovery' rules—rules governing pre-trial disclosure of information—were very lax in New Jersey, and prosecutors easily got away with withholding from the defence evidence that would be damaging to the State's case. Grand jury hearings,* for example, were held in secret. Their transcripts were usually sealed and if any testimony was disclosed, it was handed over too late to be of any use. Discovery rules are more favourable to an accused now, but . . ."

"If that's so, then how do they keep getting away with it? And why would they want to? Isn't it their job to put away the guys who really did it?"

"You would think so." Rubin chuckled at the ingenuousness of the Canadians.

"So how does that relate to the hearing in Paterson?"

"Judge Leopizzi is going to have to decide according to the standards set out in *Brady v. Maryland* whether John and I should be granted a third trial. *Brady* was a 1963 United States Supreme Court decision that allows for a verdict to be overturned if it can be shown that prosecutors withheld critical evidence from a defendant. That's how we got our new trial in 1976. To establish a violation of the *Brady* rule, the defence has to demonstrate three things. First of all, that the evidence was known to the prosecution but unknown to the defence prior to the trial. Second, that the suppressed evidence was favourable to the defence. And third, that the evidence was "material," meaning that its disclosure might have led to a different verdict, namely, an acquittal. As far as I can see, and as my lawyers have shown, we easily pass these tests with this Bello polygraph fiasco. But what do I know? I'm blind in one eye and can't see out the other."

In August, Passaic County Superior Court Judge Bruno Leopizzi issued his opinion. He ruled against Rubin and John on virtually every

*A grand jury is an American institution wherein the county prosecutor presents his unrebutted case against an accused to a jury of twenty-four local citizens, usually business owners. If the evidence warrants, the jury "returns an indictment" against the accused, who must then stand trial on these formal charges.

point. The judge decided that although, technically, information about Bello's polygraph test was known to the prosecution and unknown to the defence, none of it was "favourable" to the defence, nor did its withholding indicate bad faith on the part of the prosecution, nor would its disclosure have made any difference in the outcome of the trial. As far as he was concerned, the trial he had presided over in 1976 had been a fair one; another trial was absolutely unwarranted.

Rubin, Lesra and the Canadians were stunned. Not that they'd expected Leopizzi to rule in Rubin's favour, but they'd hoped he would. The timing had seemed right. DeSimone had recently died; perhaps the case could be laid to rest too. But Judge Leopizzi had been able to disregard those facts that didn't suit his unwavering belief in Rubin's guilt.

To Leopizzi, it didn't matter that the prosecution knew the polygrapher had found Bello's in-the-bar scenario to be the truth and that the prosecution nevertheless had Bello testify to the opposite story at trial. Leopizzi found the prosecutors to have been acting "in good faith" at all times.

It didn't matter that four former members of the prosecutor's office and two journalists testified that they were aware Bello had unequivocally "flunked" the test (the news had spread like wildfire through the prosecutor's office) and that the prosecution of Carter and Artis was in jeopardy until the polygrapher made his misleading written statement. Leopizzi dismissed their testimony as "rank hearsay."

It didn't matter that two prosecution members had resigned in disgust, one of them an assistant prosecutor who stated that "the behaviour of the prosecutor's office stunk" and "the case stunk" and should never have gone to trial. Leopizzi declared such accusations to be "simply incredible" and the product of base "personal reasons" and "active minds."

It didn't matter that a prime reason for the State's testing Bello in the first place was to settle the question of his location at the time of the shooting—Leopizzi pronounced that where Bello was before and at the time of the Lafayette Bar shooting was an irrelevant and meaningless red herring invented by the defence. All that mattered to Leopizzi was that the polygrapher believed Bello when he said he saw Carter and Artis at the scene outside the bar, after the shooting.*

Is that, wondered the Canadians, what being a "fact-finder" meant?

Hope rested once again with the State Supreme Court, which had retained jurisdiction in the matter. It was now up to the seven justices to review Judge Leopizzi's "Findings of Facts" and "Conclusions of Law," and they still had the many other issues in Rubin's appeal to rule on. The lawyers for Rubin and John wrote a massive but cogent 206-page brief, highlighting relevant testimony from the hearing, dissecting Leopizzi's 80-page opinion fallacy by fallacy, and pointing out the numerous instances of the lower court's bias. Accompanying the brief was a two-volume appendix of hearing exhibits. The prosecution submitted its brief and appendix on behalf of the State. The voluminous record in *State v. Carter* thus increased, as did the cloudiness of the issues. It had now been fifteen years.

You had to take it, Rubin said, day by day.

One day in the fall of 1981, Earl Martin called Toronto with some bad news for his son. After speaking to Lesra, he asked to speak to Terry. Earl's mind was racing. He was worried that the Canadians would now be afraid of Lesra, think he was from bad stock or something. Maybe they'd want to kick him out, send him back to the States. He hoped they wouldn't do that. His family didn't have an apartment to live in any more. They were staying at Lesra's aunt's house for a couple of days, then they were going to a welfare hotel. It wasn't a good time for Lesra to come home. He didn't have a home to come to.

As Terry took the phone, Lesra recalled when he was little, his family had a house in Queens and there was a fire; they'd got burned out and had had to stay in a hotel. People on welfare—black people—had to come in through the back door. Lesra had never forgotten how

---

*Harrelson believed Bello was truthful when he said he was in the bar and didn't see Carter and Artis, but he saw them outside the bar later, after the shooting. However, scores of people (including Bello) saw Carter and Artis outside the bar after the shooting—when they were brought to the scene by the police.

that felt. But what his father had just told him was so much worse. Lesra now thought of his older brother Fru, how Fru had always been there, teaching him and his younger brothers how to defend themselves, how to fight. Fru knew the streets and he knew the dangers. He had taught them what they'd needed to know.

Terry could tell that Earl had been drinking; his speech was rambling but not incoherent. He told Terry that his oldest son, Fru, had got into a fight with a friend in the Martins' apartment. It was over a hat or something. The guy had stolen it and refused to give it back, and then he'd laughed at Fru. Before anyone knew it, the other young man was dead. Hit over the head with a bat or a bed slat or something. Fru didn't mean to kill him. It was an accident. Fru didn't even try to run. He just sat there on the floor and waited for the cops to come and take him away. Now he was in the Brooklyn House of Detention for Men.

To make matters worse, the family of the deceased had driven by the Martins' house, wanting revenge. They had guns. They fired shots into the apartment building, lots of shots. Everyone, including the neighbours, had to flee. But Earl's family could never return. It would be risking their lives.

"Terry?"

"Earl. I'm so sorry, Earl. I don't know what to say."

"Terry?"

"Yes, Earl?"

"Terry, I just want to know . . . I just want to know . . . can I still come up there sometime for a visit?"

"Of course you can, Earl. Any time."

"I just wanted to know if . . . I can come up there and see y'all again?"

"You know Earl, you're always welcome in our house."

"And I could come and stay up there wich y'all?"

"Any time you want to."

"That's all I want to know."

After seemingly endless months in a welfare hotel, Lesra's family found an apartment on Covert Street in Bedford-Stuyvesant. This place, if anything, was in worse shape than the one they had left on

Linden Street. Still, they were thankful to have their own roof over their heads.

Fru pleaded guilty to manslaughter and was sentenced to New York State Prison for five to fifteen years. Lesra now had someone else to correspond with in a penitentiary, and a larger burden of guilt to bear: neither Fru nor the person he killed had the chance that Lesra had.

12

Late one evening in December, while the Canadians were preparing for a Christmas trip to visit Rubin, Lisa received an anxious phone call from Vickie, a woman she had met on the visits in New Jersey. Her husband, Snookey, an inmate at Trenton, had just called and told her to alert Rubin's friends in Canada. "Snookey," Rubin had said, "was the kind of guy who always had his ear to the ground. And if anything untoward happened, he'd be the first to know." Now Snookey had seen Rubin, in handcuffs and shackles and under armed guard, being removed from the penitentiary.

"What are you saying, Vickie? I was just talking to him, not an hour ago. There was nothing happening."

"I ain't lyin', Lisa. That's what Snookey told me. He said to call you quick. That's all I know."

Terry immediately called the prison mailroom and asked where they had taken Rubin. He was told that Rubin Carter was in his cell in his wing. When Terry said he'd been informed that Rubin had been taken out of the institution, they said he'd been misinformed. But this was not the first time the prison had "lost" Rubin.

Terry called Myron Beldock in New York but couldn't get him. Leon Friedman was not in either. Finally he got hold of John Artis's lawyer, Lewis Steel, and introduced himself as a friend of Rubin's. When Steel was apprised of the situation, he said, "Listen, if they're going to do anything to him, it's already been done!" That left the Canadians anything but reassured. Rubin had told them the greatest danger a prisoner faced was having nobody on the outside aware of what was happening to him on the inside. The authorities were much more careful with inmates who could contact outside help.

Steel tried calling the prison but by then its office had closed. He told Terry he would have Beldock call Trenton the next morning and try to find out what was going on.

Lesra and the Canadians were scared. They couldn't get any information. They hoped Rubin was still alive.

Forty-two more hours went by before the telephone rang and an operator asked if they'd accept a collect call. Through a fuzzy connection they heard Rubin's distant voice.

"Are you all right?" they asked frantically. "Where are you?"

He told them not to worry, and for the moment, they were relieved. He said he didn't have any phone privileges where he was; he only got this call because one of the guards had recognized him and he'd told the guard he had to contact his lawyer to get him out of there. He had called Canada instead.

"Where are you?"

"I'm in the Psychiatric Hospital for the Criminally Insane in Trenton. The Vroom Building. In the hole."

"What?"

"I was charged with inciting a riot with three other prisoners."

"I don't believe it!"

"Well somebody apparently does! Got to get off here now! I'll write you a letter. Take care!"

And he was gone again.

Although unsure of the date (he thought it was Wednesday, December 9), Rubin was sure of the return address of his letter: Hell itself. He had been trying for days to get hold of pencil and paper and now that he had, he was writing in total darkness and had to get off his bed and go to the door in order to see what he'd written. He wanted his Canadian friends to know that he loved them and missed them and probably wouldn't be able to see them again for at least 15 days, the time he was now sentenced to spend in the godforsaken hole of the Vroom Readjustment Unit.

It wasn't until Rubin's second phone call, many days later, that the Canadians learned the details of his ordeal.

On the evening of December 5, Rubin had been sitting on his bed, reading, when a guard suddenly yelled, "Everybody stand! Put your hands on the bars!" Rubin stayed where he was and continued to read. When the guard got to his cell, he told Rubin to get up. "This is a standing count."

Rubin ignored him. It had been ages since he had been required to stand for a head count. Prisoners had fought that rule and won the right not to stand except in a bona fide emergency (after an escape, for example). Nothing had happened to indicate this was an emergency. Counts in prison are routine: there was one every couple of hours, and always after a staff shift-change. The purpose of a count was to ensure everyone was where he was supposed to be. The guard could see that Rubin was there in his cell in plain view. He nevertheless told Rubin to either stand or face charges. Rubin remained immobile on the bed. The guard continued his count. He found three others in the wing who also were unco-operative: one was on the toilet in his cell and couldn't get up, and two others had been asleep and hadn't stood quickly enough.

The count completed, the guard and several others returned to Rubin's cell. They ordered him to strip, to turn around with his back to the bars, to bend over and "spread 'em." After a guard looked up his rectum, Rubin was told to put his clothes back on and turn around and put his wrists through the bars. They handcuffed him, opened his cell door, shackled him, put a restraining belt around his waist and attached his handcuffs to the belt.

He and the three other prisoners were accused of refusing to obey a guard's direct order (Prohibited Act No. 256), of conduct which disrupts the orderly running of the institution (No. 306) and of engaging in or encouraging a group demonstration (No. 253)—one guard said someone had yelled to the other inmates in the wing, "Don't stand up! Put your dicks on the bars!"

He was transported in a state vehicle to the sinister-sounding Vroom Building (named after the nineteenth-century New Jersey governor Peter D. Vroom, who was interested in penal reform). Somewhere in the bowels of the basement, Rubin was led into a hall of cells, which had steel mesh affixed to their fronts to prevent prisoners from reaching out and grabbing guards or throwing things at them. Outside one of these unwelcoming vestibules they stopped and removed Rubin's shackles, belt and cuffs. By this point, Rubin had been strip-searched three times.

A choking stench escaped from the darkness. Rubin turned to one of the guards. "Clean out that fucking cell before I go in there!"

The guard laughed. "That's not *your* cell that's stinkin'," he said. "That's the guy next door to you. He hasn't showered in months."

Although Rubin was used to some foul odours in his years behind bars—prison air is always rank—he was almost sick to his stomach. Nevertheless, as he settled into the darkness of this new environment, he empathized with his neighbour. "I smell you, brother," thought Rubin, "but I hear you too!" Rubin understood that the poor son-of-a-bitch had been reduced to filth as his only form of protest. His not washing was an act of defiance; he was exercising his last shred of "control" over his own body.

Later that night, Rubin heard a distant rhythm in ominous crescendo. It was the thumping of guards running slowly in formation, approaching closer and closer. Each guard was wearing a helmet, carrying a shield, immune and completely anonymous in full riot gear. Like some multi-peded, hard-shelled, deadly insect, it thudded past Rubin's cell and halted several cells over. There it cracked open the door, grabbed the prisoner and beat him unconscious. The marauder then beat its retreat, feet again stomping in unison, exiting the wing in decrescendo. This onslaught took place nightly. And each night it was a different prisoner who was beaten, who pleaded and moaned and was suddenly quiet.

Keeping prisoners in the hole for more than fifteen days at a stretch was prohibited by federal law, but it was easy to fall through the cracks in the Vroom Building. Two prisoners were there because they had been caught trying to escape from Trenton State Prison earlier that year. Another man, a favourite victim, had killed a prison guard nine years before and had been kept there in the hole ever since. He'd had every bone in his body broken many times over. Occasionally, after writhing in agony for hours, he would be removed to St Francis Hospital in Trenton to have his fractured limbs reset. But this did not seem to be done out of human kindness: they were mended only to be rebroken at some later date.

Rubin was enraged and overwhelmed by the reality of his powerlessness. He had to witness, to listen to this brutal punishment each night. Each night, as the thumping drew near, he expected his turn to be next. And each night, it sickened him to have to hope it would not. He had to check such thoughts. If the sadistic squad passed him by, it only meant that one of his miserable neighbours was to be its next victim. He could not wish that on anyone. Those beaten and demoralized men were suffering enough. No one deserved such torture.

Rubin couldn't help but think about what he would do if they ever did stop at his cell. He knew in his heart that he'd never let them brutalize him the way he'd heard them brutalize the others. He'd fight and he'd die—simple as that. The moment Rubin recognized he was willing to pay the ultimate price, his fear of the jackboots halting at his cell receded.

One night when the riot squad came, there were the usual noises. As the guards entered the wing, Rubin could hear their voices echoing as they worked one another into a frenzy. This time, though, their favourite prey, the guard-killer, was ready.

"Owwwww! What the fuck!" screamed a guard. "Owww! He's got a brick!"

Rubin, earlier in the day, had heard the guy trying to pry a brick loose from the cell wall. His success made the marauders more furious, more vengeful. They beat the prisoner unmercifully, but not before he himself had done some damage—at least to a guard's riot gear.

The next day Rubin overheard two of the guards laughing about how Officer So-and-so was taken to St Francis for a cracked helmet, and how his wife had showed up screaming hysterically about the danger of working in a prison. "Something oughta be done," she'd insisted, "to protect correctional officers from those animals behind bars."

On December 9, an inmate who acted as a paralegal liaison with the administration came to escort Rubin to "courtline," the three-officer internal "court" that adjudicates disciplinary charges. Rubin surprised his escort by explaining that he wasn't going.

"Look, brother," said Rubin, "they'll do exactly what they want to do whether I'm present or not. I won't be part of it. Tell them I'm busy."

Rubin had been through this charade before. In 1974 he'd been elected Director of the Inmate Council in New Jersey's Rahway State Prison. The council had sought to restore dignity and human rights to all prisoners, to have prisoners make meaningful decisions and take responsibility for their own lives. That way there was a chance that when they re-entered society, they'd do so as competent human beings, capable of governing themselves and, therefore, less of a threat to others and less likely to end up back in prison.

The council instituted a number of sorely needed prison reforms that were both popular and successful. But the council's ability to get prisoners to act co-operatively was seen as subverting the smooth running of the institution. Normally, "order" was maintained by having different factions constantly fighting and at each other's throats: blacks against whites, Hispanics against blacks, Moslems against non-Moslems, bikers against everybody. When Rubin addressed an unauthorized meeting one night, criticizing the institution but calling for peaceful means to a better end, he was taken to a courtline and found guilty of "inciting." He was then sentenced to confinement in the Vroom Building for an indefinite period.*

After ninety-two days in the Vroom, Rubin succeeded in having the matter heard by a federal court. The court ruled that Rubin's due process rights had been violated, that "inciting" was not a recognizable offence under the disciplinary rules, and furthermore, that the verdict and punishment were decided before courtline was even held. Rubin was sent back to the prison's "general population," but not to Rahway where he could continue his work in prison reform. Instead he was to experience the more oppressive maximum-security conditions at Trenton.

---

*As Princeton University social scientist Gresham M. Sykes wrote in his 1958 study of Trenton State Prison, *The Society of Captives:* "Centers of opposition in the inmate population—in the form of men recognized as leaders by fellow prisoners—can be neutralized through the use of solitary confinement or exile to other state institutions. Just as the Deep South served as a dumping-ground for particularly troublesome slaves before the Civil War, so too can the . . . mental hospital serve as a dumping-ground for the maximum security prison."

That was almost eight years ago, thought Rubin, and his lawsuit against the New Jersey Department of Institutions and Agencies for that first illegal confinement in the Vroom, *Carter v. Klein et al.,* Civil Action No. 74-774, was still pending.

Now here he was, back in the Vroom. The inmate-paralegal reported to courtline that Carter refused to defend himself against the charges. Rubin was found guilty on the 306, the disruptive conduct charge, for which he was sentenced to a year in the Vroom Readjustment Unit and the loss of a year of commutation time. The 256 refusing-to-obey charge was dismissed as repetitive of the 306. And there was a not-guilty finding on the 253, the "group demonstration" charge. (It turned out that no one could remember anyone urging the others not to comply with the standing count or to do anything with their "dicks.")

To most inmates, these sanctions would have been a considerable tragedy. But for Rubin, with three life sentences to serve, this year tacked on to his sentence was meaningless. He was hoping not for parole but for vindication and he was under no illusion that if he couldn't achieve it, they would make him serve his full term anyway, good time or no.

As for his year in the Vroom, once his fifteen days in the hole were over, things improved considerably. Rubin was moved to another part of the building, and for the first time in two weeks he was able to shave and look in a mirror. He looked gaunt, the lines of his face drawn tight, his eyes tired. He had not been physically beaten, and had long ago steeled himself to the kind of suffering he witnessed in the hole, but he couldn't deny that these experiences had exacted their toll.

He was now in an isolated, sterile unit of about a dozen cells, the latest in prison design. No one was let out of their cells for any reason; it was twenty-three-and-a-half hour-a-day lock-down. Food was slid through an opening in the door, "delivered," according to the "Reduced Mobility Units' Supplement" to Trenton State Prison's *Inmate Handbook,* "via a cell-based modality." It was like being entombed—no movement, no stimulation, just silence.

For most inmates, a year's stint in there was living hell, the worst punishment the administration could distribute. To Rubin, who rarely left his cell, this kind of jailing was normal. In this building, moreover, his cell was bigger than his five-by-seven-foot cell in Trenton, and it was new and clean. It had one of those shiny, stainless-steel sink-and-toilet units that Rubin found positively space-age. And although contact visits were not allowed, he had lots of access to a phone. If it wasn't quite heaven, for Rubin at least, it was a hell of a lot closer to it than what he was used to in Trenton.

The guards here, Rubin noticed, were peculiar. They ignored the prisoners totally. When your laundry hadn't returned from wherever laundry went in the building and you asked when you could expect it, no one answered. No matter what question was asked, no one responded. No request was granted with the exception of the telephone. Each prisoner had a jack in his cell and eventually a guard would bring a phone around. Other requests weren't denied, they just went unanswered. No one acknowledged anything or anyone. Rubin had seen neglect many times in prison, but here in the Vroom it had been elevated to an art form.

Rubin had the telephone and the Canadians to talk to, and he allowed them to jail with him. On a typical day in the Vroom, they'd be on the phone for six to eight hours. (The Canadians were fortunate they could manage, at least for the time being, such outrageous telephone bills: January's long-distance bill was $4,238.39.) This was time well spent. They were able to have consistent and concentrated discussions, and the Canadians could share Rubin's life during this latest and most incredible incarceration. They were practically right there with him, listening to the sounds of the prison, and Rubin trusted them enough not to have to deny or to put a better spin on events for their benefit. He would tell them exactly what was going on at all times. Such openness was a first for Rubin, exposing himself and the reality of life "behind the wall" day after day without reservation.

The sounds emanating from the other cells sometimes made their blood curdle. As Rubin would say, "People here aren't wrapped too tight." Few of the prisoners had family or friends left, no one to accept collect calls. Alone, it was virtually impossible to fight the dehumanization process. There was one young offender, a teenager, who had a direct line to Mohammed and Jesus. Every once in a while he would have loud conversations with them that the people in Toronto could hear. At other times, they could hear him begging, then shouting, then crying, "Let me out of here, please! Open the door! Help me, help me!"

Given that convicts are not known for being the most tolerant lot, and they usually don't much care for anyone disturbing their "peace," the Canadians asked Rubin why the other men in the wing didn't tell the kid to be quiet. Rubin answered that in a place like this, each person could understand how scared and alone the kid felt, and each one knew there might come a time when he also might not be able to take it any more. It might be *him* doing the crying, and he wouldn't want anyone cussing him out.

Just as Rubin was settling in to spending a year in the Vroom, without any warning, his sentence on the not-standing-for-the-count infraction was modified to ninety days. Rubin was removed from the Vroom and sent to the isolated Management Control Unit, the MCU, back at Trenton State Prison. This was the 1980s name for Administrative Segregation, "Ad. Seg." Other than its name, nothing here had changed from the kind of conditions Rubin had tried to get abolished in Rahway in 1974.

Here, although Rubin's access to the phone was greatly reduced and more sporadic, the Canadians continued to be his anchor to reality. Prisoners are accustomed to a certain order: mess at seven, count, out to work, back to cells, count, mess, count, back to work, over and over each day. They quickly become conditioned to such regimentation, and they define their lives by it. "The biggest mind-fuck of all for a prisoner," Rubin told the Canadians, "is to change his routine arbitrarily: not let him out of his cell, feed him at odd hours, turn out the lights intermittently, capriciously give and take back privileges." These were the methods used in the MCU—all tried-and-true techniques of torture.

Rubin wound up doing three months in that particular Trenton State country club. At the end of this time, he was told to move his things to general population. He packed into a cart his papers, books and clothes (which had finally caught up with him after his move to and from the Vroom), and moved to his designated wing. By then he was so out of shape physically (having been under constant lockdown) that it was an effort for him to walk so far, especially while toting all his worldly possessions. When he arrived at his new cell, he looked in, called the guard over and, still out of breath, told him he'd be taking his stuff back to MCU because that cell was uninhabitable. He wasn't putting himself or his belongings into that pigsty. The sink was torn out of the wall, the toilet was caked with filth and the mattress on the bed stunk to high heaven. The guard told him to get into the cell. Rubin turned on his heels and pushed the cart with his stuff on it past the guard and right back to MCU.

The prison was abuzz at Rubin's "bodacious self." Prisoners couldn't wait to tell the Canadians on their next visit how the Hurricane had looked marching without a moment's hesitation out of that wing. Nobody had ever heard of anyone refusing a regular wing over MCU. It just wasn't done, and rare was the prisoner who could get away with it.

A few days later, Rubin was told to move to 6-Left; a cell on the fourth tier in Sam's wing had become vacant. Again, Rubin piled up his things and wended his way through the prison, through the "centre," through various metal detectors and over to 6-Left. His arrival in the wing was marked by thunderous applause and cheers. The returning warrior smiled. The Rose helped move Rubin's stuff up the four flights of steps to his new cell. It had been six months since he had last seen Rubin.

13

On Rubin's return to general population, the Canadians resumed their visits with him and settled into a pattern of staying in Trenton for a week out of every month.

Although by the summer of 1982 there was still no word from the State Supreme Court of its decision in Rubin's appeal, all was not dark and foreboding. Three events lifted the hopes of Rubin, Lesra and the Canadians. The possibility of prison release was real. People they knew did manage to get out.

One of them was John Artis.

Just before Christmas, while Rubin was languishing in the pits of the Vroom, John was granted parole. He had served the minimum fifteen years of his sentence.

Unlike Rubin, who had always been confined to maximum-security institutions, John had been jailed in less restrictive facilities, like Leesburg Farm, which had no surrounding wall. He was known as a model prisoner. He had always participated in various prison activities; he had even attended college to earn his B.A. But at a news conference with lawyer Lew Steel at Rutgers University to announce his liberation, the thirty-five-year-old Artis adamantly rejected the suggestion that he had been rehabilitated.

"From what?" he asked.

It didn't seem to bother anybody that they were releasing an unrepentant man, one who steadfastly maintained his innocence and refused to accept his appointed guilt. The authorities did not care. As far as they were concerned, Rubin was the real criminal, the "ring" leader, the one they wanted. That was reflected in their respective sentences: John's three life sentences were all concurrent, Rubin had two that were consecutive.

Although Rubin would not be eligible for parole for another fifteen years (not that he imagined it would be granted him), John's "enlargement" enabled Rubin to rest easier in the knowledge that half of them had made it out.

Another state prisoner released in 1981 was Shahid Ali. An astute jailhouse lawyer, Shahid did the legal work on his own appeal and freed himself. When Rubin wrote to him in February 1982, he was working as a paralegal in the Newark law offices of Junius W. Williams, who was then running for mayor. Rubin asked Shahid if he would vet the second set of oral arguments the State Supreme Court had called for, to be heard on March 9. Rubin respected Shahid's opinion. He was intelligent, expert at law and would be able to provide an objective appraisal of the hearing.

Shahid replied, in a letter addressed to "Mr Rubin 'HURRICANE' Carter, Warrior, Freedom Fighter," that he would gladly contribute as much time and energy as he could toward helping Rubin get out. A day's trip to Trenton was little to ask.

Shahid was one of two African-Americans at the State Supreme Court that day; the other was John Artis. The arguments were intricate, and Shahid took detailed notes. He read them over the phone the next day to Terry, who then passed the information along to Rubin.

Shahid thought that Rubin's attorneys were fantastic and had done a great job. Professor Friedman had argued first, for probably close to an hour, then Beldock for ten minutes, then Steel for about thirty-five. They responded to the justices' questions persuasively. As far as Shahid could tell, five of the seven justices were definitely pro defence, and they seemed to be less than impressed with the State's case. When the State finished its presentation, lasting only ten minutes, Chief Justice Wilentz uttered incredulously, "Is that it?"

"That sounds great!" exclaimed Terry.

"I'm tellin' you," said Shahid. "You can give this message to Rubin: You know we never put all our eggs in one basket, but you got a LARGE basket now!"

Tuesdays were release days at Trenton State Prison. If the Canadians happened to be on a window visit, they would see prisoners come fresh out of the joint—looking like they'd just come fresh out of the joint—carrying their belongings in cardboard boxes, plain brown paper bags, a TV set under one arm, perhaps an electric fan in the other. That's how Mr Mobutu looked the day he got out. The Canadians wanted to surprise Mobutu. They wanted to share with him the joy of his first moments of freedom and to thank him for having taken care of Rubin when they had locked together in 2-Left.

The Canadians had never seen Mobutu but had spoken to him a couple of times over the phone and had corresponded through the mail. His letters had given them great pleasure. They were written in technicolour, the ink alternating in patches of blue, red and green, and all were signed "Love you madly, The Old Man."

His letters told them he was born March 15, 1902, in the Congo. His nephew, Joseph Mobutu, was the current president of Zaire (the corrupt Mobutu Sese Seko). His parents were an odd couple: his mother was a Pygmy, four feet, one inch tall, and his father was a seven-foot-ten Watusi; they communicated in Swahili. When he was a year old, they had brought him to America, to Trenton, New Jersey. His father's father was one of the "sandhogs" who had helped build the Holland and Lincoln Tunnels that run under the Hudson River, linking New Jersey to Manhattan. They were very poor, Mobutu wore shabby clothes as a child and spent the rest of his life trying to look good.

He either ran away from school or got kicked out and wound up in New York in 1915. There, he met a man named Alabama, and together they rode the rails, hoboing. In Seattle, in 1917, he joined the merchant marine, and spent two years as a dishwasher, then three years as a second cook, and was chef until 1975.

Mobutu stated proudly that after the age of twelve he hadn't been sick a day in his life. He still had almost all his teeth and only started wearing reading glasses at age seventy-seven—"although I always wore shades." One of his sons, his eldest, was a major, retired now at age sixty-two; another was a heart surgeon at Johns Hopkins Hospital in Baltimore; others were pimps and hustlers; and he had another who played bass slide-horn for Count Basie.

In one of his letters, Mobutu reminisced about United States Supreme Court Justice Thurgood. Marshall, the NAACP lawyer who won the landmark 1954 school desegregation case, *Brown v. Board of Education,* and the only African-American to sit on America's highest court:

Now Turkey [as Thurgood was affectionately called by his friends]—he and I went to school together. He never tease me about being raggedy. He asked me when we was small, what I was going to be when I grow up. I said I was going to get me a set of dice and a deck of cards and within a year, I would buy me a Stetson hat, Stetson shoes, a box back suit, a railroad watch, a twenty dollar gold piece on my watch chain, and I'll be on my way! So he told me that he was going to be a lawyer so he could keep me out of jail.

Mobutu was a tough old man; you wouldn't want to cross him. Neither Rubin nor the Canadians knew how much to believe of what he told them but they sure loved to listen to his stories. Undoubtedly, he had led an incredible life. He was eighty years old and had been incarcerated for the past three years. He lamented that most of the prisoners today were young punks, riff-raff. They had no respect. They didn't know how to jail. Rubin, on the other hand, was *somebody.* He had class. He knew how to respect his elders. "Rube is a good man," Mr Mobutu would write. "I love him like he was a son."

When Lisa, Terry and Sam approached Mr Mobutu in the waiting area of the penitentiary that Tuesday, he was sitting on a bench next to his beloved television set. (The Canadians smiled to themselves as they recognized the TV they'd sent to Rubin.) Mobutu was waiting for a prison official who was supposed to escort him to Asbury Park, where he was going to be staying with some relations. He was also waiting for his cheque for fifty dollars from the New Jersey Department of Corrections, the usual prison departing gift. In his brand-new, prison-issued denim outfit, he resembled somewhat the legendary blues singer-songwriter Leadbelly. He was blocky, dark-skinned and muscular, with a cleanshaven head. He didn't look a day over sixty.

Mobutu was surprised when the Canadians came up to him and called his name. He looked at them icily. It took him a minute to recognize them from the pictures that Rubin had shown him. Then his hug was big and warm.

After the Canadians registered for a window visit, they sat and talked with Mobutu for a good hour before Rubin appeared behind the bullet-proof glass. Mobutu took the opportunity to smile and wave at him, but because he was on parole, and barred from associating with "known criminals," Mobutu could not pick up the phone and speak to Rubin. Rubin beamed back, scarcely believing he was looking at the Canadians standing next to Mobutu, hugging and joking with him, at liberty. Rubin and the Canadians were thrilled for Mr Mobutu. Though their joy was tinged with sadness, it revved up their hope that some day soon Rubin would be in Mr Mobutu's position on the free side of that window.

Virtually every week during the summer of 1982, Terry would phone the New Jersey Supreme Court clerk's office and ask if a decision in *State v. Carter* had been rendered. The answer was always no. It had been a full year since Judge Leopizzi had issued his decision, almost two years since the state's highest court had heard the first oral arguments in the appeal, close to six years since Rubin had been reconvicted. Even according to "court time," this decision was inordinately long in coming. Whenever Lesra or the Canadians, whether in Canada or in the States, were out driving in a car, they would listen to an all-news station, expecting any moment to hear that Rubin's conviction had been overturned. The hours had been ticking by like days; the days like weeks; the months, years; and years were made up of 8,760 hours.

On a sunny and hot late August day in Toronto, Lesra was studying for an exam in his first grade thirteen course in summer school, American history. When the phone rang, he was inside; the rest of the household was working in the garden or sitting in the cool shade of the patio.

"Yes, I'll take it," he told the operator. "What's happenin', Rube?"

"Hey, Gus."

"Gus? Who you callin' Gus, man? It's Lesra!"

"Is that you, Lez? Damn, you gettin' to sound like a white boy."

"Giddouddaheah!"

"Where is everybody?"

"You know white folks. They're outside, sunnin' themselves." There was no responding laughter. "Rube, what's up, man? Somethin' happen?"

"Got the word from the court. . . . We've been denied . . . lost."

"Oh, no! Goddamn! No! . . . Lemme tell everyone."

"I got to go now, little brother. My lawyer is here with a copy of the opinion. I'll call back later when I see it for myself." By this time, Lesra had left the receiver and was hanging out the window of his study room and shouting, "It's Rube! We lost! We lost the appeal!"

By the time everybody reached the telephone, there was only a dial tone. Rubin was gone.

Terry called the court clerk's office in Trenton for more information. Whoever answered the phone asked Terry to wait while he checked. He came back saying the convictions of Carter and Artis had been affirmed.

"What was the vote?" asked Terry.

"Four to three."

"You're kidding!"

"I am *not* kidding," was the snarky retort.

They all saw it on the ABC television network's evening news. Having just been jolted, now they were numbed, paralysed. Max Robinson, the black co-anchor of the broadcast, announced it, a boxing photo of the Hurricane in the upper right-hand corner of the screen. A split decision. The Hurricane loses.

When Rubin called Toronto that night, he had a copy of the court's opinion in his hand.

"I'm not going to read you the majority opinion, cause it's a piece of shit. They just accepted the prosecution's contentions on every motherfuckin' issue—even the racial revenge. But there's a dissenting opinion, and it's something else. It was written by Justice Clifford."

Among its fourteen scathing pages, it said the following:

A more egregious *Brady* violation than the one presented by this case is difficult to imagine. . . .

Harrelson concluded that Bello was telling the truth when he said he was in the bar both before and at the time of the shootings. The polygraphist told members of the prosecution team shortly after the test had been completed that was his opinion, and he persisted in it in the face of prosecution efforts to convince him it was "impossible." Harrelson has never waivered in that conclusion and, as was apparent on the remand hearing, believes it to this day. . . .

The conclusion is thus inescapable that not only did the prosecution know that Harrelson's written report contradicted his findings regarding the vantage point from which Bello had supposedly made his pivotal observations, but they concealed the fact that the "wrong" test result was fed to Bello to "break" him. . . .

The inconsistency [of Bello's being in the bar versus on the street] goes to more than a witness's inconsistency in describing the physical characteristics of a defendant or the color socks he was wearing. It goes to the opportunity and ability Bello had to identify defendants and to describe their movements. Chances are that what one sees from a vantage point within a tavern as all hell breaks loose is not going to be the same as what one sees as one strolls up the sidewalk after the carnage. The defense attacks on Bello's "on-the-street" story would have proceeded from a wholly different perspective and in an entirely different framework.

Might all of this have affected the outcome of the trial? How can we say it might not have, given the real capacity for the additional information to bring about the utter destruction of by far the most important witness in the State's arsenal, with the fallout levelling the vaunted polygraphists and casting doubt on the tactics of the prosecution? Never before could defendants argue so persuasively that Bello was in all respects a complete, unvarnished liar, utterly incapable of speaking the truth. . . .

I would reverse and remand for a new trial.

Chief Justice Wilentz and Justice Sullivan authorize me to record their concurrence in this opinion.

For affirmance—Justices Pashman, Schreiber, Handler and Pollock—4.

For reversal—Chief Justice Wilentz and Justices Sullivan and Clifford—3.

Rubin read the dissent aloud to the Canadians, but his heart was not in it. He would become easily distracted, lose his place, stumble over words that would normally glide off his tongue. Given the majority's denial, it was hard to appreciate the brilliance of this piece of writing, the force and dazzle of its compelling logic. Rubin's lawyers had told him they'd never seen a more powerful legal opinion. But, thought Rubin, what difference did it make? It counted for shit. He was still in prison.

14

As Rubin's career died with his conviction, the careers of others prospered. It wasn't long after Rubin's first trial that Vincent Hull, the Passaic County prosecutor, was elevated to the status of county superior court judge. And Samuel Larner, the judge at the original 1967 trial, was appointed to a higher state court, the Appellate Division. After Carter's second trial, Prosecutor Burrell Ives Humphreys (who, in his office, proudly displayed a 1976 photo of Carter and Artis being taken back to prison) soon found himself sitting as a superior court judge in neighbouring Hudson County. And Vincent DeSimone—described by James Lieber in *The Nation* magazine as "the most influential and powerful police officer in Passaic County"—was formally promoted to Chief of County Detectives by Prosecutor Humphreys just days before Rubin was resentenced. Judge Leopizzi, in a speech he gave at DeSimone's installation dinner, sang his praises as a stalwart guardian of law and order.

Justice in New Jersey was the bailiwick of a tight-knit fraternity. So many reputations and advancements seemed to have ridden on Carter's conviction that it was hard not to conclude that keeping Carter in jail was politically expedient. The good name of Jersey justice needed salvaging from the years of adverse publicity surrounding the case. If Rubin was innocent, then a lot of people had made and benefited from some very serious mistakes.

Keenly aware of these dynamics, Rubin wrote a note to the three dissenting justices in late August 1982. Legally, it was probably considered an *ex parte* communication (coming from the defence side only, without opportunity of input from the prosecution side) and therefore improper. But as far as Rubin was concerned, there was only one side—the side of truth. He had to thank the dissenters for their courage in persevering in the face of what must have been considerable political pressure to turn away from the truth. "The ancient philosopher Diogenes," wrote Rubin, "spent his whole life searching for one honest man. I found three. Thank you."

Rubin had longed for the time when he could get his appeal out of the hands of the state and into the federal system, where local political allegiances and cronyism held less sway and the probability of impartiality was much greater. Since murder in the United States is a state (as opposed to a federal) matter, trials are held in county court and convictions are reviewed by state appeals courts. Only under severely limited and rigidly prescribed conditions can state convictions then be reviewed federally. But now, after being up and down the state ladder many times, Rubin was finally in the position to "go federal." He felt positive about federal courts, and it was on that hope that he tried to focus.

Rubin knew the key role federal courts had played in the civil rights movement in the sixties, when they intervened and forced state courts to abide by the Constitution. And he would never forget the respectful treatment he himself had received when, in 1974, he was brought from the Vroom into Federal District Court and Judge Clarkson Fisher had insisted the guards remove Rubin's shackles and handcuffs and get their shotguns out of his courtroom. No matter how dangerous Rubin was made to appear, in that courtroom he stood unfettered and felt equal before the law.

But try as he did to be optimistic, Rubin was becoming despondent. He was worried that his case had taken so many twists and turns that it would be impossible for anyone to follow. The record was monumental, the original events buried: how could an overburdened judge—even a federal judge—take the time to make sense of it? Rubin felt as if he was the only one who knew all the facts—the baseline facts before they were distorted by fictions. Only he had been there since the case's inception.

The Canadians urged him to share his knowledge with them and in response, Rubin let the record speak for itself. Since his return from the Vroom, he had been leaving packages for them to pick up at the mailroom after their visits: boxes of grand jury testimony, trial transcripts, newspaper articles, police statements and various court decisions in his case—papers he had been hauling from cell to tiny cell. After the Canadians studied these, they dug and sifted through Rubin's memory. They also did some historical research of their own.

Paterson, only seventeen miles from Manhattan, is the principal city of Passaic County and the third largest in New Jersey. In 1966 it was a decaying industrial urban centre with a population of 138,000 including 45,000 blacks and 10,000 Puerto Ricans. The Canadians discovered ominous dynamics operating in the city that had contributed to prevent an objective investigation and prosecution of the Lafayette Bar murders. Paterson was fertile ground for organized crime.

In the mid-sixties, the Genovese "family" that had long flourished there was trying to maintain its threatened hold on the lucrative numbers rackets and was battling for ascendancy in the burgeoning drug trade. The competition came chiefly from the Bonanno family, whose head, Joe Bonanno, as FBI tapes later disclosed, was "planting flags all over the world," including Paterson, Genovese's territory. The competition was intensified as blacks began to enter the ranks of the mob (a process begun by "Crazy Joe" Gallo), usually as front-men and enforcers. Passaic County was in the middle of a gangland war that no one in power wanted exposed.

By the time the shooting massacre at the Lafayette Bar occurred in June 1966, there had already been a spate of unsolved murders in the Paterson area. The public was frightened, angry and clamouring for action. The mayor, the police and the prosecutor's office were all feeling the heat.

But the last thing those in power wanted was an exposure of the seamy underworld and the war that was raging out of control. Even the FBI at the time was baldly denying the existence of organized crime. Never mind the word on the street that the Lafayette Bar was a numbers drop. Forget about the anonymous tips regarding drugs and Harlem and the suitcase full of money in the trunk of one of the victims' cars. No, it was much better for all to view the Lafayette Bar murders as simply an act of senseless brutality, one to be "solved" at all costs.

Mayor Frank X. Graves, who loved to make political hay of his law-and-order platform, put on a grand show. He described the Lafayette Bar homicides as "one of the most heinous crimes" in the city's history. He ordered 100 police officers out of a total force of 341 assigned to the investigation. He promised promotions and three-month vacations to the arresting officers. The city and a local tavern owners' association offered rewards totalling $10,500 for the arrest and conviction of the killers.

Before long, yet another violent crime racked the community and commanded attention—the sensational murder of Johnny "The Walk" DeFranco, a Paterson hood who, answering a knock at his door, had his throat slit from ear to ear so cleanly that not a drop of blood splattered on his clothes. Apparently, his superiors had suspected him not only of skimming from his weekly take in the rackets, but also of being a stool-pigeon. Even according to the mainstream magazine *Look*, the DeFranco murder was an obvious gangland contract killing, but the Passaic County prosecutor's office pointedly avoided investigating that connection. Instead, on the basis of the flimsiest evidence, they linked that murder to the random killing six months earlier of a suburban housewife, Judy Kavanaugh, and indicted five people, including the husband, to face the electric-chair.

Exploding into a major scandal involving charges of crooked cops and corruption in high places,* the Kavanaugh-DeFranco murder trials were to occupy the headlines for four years and cost the county $10 million. One defence attorney took the extraordinary step of openly accusing the prosecution of framing the defendants. The renowned

---

*In the late sixties and early seventies, the Paterson police and the Passaic County prosecutor's office were under a constant pall of charges and investigations. One probe centred on the following activities: ties between some members of the police, the prosecutor's office, the judiciary and organized crime for possible involvement in a sentence-fixing scheme for convicted criminals, narcotics traffic, gambling and even murder. Other probes, like the Governor Hughes's Commission on Civil Disorders, focused on police terrorizing and assaulting members of the black and Hispanic community and destroying their property. A consultant to the Governor's Commission described Paterson's police as "the worst in the state . . . possibly the worst in the country."

F. Lee Bailey, also acting for the defence, was so scandalized by the rampant corruption he found in the Passaic County prosecutor's office that he wrote an open letter to every legislator in the state, demanding the office be investigated: "I have never in any state or Federal government court seen abuses of justice, legal ethics and constitutional rights such as this case involved." For his efforts, Bailey was rewarded by being barred from practising law in New Jersey. The defendants were all ultimately acquitted, but not before their reputations had been ruined and their lives shattered.

In addition to the near-application of the death penalty, there were many disturbing parallels between the Kavanaugh case and Rubin's case. The main witnesses in both cases were criminals who bought their way out of trouble by testifying for the State, only to recant later on. Investigative reporters were harassed by the prosecution in both cases, and law officers lost their jobs by going against the official line and making statements like "It's a clearcut gangland case." Possibly the most frightening similarity of all was the prosecution's singular lack of concern in going after the real perpetrators; they were more interested in obfuscating matters, and they had the power to do so. And despite two separate grand juries in Carter's case having refused to indict Rubin and John, the job was finally done by the same grand jury the Passaic County prosecutor had assembled to hand out indictments in the Kavanaugh case.

In the face of such unrestrained power, truth was easily overwhelmed.

Next it was important for the Canadians to find out what actually happened to Rubin that fateful night. The pieces of the puzzle fit together into a coherent, if frightening, shape. What had begun as an unremarkable summer night had turned, without warning, into a Kafkaesque nightmare.

PATERSON, NEW JERSEY, JUNE 17, 1966*
It's 2:00 AM and the Nite Spot, a popular Paterson cocktail lounge, is jumping. There's a constant stream of traffic out-

---

*Not all conversations in this italicized section are verbatim. While many have been taken directly from statements and transcripts, some have reconstructed from memory and circumstances.

side the attractive two-storey building at the corner of East 18th and Governor Streets. Thursday night is Ladies' Night: it's when all the domestics are given a night off. Inside, there are some whites among the mostly black crowd. There's a band playing in the back room, where people are dancing. Everyone is lively and sociable, having by this time consumed a not inconsiderable amount of alcohol.

Rubin enters, wearing black pants and an off-white jacket with thin, beige stripes. He goes up to one end of the bar and asks Big Ed for the usual. The bartender pours him a vodka. Rubin takes out his wallet to pay and sees that it's empty.

"My slide's on E, Big Ed. I'll have to pay you later."

Cathy McGuire and her mother, Anna Mapes, come over to Rubin and ask if he's driving tonight.

"Not my Cadillac," answers Rubin, referring to his black Eldorado. "It's too much of a hassle to drive that car around Paterson—like a red flag to those bull cops. And I'm tired of being the target. So I rented myself a Dodge."

Rubin had leased the 1966 white Dodge Polara for several months for tax reasons. He is driving it that night because it happened to be in his driveway blocking the Cadillac, which was in the garage. Anyway he was going out on business, to make arrangements for his next fight.

"Would you mind giving us a ride home?" asks Cathy. "It's after two, and Mum has to go to work in the morning."

"Sure, streets aren't safe—specially at this time of night." Just then Rubin catches the attention of a tall, muscular black man standing at the other end of the bar, and asks the women if they wouldn't mind waiting a few minutes. "I got some business to take care of . . . Hey, Wild Bill!"

Rubin wades his way over to Bill Hardney, who is talking to a beautiful woman he introduces as Felicia. Rubin tells Hardney he wants him to come down to South America as a sparring partner for the Rocky Rivero fight. Rubin says the promotors are balking at paying for sparring expenses, but he's trying to arrange it now.

"Can we talk about this a little later, Hurricane?"

"Okay. Look, I'm gonna drive Cathy and her mother home. I'll be back in ten minutes."

Hardney turns to Felicia as Rubin slaps him on the back and, collecting the two women, leaves the tavern.

About ten minutes later, Rubin returns to the Nite Spot alone. Seeing that Hardney is still wrapped up with Felicia, he looks into the back room. The last dance of the night has been announced and Rubin watches. A young man, John Artis, casually dressed in light-blue pants and a short-sleeved, V-neck sweater, is doing a sensational boogaloo. When the music stops and the back room begins to empty, Rubin approaches Hardney again.

"Bill, I got to go home to get some money. If you come with me, then my wife won't bitch about me goin' out again. And we can talk about the South America fight on the way."

But Hardney, smiling at Felicia, says, "I think I'll wait here for you, Rube. Okay?"

On the way out, Rubin sees Artis near the door, standing beside "Bucks" Royster (a genial, neighbourhood alcoholic Rubin was fond of), who is propped up against the cigarette machine. Rubin compliments Artis on his dancing and asks him if he wants to go for a ride. Royster overhears and asks if he can tag along. "Of course you can, old buddy!" Artis asks if he can drive, and Rubin tosses him the keys. "Bucks" gets in the front beside Artis, and Rubin settles in the back, reclining.

Royster, sporting a beard and a small-brimmed straw hat, tries to stay awake as Artis (between asking Rubin for directions to his house) rambles on about how, although boxing's not his thing, he's seen the Hurricane on television, that all his friends didn't believe him when he told them he had met the Hurricane in person a coupla times before, and are they ever gonna shit when they find out he's not only been in the Hurricane's car, but he's even driven it himself! It's not the custom Eldorado, but still . . .

Suddenly, a police car rolls up alongside and motions to Artis to pull over to the curb, which he does. A white cop approaches and asks John for his licence and registration. He gives the cop his licence, but fumbles around looking for the registration.

"It's on the steering post, John," says Rubin, now sitting up.

The cop, surprised, flashes his light into the rear of the car and into Rubin's face. The cop smiles. "How ya doin', Hurricane?"

"I'm all right, Sergeant Capter. What's the problem? What'd you stop us for?"

"Oh, nothing really. We're just looking for a white car with two Negroes in it." He hands back John's licence. "But you're okay. And I still want that autographed picture you promised me for my nephew, Hurricane. I haven't forgotten."

Capter's partner, Angelo DeChellis, notes down the time: 2:40 AM.

A short time later, having completed the round trip to Rubin's house, the car pulls up outside the Nite Spot. The tavern has closed and only a few stragglers remain on the street. Rubin tells John to drive over to the Club LaPetite on Bridge Street to look for Hardney. They pull up to the club and find that it, too, is now closed.

As they sit there double-parked, deciding what to do, a cop car passes slowly. One of the cops radios to headquarters that they've got a white car under surveillance, with New York licence plates, number 5Z4 741; three male Negro occupants, two with beards. "Any of the suspects sport beards?" the cop asks. "Beards, negative," replies headquarters. They are told not to apprehend the vehicle or its occupants and to continue their search for "two coloured males in a white car." It's 2:55 AM.

The three men decide to call it a night. Artis continues to drive, and they drop Royster off at his house. On the way to Artis's, they stop at a red light, waiting for the signals to change. A cop car comes squealing up behind them. The cop is talking frantically into his transmitter. He approaches the car and starts shaking his head. It's Sergeant Capter again.

"Awwww, shit! Hurricane. I didn't realize it was you!"

Suddenly patrol cars appear from every direction, then shotguns and police revolvers, converging on Rubin and John like spokes on a hub. Rubin just stares at Capter, disgusted. Capter is embarrassed, but says nothing when a bull-faced officer approaches and orders them to remain in their car and to follow his vehicle. Seconds later, they find themselves in the middle of a five-car police escort, speeding down city streets, sirens blaring. They come to a screeching halt in front of a dilapidated corner bar, its neon sign flashing: "Lafayette Bar and Grill." The crowd of white people in the street moves out of the way, then gathers close. Rubin looks at the angry and frightened faces pressing around the car, and sees the shotguns pointing at him.

"What are we doing here?" asks Rubin.

"Get out!" the cop snarls again, now pulling the gun out of his holster. Slowly they exit the car.

"Get up against the wall! Don't move!" The cop motions with his pistol. "Just get up against the wall, and shut the fuck up!"

Rubin and John face the wall, backs to the crowd. They hear a frenzy of confused sounds: sirens wailing, people whispering, cursing, crying, Rubin's car doors being opened and closed, someone telling an officer not to forget to search the trunk. The search of the car produces nothing. Rubin and John are frisked—again, nothing. They are herded into the rear of a paddy wagon, which screeches off. John can't stop talking: "What's going on? . . . Something terrible has happened here! . . . Something horrible is going on! . . . But what's it got to do with us?"

Rubin tells him to be cool. "Don't volunteer anything, but if anyone asks any questions, tell them the truth. The cops are just playin' with me—as usual. It'll all be cleared up

soon." But even the Hurricane doesn't quite believe it; every-
thing feels wrong.

They are taken to headquarters, hustled into the building
and out almost as fast and back into the paddy wagon, which
races away. Before they know it, the wagon slides once again
to a halt. Rubin and John, surrounded by armed cops, are
hustled into an emergency operating room at St Joseph's Hos-
pital, where a couple of plainclothes detectives are waiting.
Except for the detectives' suits and the uniforms of the men in
blue, the room is all white. Doctors and nurses are minister-
ing to a middle-aged white man who has been shot in the
head; it looks like a bullet has pierced his left eye.

"Doctor, is he able to speak?" asks the detective who ap-
pears to be in charge, Sergeant Robert Callahan.

Disturbed by the intrusion, the doctor looks with hostil-
ity first at the cops, then at John and Rubin. After a moment,
he and a nurse lift the victim's head.

"Can you make out the faces of these two guys?" asks
Callahan. The victim nods, yes he can. Rubin holds his breath
as the injured man is asked if Rubin and John are the
ones who shot him. He looks at them carefully, taking his
time. Finally, he responds, shaking his head from side to side,
no.

"But, sir! Are you sure these aren't the guys? Look care-
fully now!"

"Dirty sonofabitch!" snarls Rubin to the cop, hearing the
"you-know-all-niggers-look-alike" tone in his voice. "Dirty
motherfucker!"

The victim keeps shaking his head.

In the detective bureau later that night, Rubin, still in custody,
sits in one of the windowless interrogation rooms; Artis is
alone in another. A heavy, jowly detective enters holding a
stack of yellow legal pads.

"DeSimone!" Rubin recognizes the detective from previ-
ous run-ins.

"That's right, Carter. But I haven't forgotten you, either.

How could I? You leave such a strong impression wherever you go, Hurricane. I guess all natural disasters do that."

"You fat-ass motherfucker!"

"Let's dispense with formalities—a simple 'Lieutenant' will do."

Vincent DeSimone places the pads squarely on the table, sits down and draws out his fountain pen. "We like to tackle the facts head on," he says in his gravelly voice. "And I'm gonna be frank with you. There's a dark cloud hanging over your head, Rubin Carter, and it would be wise for you to try and clear it up."

"You're the dark cloud hangin' over my head, you fuckin' bulldog! Hoverin' around like stunk on funk!"

"Boy, for an ex-con you sure got a way with words! Now, I just want you to account for your whereabouts this past night, that's all."

Rubin is silent and seething. He stares at the scar on DeSimone's pock-marked face. That is one ugly mother-fucker, thinks Rubin. DeSimone was disfigured during the Second World War, and he wears his scar proudly. It is a badge of honour, won in the service of his country, a perma-nent reminder of the high cost of freedom. He had protected his country—but for what? Rubin could see DeSimone won-dering. For this coloured piece of shit sitting here?

"Well, if you got something to hide . . ."

"Hide? From you? Hmmph! Ask your motherfuckin' cops to account for my whereabouts! Tonight, your cops stopped me not once but twice. I was trying to give a kid a lift home and suddenly we get put on display in front of a hyster-ical mob at some godforsaken place, and get taken to a hos-pital where a cop tries to talk a guy into fingering us as the ones who shot him! What the fuck is going on?"

"Take it easy, Rubin. A little slower now so I can get this all down."

"Yeah, let's get down!"

Rubin then begins telling DeSimone of his activities that night, and DeSimone makes copious notes.

"I was watching a James Brown special on TV. It ended at 10:00 PM and I didn't leave the house till just after that. I had an appointment to meet my business adviser at the Club LaPetite about the arrangements for my next prize-fight. . . ."

As Rubin continues to relate the rest of the night's events, two witnesses pass by: Patricia Valentine, a skinny, mousy brunette in her early twenties, and Alfred Bello, a short, fat punk with greasy black hair, same age, both of whom were among the crowd at the Lafayette Bar. Bello told the cops when they arrived at the scene that he saw the gunmen: they were "both coloured, thin build, about five feet, eleven inches." Valentine said that, looking out her window in the apartment above the bar, she noticed that the two men fleeing to a white car were well-dressed Negroes, both in dark clothing; that there were no lights on the car licence plate, and that the rear of the getaway car was similar to the one (Rubin's car) the police had brought to the scene later. Upon viewing Rubin and John at headquarters, each of the witnesses shakes their head, no. Valentine later that night tells her boyfriend's relatives that "Hurricane" Carter was definitely not one of the men she saw fleeing from beneath her window.

Bobby Ward, a black cop that Rubin is friendly with, walks into the interrogation room. Rubin asks Ward to tell him what's going on, what happened at that bar he was taken to.

"There was a shooting, Rube. A bartender and a patron were killed instantly. A female patron was critically wounded and probably won't live too long, and then there's the man you saw in the hospital . . ."

" . . . who told your cop friends it wasn't me," says Rubin. "But you guys still think I had something to do with this shit?"

Ward shakes his head. "DeSimone is saying if you didn't, then you won't be afraid to take a lie-detector test."

"I got nothing to hide."

Hours later, Rubin is present as the cop who has just administered the polygraph test, a Sergeant McGuire, studies the graphs. DeSimone and a few detectives are also in the room.

"Vince, here, look at this," McGuire says as he lays out several charts on the table, the other cops crowding around. McGuire points out a long straight line. This, he explains, is where Carter answered no to the question of whether he had ever been inside the Lafayette Bar. "The uninterrupted line indicates the answer is truthful. The answers to all the other questions are truthful too. They had nothing to do with this, Lieutenant. You can let them go."

Rubin and John are set free.

In the local papers and in The New York Times *the next day, it's reported that middleweight prizefighter Rubin "Hurricane" Carter (among many others) had been brought in for questioning in regard to the Lafayette Bar murders, but Passaic County Prosecutor Vincent Hull says the questioning was merely routine: Carter "was never a suspect."*

Rubin and John testify voluntarily before a grand jury at the end of June, and are completely exonerated. In July, Rubin leaves for South America for his fight with Rocky Rivero. He is sure that his entanglement with the Lafayette Bar murder investigation is over. In his mind, it is just one more "botheration" by the Paterson police because of his attitude and outspoken civil rights stance.

After that bout in August, he returns to Paterson. He talks to Teddy Brenner, the matchmaker at Madison Square Garden, and starts negotiating a deal for a title fight. Emile Griffith, who the Hurricane had knocked out in the first round of their bout, is now middleweight champion.

In October of 1966, the cops swoop down on him for keeps. Thanks to new statements from Valentine, Bello and Bradley, given four months after the night of the shootings, Rubin and John are arrested and charged with triple murder. In May 1967 they are tried and convicted.

"But," exclaimed the Canadians, "how were you convicted if you had an alibi? People were with you the whole night! How did the prosecution discount that fact?"

"You read the transcripts of Ray Brown's testimony from the second trial, didn't you?" replied Rubin, rhetorically.

Yes, they remembered. Raymond A. Brown, Sr., a prominent and highly respected New Jersey attorney, had represented Rubin at his first trial. Brown, under oath at the retrial, gave a clear picture of what happened to Rubin's alibi witnesses. There were many people who told Brown they could support Rubin's alibi, "but they were terrified and would not come forward and undergo . . . the same kind of travesty and the same kind of crucifixion that Rubin Carter suffered." As for the witnesses who did come forward, Brown was obliged by discovery rules to disclose their names to the prosecution (which meant, to DeSimone). As soon as he did, DeSimone "proceeded to contact them and then they would disappear."

"For example," Rubin elaborated, "Bill Hardney, my sparring partner—they ran him out of town by resurrecting some old child-support charges against him. Royster hid out in an attic until the trial, and when he testified, they tried to make it look like he was too drunk to know what had gone on that night. DeSimone got Cathy McGuire and her mother alone in a room and scared the hell out of them, screamed at them how he'd 'tear their black asses up' if they testified. Then he got them to sign a statement that had the wrong date for when I drove them home, so even though they testified for me at trial, it was confusing for the jury. At the second trial, it got even worse. By that time, Cathy was engaged to a Paterson detective, and she swore it was another night I drove them home."

"But you didn't fit the descriptions! You and John were never even alone together until Sargeant Capter stopped your car the second time, long after the murders had been committed!"

"That's right. It was only when we dropped off Royster twenty minutes after we were first stopped by Capter that we then became 'two Negroes in a white car.' And that's all they needed.

"But these are details," continued Rubin, tired of regurgitating minutiae in the face of the larger lie. "Let's get down to the basics.

Think of the absurdity of this. According to the State's case at both trials, the prosecution claimed that on the night of the shooting they already had in hand the following evidence against me: they had, they said, a positive car identification from two people, Bello and Valentine; they'd found one bullet and one shell in my car that matched the calibres of those used at the Lafayette Bar; they had a description of the assailants which 'approximated' John and me; DeSimone claimed that John and I gave him inconsistent statements of what we did that night; and we failed our lie-detector tests. If that was so, why did they release us, tell the press we weren't even suspects, go on to clear us before a grand jury and let me go to Argentina, which has no extradition treaty with the United States? Would they have done that in the face of this mountain of incriminating evidence they later alleged they had in their possession that night? This, remember, was 1966. These were times of real racial paranoia. If they'd had the merest suspicion that John and I had really gunned down four white people, can you imagine what they would've done to our black asses?"

"So that means they manufactured that evidence later."

"Is there any other conclusion?"

So how, Rubin and the Canadians wondered on the phone one day, could Rubin get a court to go back to the actual events of the night of the crime, when he was exonerated by all witnesses? To go back to the original grand jury investigation in which DeSimone himself stated "the description of the assailants is not even close" to Carter and Artis, before the descriptions started changing? To the grand jury that was told by DeSimone that Carter and Artis had passed their lie-detector tests, before the prosecutors claimed to have lost the original documents?

"Let's make a chart, Rube," said Lisa, sensing that his energy was flagging.

"A chart of what?"

"Your case. For the federal court. We can start at the night of the crime with everybody's original statements to the police and then trace how their stories change from there."

"How you gonna do that?"

"*We're* gonna do it, together."

"Have you any idea how much paper this case has generated over these fifteen years? You haven't seen a fraction of it. Lord, woman, you come up with some crazy ideas sometimes."

This crazy idea occupied Rubin and the Canadians for six full weeks. They made a huge chart, about nine feet by three feet. Down the left hand side they placed the names of all the major witnesses. Across the top they put, in chronological order, the various hearings and trials, starting with the night of the crime, June 17, 1966, and continuing through the grand juries, the first trial, the recantation hearing, other hearings, the second trial, and ending with the Bello lie-detector hearing of 1981. Under each heading they entered the salient features of everyone's record testimony. Only Bello had all fourteen of his boxes filled in across the board, each one with a different story.

This endeavour required enormous concentration and effort. Every day, Rubin would dig out more transcripts and read them over the phone to the Canadians, who recorded the important sections on tape and then summarized them in point-form on the chart. Between the taping, typing, transcribing, synthesizing, laying out and lettering of the chart, everyone in the Toronto house was involved. By the time they finished they had what they hoped could be used as an exhibit in federal court. It demonstrated clearly that all the evidence on the night of the crime exonerated Rubin and John and that the stories of the State's witnesses had "improved," and had kept improving through the various proceedings over the years to the advantage of the prosecution.

One trend which became clear was that the more that suppressed evidence came to light, the more it became necessary for the prosecution to fill the huge holes and contradictions in its case by focusing attention on other areas. For example, as the credibility of Bello's testimony decreased, the importance of Patricia Valentine's corroborative testimony increased. Valentine lived above the Lafayette Bar and claimed to have seen the rear of the getaway car as it sped away from the scene. The chart showed the following evolution in her testimony:

June 1966, original statement to the police: The rear of the Carter car was "similar" to the rear of the getaway car.

May 1967, first trial: The Carter car had "the same kind of tail-lights" as the getaway car, but she "was not specifically identifying" it as the same car and had not done so to the police at the scene.

December 1976, second trial: The Carter car was unquestionably the getaway car and Valentine now testified she had told the police that "fact" immediately at the scene—"There is no doubt."

Similarly, as it became apparent at the retrial that the shotgun shell the police claimed they'd found in the trunk of the Carter vehicle on the night of the shooting was actually evidence that had gone "astray" from ammunition collected by the police from the scene of an earlier crime, Valentine was called upon to bolster the State's case. She now claimed she'd been present in the police garage when the detective searched the trunk of the Carter vehicle and found the shell (and this was *after* the car had been searched at the scene). The chart showed this was not only unsubstantiated by, but contrary to, all testimony and records over the preceding ten years.

In the fall of 1982, the Canadians packed up the chart and sent it from Toronto to Myron Beldock in New York. At the same time, so nobody would forget, Rubin typed up and sent his lawyer a list of a score of demonstrable instances of wrongdoings on the part of the prosecution (suppression of exculpatory evidence, intimidating witnesses, falsifying evidence). This list alone took up five full pages of single-spaced, marginless typing.

Rubin felt relieved once this task was done. He now knew it was possible for others to follow the convolutions of his case and not lose sight of the undoctored, original events.

Beldock was surprised by the oversized parcel a courier delivered to his Fifth Avenue office one October day. He didn't know anyone in Toronto who would send him such a thing. It was neatly wrapped in a black portfolio case.

"What in God's name is this?" he asked himself as he pulled the chart from its container and recognized the headings. With the Supreme Court denial, he too, had been feeling Rubin's case was just this side of hopeless. "My God," he thought, "the amount of work that must have gone into this!"

As he later expressed it in an interview with William J. Dean, the executive director of Volunteers of Legal Service, Inc., "Carter produced a massive analytical document of all the wrongs that had been done to us. I could not face reading it, but its very production was like a kick in the pants and got us going again. Carter made me into more than a lawyer. Now I was representing a principle, not just a case."

15

Rubin was unaware of the energizing effect the chart had on Myron Beldock. As far as Rubin could see, absolutely nothing was happening with his case and it appeared to him as if nothing ever would. He knew there was one piece of unfinished business left in the state, but he didn't know it was holding them up from proceeding federally.

At the 1981 hearing before Judge Leopizzi, Rubin's lawyers had tried to develop some potentially explosive new evidence originating from a former prosecution member named Richard Caruso. Caruso had been an investigator on the Carter-Artis task force, formed after the first trial verdict was overturned in 1976 to see whether the evidence warranted a second trial. After three months, Caruso asked to be removed from the task force and reassigned, or he would "blow the whistle." He had discovered that the reinvestigation was a charade. Caruso was reassigned.

Despite DeSimone's extraordinary directive to all investigators on the task force *not* to make any notes, Caruso did, and kept them. For the first time in the case, the defence was presented with the tantalizing prospect of getting raw, uncensored information from the prosecution's own investigation. Beldock had tried to have Caruso's notes turned over to the defence and exposed at the 1981 hearing, but Judge Leopizzi wouldn't hear of it. The last thing the judge wanted to do was open up this can of worms and another possible appeal issue. As far as he was concerned, the defence was always grasping at straws. Leopizzi refused to order Caruso to turn the file over to the defence, and severely limited Beldock's questioning of Caruso on the matter. Beldock, desperate to protect the Caruso documents, asked the court to seal them, to prevent their disappearing or being tampered with before the defence could examine them.

"I am going to seal the whole file, Mr Beldock," pronounced the judge. "I will seal it nice and tight, gentlemen. It will be a pot of gold—no?"

Beldock then had to petition the New Jersey Supreme Court to have the file opened and available for scrutiny, but the Court had failed to address the matter in its August 1982 opinion. Beldock had to re-petition the Supreme Court to renew his request. There was bound to be some juicy stuff among the papers in that file. Months later, they were still waiting for an answer.

As the days dragged on, Rubin brooded over his repeated rejections in the courts. It became increasingly difficult for him to keep his head above water and not sink into a well of despair. The Canadians did their best to buoy him up, to keep his mind occupied. When not visiting in person, they spoke daily over the phone.

Over the years Rubin's interest in boxing had waned. It belonged to a past life that seemed to have no bearing on his present one. But whenever the subject came up in conversation, Rubin's knowledge of and expertise in the sport would come pouring forth. Such was the case when tragedy struck the World Lightweight Boxing Championship between Ray "Boom Boom" Mancini and Korean boxer Duk Koo-Kim, and Duk Koo-Kim was knocked out and rendered comatose. Safety in boxing instantly became a main topic on the news. There was talk again that boxing was such a dangerous sport, it should be abolished altogether.

Rubin watched replays of the knock-out blow on television and remembered vividly his own experience with a similar type of head injury to one of his sparring partners, who had fortunately recovered.

He told the Canadians that he had observed through the years that life-threatening injuries are not caused only by the force of the blow itself, but by what happens when the fighter falls to the canvas. In many instances, the back of the fighter's neck strikes the lowest strand of the ropes, which, given the velocity of the fall, delivers a tremendous whiplash effect directly to the nexus of nerves at the base of the skull. Such force on so sensitive a spot could easily cause brain trauma and produce blood clots, which ultimately could bring about the death of the fighter.

What Rubin said seemed to make sense to the Canadians, as they too observed replays of the knockout to Duk Koo-Kim, who for some time languished in a coma, and later died. The base of his head had indeed struck the bottom rope.

"My theory can easily be proved or disproved by examining the film footage of other bouts where serious injuries occurred, like those that brought about the deaths of LaVern Roach, Sugar Ramos and Davey Moore. And if my observations are borne out, then the solution is simple. All that needs to be done is to loosen the turnbuckle and move the lowest strand of the ring ropes—you don't touch the others—so that it sits six or eight inches out toward the outside apron. That would completely eliminate the possibility of a fighter's head or neck striking that portion of the ropes, and yet still serve its original purpose of preventing a downed fighter from falling out of the ring."

"That sounds like a great idea," said the Canadians. "But isn't it kind of a band-aid solution to a larger problem—the nature of boxing itself?"

"You know I have no interest in defending boxing. It is a violent sport, no question about that. But people aren't going to stop using it as an avenue to improve their lives, to get out of ghettos, to make some money, get some respect. How can I tell anyone they can't do that, that this door should be closed to them, when the doors to university, where they should be going, are *already* closed to them, Lesra notwithstanding? No, it's not boxing but boxers that I'm concerned about—prizefighters. I love prizefighters. They're good people, warm people, generous, big-hearted people. These people should be protected in every way possible."

"So what are you going to do about it?"

"What *can* I do?"

While Rubin was watching the morning news on television, what to do became clear. Angelo Dundee was on a sports segment, discussing boxing safety. He was a man who Rubin had always respected, the trainer and manager of (at that time) ten world boxing champions, including Muhammad Ali, a man who cared about his fighters. His suggestions were for mandatory standing eight-counts, properly fitted mouthpieces and gloves with safety thumbs. These ideas were good, thought Rubin, but there was one Angelo hadn't come up with.

At the urging of the Canadians, Rubin set aside his powerlessness and started typing: "Dear Angelo." He concluded the letter with a question: If this works, why has such a solution not been proffered before? Because, answered Rubin, we are all prisoners of some sort. In this case, we are "prisoners of our own assumptions." Our assumption is that the ropes protect the fighter, therefore we cannot conceive of the fact that they could injure him as well.

"He's my best friend," Angelo Dundee later told *Washington Post* reporter John Ed Bradley, as he proudly displayed Rubin's letter and diagrams for a redesigned boxing ring. "They put him in prison for life for supposedly killing some people with a gun. My best friend, the Hurricane. And he's got an idea."

The reporter read the November 17, 1982, letter from Rubin that Dundee proudly kept on file in his Miami office. His eyes lit upon the paragraph at the top of the third and final page:

> . . . This slight adjustment of the bottom strand . . . can only add to the integrity of the sport . . . the safety of its participants . . . is paramount . . . it would be visually imperceptible and the cost negligible.

As Bradley revealed in the opening paragraphs of his article on the front page of the *Washington Post*'s sports section, he was as impressed with the eloquence of Rubin's presentation of the idea as Dundee was with its substance.

Rubin also sent copies of his ring-safety proposal to others, including illustrious attorney and sports aficionado Edward Bennett Williams, with whom Rubin had been acquainted for years.* Williams thought his idea had "tremendous merit" and asked for Rubin's permission to pass it on to Jose Sulaiman, then president of the World Boxing Council. His idea—the Canadians dubbed it "the Hurricane rope"—was well received and considered, at the very least, worthy of investigation.

Such positive feedback, however, rather than making Rubin feel more hopeful, drove him deeper into despair. The act of reaching out, peeking over the penitentiary wall, made him feel the fact of his imprisonment even more keenly. His association with Lesra and the Canadians was now a constant reminder of his confinement. What if he should never be released? His appeal had been denied first by Judge Leopizzi and then by the State Supreme Court, when everything had pointed to his imminent freedom. What if he could no longer do the time? With hopes so raised, how could he not have been disappointed? He knew better—he had learned to protect himself so he *could* do the time. It was easier not to feel, not to care, not to interact, and above all, not to need.

Now he was really fucked up. Now he was tormented by hope.

December 1982: another Christmas was approaching. Christmases had always marked major turning-points in Rubin's life. It was just three days before Christmas in 1976 that he had been reconvicted and thrown back in prison. Two Christmases ago Lesra had first come to see him. Last Christmas was when he was shunted off to the Vroom Building.

This Christmas, Rubin seized the reins. He stopped calling Toronto. He had had enough.

---

*In the early sixties, Williams had offered Rubin a contract to play football for the Washington Redskins. Rubin was flattered, but refused. He thought you had to be crazy to play football; it was too dangerous, too easy to get hurt. He said he'd rather take his chances in the ring, one on one.

16

Lesra and the Canadians were devastated by Rubin's withdrawal. They had grown so close to Rubin, had shared his life so intensely, that the abrupt loss of contact with him stung them to the quick. At first they could hardly speak about it. Their phone was strangely quiet. The laughter and chatter that usually animated their house ceased, and instead there was a deep and grieving silence.

Understanding why Rubin had cut himself off was not easy. It didn't appear to make sense. It had come at a time of brightening prospects, forward momentum. They were about to go federal, with the strong dissenting opinion and the chart ready in hand. They had been looking forward to being together over the Christmas holidays. For months, Lesra had been working in his spare time with Michael, stripping down and rebuilding a classic 1970 Mercedes-Benz which they had planned to drive down to the States; now there was no joy in having finished the job.

With Rubin not responsive, the group knew there was no way they could bridge the relationship. He, or rather, his conditioning, was in control. He was behind an impenetrable wall; he had locked himself down in a maximum-security prison nobody could break him out of.

So they did what they always did when action was futile; they did nothing.

The Canadians, now involved in the business of renovating houses, made sure that Lesra and Marty got their high school diplomas and were ready for university.

To get into a university in Ontario, a Secondary School Honour Graduation Diploma (SSHGD) was required. This diploma was granted upon completion of six credits at the grade thirteen level, a sort of college preparatory year akin to A-levels in Great Britain. Between correspondence courses, and night- and summer-school classes in biology, English, history and sociology, Lesra and Marty were each expecting to have six credits and their diplomas by the end of the summer of 1983. Their marks were excellent, and they were hoping to get into the University of Toronto. Marty wanted to study archaeology; Lesra's interest lay in anthropology. For Lesra, U of T's downtown campus had held a special meaning ever since his first trip to Toronto: not only was it where his Canadian tutors had gone to school, it had been his vantage point for the Caribana parade.

The problem was that, in order to be accepted into U of T, it wasn't good enough just to have an SSHGD with a high grade-point average; the credits had to be distributed over a certain range of subjects. Lesra and Marty had the marks, but they were going to lack the one credit required in either mathematics or a foreign language. Although Lesra's knowledge of basic mathematics was excellent, he did not have the background to study it at the grade-thirteen level. Similarly, although he had taken a year of Spanish, he needed a minimum of another year before he could take it at the advanced level.

One of the group, Gus, who in the late sixties had been the assistant registrar at New College in the University of Toronto, broached the subject with Colin Dobell, an officer in the university's Faculty of Arts and Sciences Department of Admissions. Colin was fascinated by the unusual backgrounds and educations of both Lesra and Marty. He thought that Innis College, an innovative college within the university, would suit them well and suggested they make an appointment with the registrar and explain why they lacked one of the prerequisites and why they thought the rules should be waived in their circumstances.

The registrar was impressed by both youths, by their written applications and sample essays, as well as by their personal interviews. They were both very verbal, highly articulate, and there was no question that they were ready for university studies. Lesra made the argument that since Black (Non-standard) English was, for all intents and purposes, a foreign language—indeed, he had been taught Standard English as if it were a second language—then his knowledge of and fluency in Black English should count toward the foreign language requirement for admission to the university. Marty, in turn, explained that while his dyslexia prevented him from obtaining advanced math and language credits, it did not prevent him from doing well in other subjects. He was confident he could be successful at university, particularly if his professors gave him oral exams or allowed him more time on written ones.

The registrar accepted them both, provided their final grade thirteen marks were as good as their interim ones. They were euphoric. For both of them, a dream had come true.

Lesra and Marty, nineteen years old and twenty, hung out together, going to discos, movies, parties and doing odd jobs. They did a lot of hanging out around the house, too, and their closest friends—Sean (who was white) and Earle and Junior (both black)—were there so often that they felt like part of the family. In spite of not having gone to regular day school, Lesra and Marty were popular and had a lot of friends. They were both intelligent, good-looking, easy-going but serious people. There was the added cachet of Lesra's being a black American from New York—probably the ultimate in cool. And Marty's closeness to Lesra reflected well on Marty: to be "tight" with a black friend, Marty must not only be hip, but trustworthy.

There was one night-school class, a grade thirteen course in English literature, that Lesra and Marty took together. Although the class was fairly large, people couldn't help but notice them. Certainly it wasn't long before Paulene did. She wondered who these guys were who were black and white and seemed inseparable. She had overheard Marty tell someone that Lesra was his brother from New York. They both radiated self-assurance and were the most vocal students in class. They played off each other, one often finishing a point the other had begun. They dissected books like tigers on fresh game.

Paulene had never seen anything quite like them and loved listening to them. She was black, had been born in Jamaica, grown up in London, England, and had recently emigrated to Canada on her own. When she started the English class, she had been in Toronto for only a few months and was trying to further her education.

She had been a nurse in England; in Toronto she was employed as a nanny, the only work she was allowed under Canadian immigration rules. She was disenchanted with Canada, finding her job exploitive, and was seriously considering going home.

One night, the whole English class went to see a play they were studying. After the performance, Lesra and Marty offered to walk Paulene to the bus stop. They talked about the play, then asked Paulene about her background, what she thought of Canada, and so on. She found herself able to talk with them freely and effortlessly.

Paulene, finding strength and support in her two new friends, decided to stay in Canada and slog it out. She and Lesra started going out together. Paulene was Lesra's first true love, and she soon joined the group. Going to school in Canada was indeed bringing unexpected rewards.

"What's happening, stranger?"

This was the first time the Canadians had heard Rubin's voice since the previous December—almost eight months. "The Rose needs help," he said, "with his case."

Rubin sounded wary and sheepish. He didn't want to talk about himself. This was a "business call."

The Canadians were happy that Rubin had opened the door. They didn't push it. They spoke about Sam South's case.

Rubin and "the Family" had earlier worked together on the appeal of Sam's murder conviction and his thirty-year sentence. Sam had been unhappy with his lawyer (both at trial and with his appeal work), had fired him and decided to start again *pro se* (on his own behalf), with the assistance of Rubin's legal know-how. Sam had given Rubin and the Canadians copies of all the documents in his case, including the trial transcripts. They had found his papers comparatively easy to digest; they numbered in the hundreds, as opposed to Rubin's, which were in the tens of thousands.

There was no question that his trial, which had lasted only a few days, had been unfair and that he had been inadequately represented. Had his lawyer done even a modicum of investigating, it is hard to imagine that Sam would have been found guilty. Sam's lawyer could have easily established his alibi by using the computerized lottery tickets (showing time and place of purchase) that Sam had been buying at the time of the murder. And the State's key witness testified that when she met Sam in a bar four days after the crime, he told her he was glad he'd committed the murder; problem was, at that time, Sam was miles away in another town with his probation officer.

Rubin and the Canadians had catalogued all the areas and arguments they could think of in Sam's case to show "ineffective assistance of counsel," which was the legal umbrella under which Rubin had decided every point had to be pegged. He knew it was almost impossible to win an appeal on this ground, but Sam had forfeited the other issues his lawyer previously raised in his aborted appeal. Rubin was then going to type up a brief in the proper form—a procedural history of the case, a statement of facts and then the legal arguments, citing precedents, constitutional grounds (violations of Sam's Sixth- and Fourteenth-Amendment rights), the legal tests to be applied and how Sam's case meets those standards. It was going to be a motion for a new trial, or at minimum, for an "evidentiary hearing" to place onto the record the evidence that Sam's lawyer had failed to bring out at trial.

By the time Rubin resumed calling Toronto, he had completed a draft of the brief, but wanted to be sure that it was as good as it could be. He didn't want to be solely responsible for it if it wasn't. He was wondering whether the Canadians would look at it, to make sure that he hadn't left out any of the facts and that the writing was polished. It had to be perfect before it was submitted to the court. Sam deserved only the best.

They agreed.

Over the next weeks, they worked together on Sam's brief, mostly through the mail, papers winging back and forth across the Canada-U.S. border. By the time they were finished, they had a sixty-five-page brief (excluding exhibits) ready to be filed in court. Rubin's legal arguments and use of precedents were masterful, and their factual foundation was unassailable. The Rose was touched by all the care and energy that had gone into it. He thanked Rubin and "the Family" profusely.

It was fall 1983 when Rubin started to get down to the business of himself. It was as if he had spent the year in limbo. He had seen nothing happening in his own case for almost a year. No papers had been filed in federal court. Although his lawyers had finally obtained access to the Caruso file, Rubin had not yet had a chance to see it.

And it was time to come to terms with his feelings about the Canadians. He loved them, but they infuriated him with their care. Worse, they showed him that *he* was caring, and that made him feel vulnerable. He hadn't wanted to have to care. It was easier instead to resent them for interfering in his life, for questioning him, for "making" him respond, for "forcing" him to poke his head above the penitentiary wall. But what is easiest is not always best, Rubin knew.

That's what the year apart had shown him, and he finally called and told the Canadians so. He now accepted the fact that he trusted them and needed them. He trusted them to understand. He needed them so he could be free.

They asked him, "If the doors to the prison were opened would you walk out? Could you leave there?"

It was an odd question, but Rubin understood where it was coming from. It brought to mind Franz Kafka's words from *The Trial*: "It is often safer to be in chains than to be free." Rubin recognized he had been a prisoner for the majority of his life. He was a professional prisoner, a master at it. He knew how to lock down, how to do time. Now he knew he could no longer play it "safe." To be free he had to try something different.

Yes, more than anything now he wanted to be free. It wasn't just words. It wasn't just a stance. He meant it. Yes, more than anything. Yes, he was willing to do whatever was necessary to get out. He was willing to commit himself wholly. He was ready to walk through that door.

He answered: "Yes."

William towering over "I ain't got no neck" Lesra in Toronto, beside "painted" birch tree. Summer, 1979.

The home Lesra leaves in Brooklyn.

The home Lesra comes to in Toronto.

Except where otherwise indicated, all photographs are reproduced by courtesy of the authors.

Rubin Carter, second from right, a Ranger in the U. S. Army, stationed in Germany, 1955.

The Hurricane at work, December 1963. Carter KO's Emile Griffith in the first round. Griffith later becomes world middleweight champion; Carter later becomes #45472.

*Lesra and his Canadian family.
Each step, starting from the
bottom, right to left: Lesra, Lisa,
Sam; Gus, Marty, Mary; Kathy,
Terry; Michael.*

*Lesra reading the discarded copy
of Rubin's autobiography bought
at the library sale.*

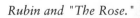

Rubin and "The Rose."

Trenton State Prison, 1981. Rubin, wearing his new slippers and velvet robe, accepts a little softness in a hard place.

Lesra (right), his younger brother, Leland, and Marty. Toronto, 1984.

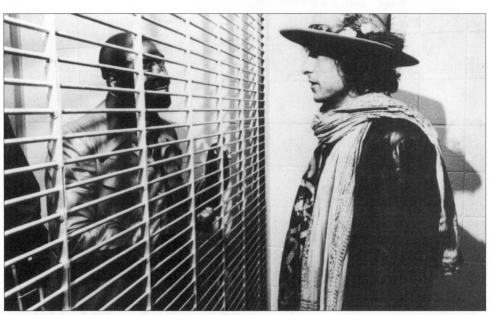

Bob Dylan greets his friend Rubin Carter in a New Jersey prison, where Dylan and his Rolling Thunder Revue are about to perform his song "Hurricane" for the prisoners. December, 1975. (Ken Regan/Camera 5)

Rubin "Hurricane" Carter, cause célèbre, with Dyan Cannon and talk-show host Mike Douglas at Trenton State Prison, 1975. (Photo: The Times, Trenton N.J.)

After the marches, protests, and appeals, the N. J. Supreme Court throws out the 1967 convictions, and Muhammad Ali celebrates with Rubin Carter and John Artis on their first day of freedom, March 1976. (Photo courtesy of Howard L. Bingham)

Vincent DeSimone (second from right) sworn in as Chief of County Detectives after 1976 Carter/Artis convictions. (Photo: Paterson Museum)

Passaic County Superior Court Judge Bruno Leopizzi presiding. (Photo: The News, *Passaic, Cty.*)

The State's star witness, Alfred *"not to my recollection"* Bello, testifying in 1981. (Photo: The News, *Passaic, Cty.*)

Teamwork. Rubin thanks his dedicated attorneys, Myron Beldock (left) and Professor Leon Friedman. (Photo by Ed Quinn)

More teamwork. John Artis, Myron Beldock, and Lewis Steel. (Photo: Associated Press)

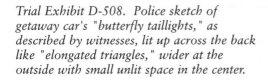

Trial Exhibit D-508. Police sketch of getaway car's "butterfly taillights," as described by witnesses, lit up across the back like "elongated triangles," wider at the outside with small unlit space in the center.

A 1966 Dodge Monaco's taillights correspond exactly with all descriptions of the rear of the fleeing car. (Neither this nor the following striking visual evidence was able to be used in court.)

By contrast, the 1966 Dodge Polara, the car Carter was driving that June night, lights up only at the extreme ends.

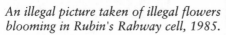

Lesra and Paulene at Lake Ontario, 1984.

An illegal picture taken of illegal flowers blooming in Rubin's Rahway cell, 1985.

Earl and Alma Martin at their son's Toronto home, 1986.

Christmas in Rahway apartment, 1984. From left: Marty, Tina, Dorothy and Isabell.

Sporting a sheepskin coat, Rubin is escorted to federal court for his 1985 release hearing. Steel jewelry courtesy of N. J. Department of Corrections. (Photo: Corbis-Bettmann)

U.S. District Judge H. Lee Sarokin. (Photo by Dave Hornor)

Rubin, flanked by the authors, Sam (left) and Terry, at home in Canada, 1992.

"And when it's all over I'd just as soon go on my way... And ride a horse along a trail"
(from "Hurricane"). Rubin and Red Cloud in December 1986.

PART THREE
PREVAILING WIND

The crooked shall be made straight
And the rough places plain;
The pools shall be filled
And the worn renewed;
The needy shall receive
And the rich shall be perplexed.

So the Wise Man cherishes the One,
As a standard to the world:
Not displaying himself,
He is famous;
Not asserting himself,
He is distinguished;
Not boasting his powers,
He is effective;
Taking no pride in himself,
He is chief.

Because he is no competitor,
No one in all the world
Can compete with him.

The saying of the men of old
Is not vain:
"The crooked shall be made straight—"
To be perfect, return to it.

—Lao Tzu, "Poem 22"
THE WAY OF LIFE
Translation by R.B. Blakney

17

When Americans think of Canada—if they think of Canada at all—it's usually in terms of weather fronts that every once in a while invade their borders and "freeze their butts." In the autumn of 1983, there was a northwesterly wind that swept south over the Great Lakes and wound its way down to Trenton, New Jersey, seeking out a brother storm that had been stationary, gathering up momentum, and was now ready to move. To Rubin's persecutors, the prevailing wind was to be a most major pain in the ass.

Rubin had entered his eighteenth year of unjust incarceration when he and the Canadians became single in purpose and decided to go for broke.

The "kids" were taken care of. Lesra and Marty had successfully completed grade thirteen and received their Secondary School Honour Graduation Diplomas. Lesra was honoured as an Ontario Scholar for his superior academic performance. He had his diploma and scholarship certificate framed and sent to his family's home in Brooklyn. Lesra and Marty were now both happily ensconced at the University of Toronto.

The Canadians were going to split into two groups. One group, which included the university students, would stay in Toronto. They planned to sell the house and move into a smaller place, and support the second group, which would go down to the States to get Rubin out. Being in New Jersey would be cheaper, less draining and safer than travelling back and forth all the time. It would give Rubin more and closer support. And it would allow them to concentrate fully on his case and do whatever was necessary to speed things along.

Rubin was staggered that they'd even consider such a course of action. The Canadians were in for the long haul. In their aging but rebuilt Mercedes sedan, they drove across the border and down to New Jersey. The pioneers were Kathy, Michael and Lisa.

In many respects, New Jersey is a superlative state. Dubbed the "Garden Colony" in 1760, the richness of its soil and beauty of its countryside then rivalled England's. Over two hundred years later, New Jersey is now the most densely populated, most industrialized, most polluted state in the United States. It ranks highest in number of hazardous waste sites, automobiles and miles of highway per capita. It employs more police per person than any state in the union. To outsiders, the state appears to be little more than a tightly patrolled, smokestack-flanked commuter highway between Philadelphia and New York City. Nevertheless, its licence plates unabashedly proclaim New Jersey, the "Garden State." And the Canadians were about to go weeding.

With the Quality Inn in Bordentown as their base, their first task was to find an apartment. According to the ads in the Trenton newspapers, there seemed to be a lot of apartments for rent in the area, but whenever Kathy or Michael called these places, no one knew for sure whether or not there were any vacancies. The Canadians would be asked to come in and "talk about it" in person. They found this rather odd. How, they wondered, was it possible for a building superintendent not to know whether he had apartments available? Peculiar, too, was the invariable answer to their question of what kind of area these possibly vacant apartments were in: "Safe." They had expected words like "suburban," "residential," or "commercial." The Canadians were to find out that "safe" meant "white."

When they showed up to look at the apartments, there was no longer any debate as to availability. There were apartments aplenty. More than one landlord willingly explained the necessity of a code:

"You can't tell over the phone who you're talkin' to any more, so you tell everybody to come and see you in person. It's against the law to not rent to 'them,' but what are 'they' gonna do about it, when you tell 'them' there's no vacancy?"

"If you knew why we're here in Trenton," mused the Canadians, "this well of vacant apartments would dry up quick."

They rented in a low-rise building of what were euphemistically called "garden apartments." It was in an area that was fast becoming an all-black neighbourhood, in Ewing Township, about a twenty-minute drive north from the prison.

After they settled in, they invited over Isabell Carter (no relation to Rubin), a black woman they'd met at the prison, where she visited the father of her two girls. She was a warm, outgoing, no-nonsense kind of person in her late twenties who lived in the same township, not far from the Canadians. They became fast friends with Isabell and her two daughters, Dorothy, aged nine, and Tina, who was seven. Dorothy ended up spending a lot of time at their apartment. The Canadians weren't aware how unhappy this little girl was making their fellow tenants until they were met with cold stares and realized there wasn't a single black person living in the building.

One night they were awakened by shouting from downstairs. The couple that lived in the apartment below were quarrelling. They were the well-scrubbed pair who dutifully dressed up and went to church every Sunday. The Canadians couldn't help but hear what the argument was about. The wife was making it known how miserable she was with the way her husband had been treating her, her voice rising as the social status of her carefully chosen nouns diminished.

"I am not your child," she screamed. "I am not your dog. I am not your nigger!"

On top of all this, the thing the Canadians needed most—the means of communication to Rubin, a phone line—was proving unexpectedly difficult to get. After long delays, and many calls to the phone company, an installer finally appeared. When asked what the hold-up had been, he hesitated, hemmed, then hawed, then said, "Well, you see you're in a yellow-jacket zone," as if that explained it.

"You're not talking about wasps or bees, right?" asked Michael.

"No," the installer laughed, "I shouldn't be telling you this, but it's a description of your area. It's considered unstable. You get low priority and high security deposits. You got a lot of blacks around here—in fact, this building's surrounded. But, hey, you're lucky you're not in a red-line zone, like, say, downtown Trenton. You'd be waiting for months to get your phone."

It was in this atmosphere that the Canadians decided not to hang out their law firm shingle, "Carter and Partners," but to go about their business quietly.

After the apartment was established, Michael and Kathy, who were needed for the renovating work in Toronto, exchanged places with Sam and Terry, who were the most familiar with the details of Rubin's and The Rose's cases.

They first had to tie up some loose ends in The Rose's appeal. They had hired an investigator, Herbert Bell, to obtain affidavits from witnesses as proof of the exonerating evidence that was available but which The Rose's lawyer had failed to investigate. Bell, an African-American in his early forties, was apprised of the facts of the case, what was required of him, the kind of people involved and so on. He soon had the affidavits they wanted. Rubin, Terry and Sam then wrote a supplementary brief for The Rose, explaining the significance of the new evidence and asking to have his conviction overturned.

With that work completed, it was time again to turn their attention to Rubin's case. Rubin had just received a copy of the long-awaited Caruso file from Myron Beldock. As eager as Rubin was to study the documents, he left them for the Canadians to pick up at the prison mailroom. They photocopied the nearly two hundred pages and mailed them back in to Rubin. This was the awkward procedure they had to follow throughout.

Together, Rubin and the Canadians painstakingly scrutinized the Caruso information, analysing various typed statements and decipher-ing his cryptic shorthand. It made for exciting, if somewhat detailed, reading. This was indeed "a pot of gold." Not only did the file contain Caruso's notes from his work on the 1976 Carter-Artis task force rein-vestigation (notes that the prosecution had all along denied existed), it also contained the report of another State-employed investigator (this one named Thompson) who, in the course of his own investigation earlier that year, had uncovered a dimension of the case that was, until now, unknown to Rubin. Suddenly a whole new cast of characters appeared, and familiar characters were playing altogether new roles.

To say that the new information shocked Rubin and the Canadians would be to put it mildly. They were floored. Of course, Rubin knew all along he had been set up, but now he felt as if he'd been doubly suckered. What, wondered Rube, had made him "believe a fuckin' thing the prosecution had said about anything?"

All along, the prosecution had presented a simple picture:

In June 1966, Patricia Valentine was living alone in her own apartment, a mother with one small child, struggling to make ends meet, working as a waitress in a restaurant opposite the courthouse. The night of June 16-17 was still and summery. After putting her child to bed, the mother had fallen asleep on the living-room couch while watching TV.

Suddenly a loud noise disturbed her peaceful slumber. She thought she had heard the front door of the Lafayette Bar and Grill downstairs open and close. She heard two more bangs and thought Jim Oliver, the bartender, must be having trouble closing the door. Valentine was now wide awake, her television still on, the test pattern showing. She figured it was around 2:30 AM. She got up and looked out the front window of her second-floor apartment overlooking East 18th Street to see whether the bar's neon sign was still lit. It was, but she saw nothing else. Then she heard a woman's anguished cry:

"Oh, my God! No! No!"

As if by instinct, Valentine dashed to a side window overlooking Lafayette Street and saw two black men running from the sidewalk (under her window) to a white car parked out from the curb. Both men were well-dressed in dark clothing, sports jackets; one was wearing a fedora. She didn't see their faces, but could tell from the back of their necks that they were "coloured." She continued to watch as the white car peeled rubber and sped away in the darkness. It had distinctive triangular tail-lights that lit up like butterflies.

The defence had never had reason to doubt the veracity of this scenario. But the information sealed by the court in the Caruso file, including Thompson's report, dispatched this story to fairy-tale heaven.

During the course of his investigation, Thompson found out that on the night of the Lafayette shootings, contrary to the State's case, Valentine had not been alone, sleeping. She and her roommate, Sandy, had been drinking and partying with two neighbours, Louise and Avery Cockersham, in their house next door, at 257 Lafayette Street.

Apparently, Valentine was not the paragon of virtue the prosecution had depicted. In June 1966, she did not live alone and neither was she employed. According to statements obtained by investigator Thompson, the apartment above the tavern actually belonged to Valentine's friend, a twenty-year-old woman named Sandy, with whom Valentine and her child were staying. It seemed that Ray, the father of Valentine's child, was also living there—he worked nights—and Valentine's married boyfriend, Steve, would come over about five times a week (when Ray was at work) and stay for an hour or so, sometimes all night.

Thompson interviewed Louise Cockersham in 1976; by then she was divorced from Avery. She confirmed that Valentine and Sandy had been partying with her and Avery in her house that night. Sometime after eleven, Louise left and walked next door to the Lafayette Bar to buy a bottle—a fifth of whisky. Six white people were in the bar, she said. Aside from the four (soon-to-be) shooting victims, who were regulars, there were two guys she didn't know. Louise returned home with the bottle and she, Avery, Valentine and Sandy continued drinking, playing records and dancing. After a while (Louise guessed it was around one) Valentine left and went back to Sandy's apartment above the bar. Sandy stayed with Louise and Avery, drank a couple more drinks and left about an hour later. Shortly after that, while Louise and Avery were preparing to go to bed, they heard the gunshots. Louise said Avery looked out their window and saw people running.

Louise suggested that the investigator speak to Sandy. "She saw more than any of us and told Pat [Valentine] not to mention her name to the police."

After some effort, Thompson "made telephone contact" with Sandy. She denied ever being inside Louise's house and said she only knew Louise and Avery Cockersham from seeing them enter the Lafayette Bar. When informed that Louise had said that Sandy *had* been at her house, Sandy swore she'd never been there.

Then Thompson went to see Sandy in person. She "was extremely nervous [sic] and evasive." Sandy said that, on the night of the Lafayette shooting, she wasn't home. She had gone to her mother's house and was there by ten or ten-thirty. She repeated that she was never in Louise's house and only found out about the shooting the next day. Thompson told her that what she was saying was totally contrary to the sworn statement he had received from Louise.

Thompson went once more to see Louise, and she reaffirmed her story. He called Sandy again.

Sandy now said that, "after thinking it over, [I] was, in fact at Louise's home" on the evening in question. She admitted, "Louise had invited [me] and Pat [Valentine] over," that they spent the night drinking and dancing, and that Louise did leave and go to the Lafayette Bar to buy some more liquor. Sandy said that Louise said, when she returned with the bottle: "Jim, the bartender, was at it again. He was drunk and had a butcher knife in his hand and he was waving it . . . two black men walked into the bar . . . [Jim] refused to serve them and threatened them and stated . . . he doesn't serve niggers in the bar and for them to get out." Sandy said Louise told her she recognized one of the men to be Rubin Carter. As he was leaving the bar, he "stated that he would return."

Sandy continued to insist that she spent the night at her mother's house and was there by 10:30 P.M., even though she simultaneously verified that she did not leave Louise's until after Valentine had left, and that Valentine had left at about 1:00 A.M. (because "her boyfriend Steve was going to come over"). In a subsequent sworn statement, however, Sandy admitted that when she left Louise's in the early morning hours of June 17, she went back to her own apartment above the Lafayette Bar.

Thompson next interviewed Pat Valentine's boyfriend, Steve. Louise had told Thompson that Steve "would have knowledge of the shooting." Steve admitted that he was dating Valentine frequently at the time, that sometimes he did stay all night with her, but that he could not recall whether he was with her on the night of the shooting.

Steve opined that he "might have a mental block" about this matter. Thompson noted that Steve was "anxious, evasive, and afraid," "contradicted himself in many ways" and was very concerned to know what Pat Valentine had said. When pressed, he "refused to state whether he was, in fact, at Pat's house on the night in question." He said he was married and didn't want trouble. He also "led [Thompson] to believe . . . that Pat's other boyfriend [present husband]" and a woman named Ruth may have been there as well.

In 1976, Thompson was also able to locate Avery Cockersham; he was languishing in a North Carolina hospital, dying of a cancerous brain tumour. There, Thompson interviewed Avery's current wife, Fanida. She said that Avery had spoken to her about the Lafayette Bar shootings, and that he had indeed looked out when he heard the shots. He had seen two men running from the bar, and had been able to recognize who they were. They were *not Carter and Artis*. Avery himself was too ill to verify this account for Thompson.

As to Pat Valentine, Thompson was able to speak to her only by telephone. Her initial answers to his questions were identical to Sandy's initial answers: yes, she knew Avery and Louise Cockersham, but "she swore to God that she had never been in Louise's house." When Thompson advised her that his "investigation revealed that she was, in fact, there . . . she became very evasive, anxious and hostile" and abruptly terminated the phone call. Thompson was unable to question Valentine further; no one in the prosecutor's office would tell him her whereabouts, except that she was some place in Florida.

Thompson's report ends with the conclusion that the witnesses were not revealing their entire knowledge of the shooting at the Lafayette Bar and Grill, and that they were withholding material information.

According to his file, investigator Richard Caruso then entered the picture, and things got even juicier.

The first words on the first page of Caruso's handwritten notes were revealing: "First concerned about atmosphere, sincerity, etc. when Chief interviewed me for job." He was referring to Chief of County Detectives Vincent DeSimone. Caruso's work in the Carter reinvestigation troubled him. "Some information came too easy, some was impossible to obtain (Chief's file). I was concerned with key testimony and red flags—secret meetings, code, notes. Pat Valentine and Al Bello—not pressed for truth."

When the case was re-opened in March 1976, the official prosecution line was that in the interest of impartiality and justice, Vincent DeSimone would not be actively involved, because he personally had been the most incriminated by what Bello and Bradley had said in their well-publicized recantations and, therefore, had a vested interest in the outcome. Caruso was to find that DeSimone was nevertheless running the show from behind the scenes.

In attempting to obtain information from the owner of the Lafayette Bar, Caruso stumbled upon a code that a clique of witnesses (including Valentine) and certain members of the prosecutor's staff shared with DeSimone. This code was apparently used to identify those who were aggressively anti-Carter and to avoid open discussion with those not so partisan. Caruso learned that witnesses had been alerted and coached before he had a chance to question them, and that they were deliberately withholding information. As the owner of the Lafayette Bar admitted to him, "Vince [DeSimone] told me not to say certain things."

There was a lot about the case that disturbed Caruso.

There was no hard evidence. Many witnesses were not available. On one page of his notes, under the heading "Requiescat in Pace," was a list of deceased witnesses. By July 22, 1976, they numbered thirteen; one of them was Avery Cockersham.

Caruso rejected the officially sanctioned story of Valentine's activities on the night of the shooting. Given Thompson's findings, there was strong reason to believe that, when the shootings occurred, Valentine had been drinking heavily and was not alone but with her married boyfriend and probably others. The physical evidence (the location of tire marks), Caruso concluded, was "inconsistent with her testimony" and contradicted her ability to see from her window what she said she saw. Caruso noted that Valentine had bought a home in Florida, and he couldn't help wondering where the previously unemployed mother got the money. He found out that DeSimone had met secretly with her in Florida, reviewed photographs and rehearsed her testimony for the second trial. Caruso's notes described her with the following string of adjectives: "unscrupulous, immoral, psychotic, biased, rehearsed."

Caruso also discovered the presence of another witness at the
Lafayette Bar, another woman named Pat. She was a friend of Valentine's and had been dating none other than Alfred P. Bello. In June
1966 she was also dating Valentine's live-in boyfriend, Ray, having
lost her previous boyfriend to Valentine's flatmate Sandy—all this
while her own husband was away in the service. Incredibly, this Pat
was the niece of a Passaic County Judge and related to a county detective as well. She was a part of the "network" that Caruso, try as he
might, could not get close to.

After three months of being thwarted at every step, it became clear
to Caruso that the prosecution was intent upon proceeding to a second
trial, regardless of what the evidence showed. Accordingly, as evidenced
in his notes, Caruso "demanded to be removed or expose. They said
OK. But I would never be allowed to *reveal*/testify as I was privy to
Pros. case. [Assigned to] file room until I resigned. Respect for obligation to [three named colleagues] is why I didn't make more waves."

Caruso's file also contained a newspaper article about allegations
against the Passaic County prosecutor's office for ignoring charges of
police misconduct in Paterson. This was preceded by a page of notes
about the Knapp Commission (regarding police corruption in New
York City) with the following remark penned in: "Evidence has shown
reprisals against people, including policemen, who report police misconduct."

Rubin and the Canadians felt like they'd just been hit by a ton of
bricks. They might as well be starting the case all over again. The chart
they had made together was not to be the final word. It had become
obsolete. Here was hard new evidence, straight from the horse's (prosecution's) mouth.

It was clear why DeSimone had tried to censor the activities
around that bar, Paterson's own little Peyton Place. He needed these
witnesses kept hidden; they would wreak havoc in the State's case. It
was imperative that Pat Valentine be a credible witness, because from
the beginning it was acknowledged that Bello wasn't. Valentine was
necessary to complement Bello's story and corroborate his alleged car
identification. She had to be clean. And the others? *They* might have
seen what Avery Cockersham saw—or rather, who he did *not* see.

Rubin called Beldock several times and fired off letters to him with lists of questions and requests for further documents. The Canadians wanted to know if the defence had ever been alerted to the existence of these new players. Did Beldock have any "discovery"—any police notes or statements—on Louise and Avery? Anything more on Valentine? The other Pat? What about Sandy, Steve, Ruth or Ray?

"Who *are* these people, Myron?"

"Rubin," said Beldock, "we got dribs and drabs very late into the trial, and the few people we were able to contact were so hostile that we thought they might do us more harm than good."

Rubin pointed out to Myron what was becoming abundantly clear to him and the Canadians: they need not be concerned if, at first glance, some piece of evidence appeared to be damaging. For example, if Sandy had really said Louise said that Rubin was in the bar and had promised to return, Louise herself would have been subpoenaed and brought into court as the State's star witness. The fact was, what she really told investigator Thompson, and what he verified in his report, was that she observed two strangers, two *white* men in the bar; and this was information the State did not want brought forward.

Carter and Partners seized upon other questions raised by their reading of the Caruso file. For one, they were intrigued that there seemed to be a black man living in the same building as Louise and Avery. Who was he? The presence of a black man living in that neighbourhood would undermine a key plank in the State's motive theory, namely that the Lafayette Bar was a "natural target" for a racial-hatred killing because it was located in an exclusionary white enclave where blacks were not welcome.

To say that the Caruso file inspired Rubin and the Canadians would be an understatement, and their excitement was conveyed to Beldock. Rubin was fed up with prisons of any kind, including the prison of ignorance. Now he wanted to know, to know every detail about his case, to know what really happened. He was ready, he warmly announced to Myron, his lawyer and friend, and asked him if he was ready too. "We're on the move again," declared Rubin. "We're going home."

18

Christmas 1983 again brought the unexpected for Rubin, although this time the unexpected was welcome. It arrived with a warm note from one of his New Jersey attorneys, Louis Raveson, a professor at Rutgers School of Law.

"It was a long time coming," wrote Lou, "but I think it was an important victory. Enclosed are the money orders for your judgment against the State. The total is $2,760."

Rubin had actually won something. He had won his civil suit, *Carter v. Klein,* against the prison authorities for his unlawful transfer to the Vroom Building in 1974 in conditions that a federal judge termed "far more onerous than conditions in the general population at TSP [Trenton State Prison]." It was official now, legal fact. "Carter was deprived of a right secured by the Constitution of the United States" and those "who deprived him of that right were acting under color of state law at the time," wrote U.S. District Judge Dickinson R. Debevoise in his ruling.

So the authorities had to eat crow and shell out some money, "compensatory damages," in the process: thirty dollars a day for each of the ninety-two days Rubin had spent on bread-and-water in the

Vroom. They were also ordered by the court not to penalize Carter as a result of his illegal removal to the Vroom or to have it reflect negatively on his prison record.

Although the award was piddling consideration for such an outrage, came almost ten years after the event and did not touch on the sticky fact that Rubin should not have been *anywhere* in the prison system in the first place, the win was a major psychological boost. The victory was in the victory. Rubin had been right in proving he had been wronged. Clear the scoreboard and start tallying from here: Carter, 1; State, 0. Success was a matter of perseverance.

Sudden and unexpected transfers are part of a tried and true method of demoralizing inmates. A prisoner's cell is never his own, never a safe place. Capriciously and without notice, his "house" can be raided and torn apart. In a flash, he can be shipped out to another institution, what's left of his belongings trailing behind him weeks later, his letters and photographs torn up or missing, his TV smashed. And in its wisdom and compassion, the system of "corrections" ensures that the weakest are always the worst abused. Contrary to a common perception that prisoners lead lives of relative comfort, if not luxury—all meals prepared for them, school or work during the day, relax in the recreation room, read or watch TV evenings in their cells—life behind bars is life on the edge.

A couple of weeks before Christmas, Rubin told the Canadians that several "young boys" had just been brought into Trenton State Prison from the Bordentown Youth Correctional Institution, a medium-security reformatory for youthful offenders. It had been another middle-of-the-night shipment. Its purpose was educational. Goon squad guards would terrorize the kids and beat them before sending them back.

"These *inmates,*" said Rubin, consciously using what he considered a pejorative word and sarcastically imitating a guard's nasal voice, "they need to be given a taste of what it's like 'behind the wall.' This is no fun-house. This will teach them to keep their place. It'll show them the kind of special treatment waiting for them here if they step out of line in Bordentown."

The mention of Bordentown reminded the Canadians to tell Rubin that a Canadian youth named Bruce Curtis had recently been incarcerated there.

"In Bordentown—here in Jersey? For what?"

"Murder."

"Have mercy."

The Canadians had read about the case in the papers. In 1982, at the age of eighteen, Bruce had graduated with straight "A"s from an exclusive prep school in Nova Scotia and had been planning to study astrophysics at Dalhousie University in the fall. His nightmare began during that summer while he was vacationing at the home of a friend, Scott Franz, in Monmouth County, New Jersey. Franz shot and killed his abusive stepfather, and Bruce shot Franz's mother—by accident, he has consistently maintained. At the trial, Scott Franz testified against Bruce, and Curtis was convicted of aggravated manslaughter and sentenced, in New Jersey's generous style, to twenty years in State Prison. By now the Canadians had some understanding of the meaning of such a fate for a high school kid from rural Nova Scotia. They asked Rubin if there was anything he could do to help protect him.

Rubin sent out a message through one of the Bordentown prisoners who had been temporarily moved into Trenton. He told him to spread the word that if anyone laid a hand on Bruce Curtis, they would have to answer to the Hurricane. Nowhere in the prison system would they be safe. Rubin's reputation was legendary. He had only to open his mouth in displeasure and drastic things could ensue, as the Canadians were soon to find out.

Rubin then sent Bruce a Christmas card. Beyond the usual message of peace on earth and goodwill toward men, Rubin wanted Bruce to know that he was not alone and that there were people watching out for him.

This was the first Christmas the Canadians were able to spend with Rubin. Visits at Trenton were now held in a new building, a shining example of the latest in prison architecture—red brick with windows so narrow they didn't need bars, and rabbit warrens of small, isolated units. The edifice, which allowed the number of Trenton's inmates to swell from twelve hundred to two thousand, had raw cinder-block walls and an abundance of metal trim painted in primary colours, blue and red. This up-to-date pride of prison design was attached to the old prison, like a post-modern excrescence grafted onto nineteenth-century roots, and the building's newness was instantly tarnished by the beat-up furniture (not to mention prisoners) rifled from the antiquated wings.

The new visiting hall was a large room. Here, prisoner and visitor were forced to sit in hard, immovable plastic chairs, side by side, rather than face to face, as before in the death-house. Where prisoners and their wives or girlfriends were formerly allowed to touch as long as they kept both feet on the floor, now prisoners were reprimanded and threatened with charges if they kissed or even hugged their visitors, except at the beginning and end of the visit. Guards circled constantly.

Christmas Day in 1983 fell on a Sunday, a regular contact visit day. Being Christmas, more children came than usual.

The visitors had already settled into their seats when Santa tried to make a stealthy entrance. This was difficult to do, as he was wearing red velveteen pants, a red jacket bordered in white fluff and a red hat. He was also wearing black leather motorcycle boots with a three-inch heel and toting a white mesh sack through which gaily-wrapped packages of candy could be seen. He was the shortest, scrawniest, sallowest, meanest-looking Santa imaginable. Although himself an inmate, he sat down on a bench next to a couple of guards, away from and opposite to the prisoners and their visitors. He placed his sack carefully onto the floor between his boots, then crossed his legs.

"Daddy daddy! There's Santa! I'm gonna . . ."

"Don't you go near that Santa, boy!" said a wary prisoner. "You stay away from him, you hear?"

There was a similar exchange with a number of other children and their fathers.

After much squirming and wriggling, one child managed to escape from her parents' clutches and ran up to Santa. The girl stopped about two feet from him, hoping her presence would elicit, if not some presents from his sack, at least a "Ho! Ho! Ho!"

Santa wasn't going for that. He ignored her. He kept his eyes wandering about the room, above the visitors, beside the visitors, behind the visitors, everywhere but on the child. The girl stood there patiently waiting, but Santa knew how to wait better than she did. The little girl left, empty-handed. (This Santa was 1983's precursor to 1990's Homey D. Clown from the television show, "In Living Color"—only without Homey's political savvy.)

"How come *he* got to be Santa?" asked the Canadians, thinking what a great Santa someone like Zig, with his big, warm smile and massive frame, would have made.

"It's no accident," answered Rubin. "He was hand-picked by the administration. They got exactly who they wanted."

Sure enough, when Santa left the visiting hall that day, his sack was not one ounce lighter.

The January slush from the New Jersey Turnpike splattered the car's windshield and painted the landscape grey as Terry and Sam drove the sixty miles northeast to Manhattan for an unusual Fifth Avenue shopping spree. They had a long shopping list, which would require the whole afternoon to fill. They weren't going to Tiffany's or to Saks, but to Beldock, Levine and Hoffman's at Fifth and Forty-sixth. They had an appointment to meet Myron Beldock at twelve-thirty.

"Now that I'm rich," Rubin had told the Canadians, after receiving the "enormous bounty" from his lawsuit, "let's do our own investigation. We can hire an investigator and use Caruso's file as our starting point. I want to know what really happened at the Lafayette Bar that night. With this money we can send someone down to North Carolina to find Avery Cockersham's second wife, Fanida. Maybe talk to his doctor and nurse—see if they heard anything. Pay a visit to Avery's first wife, Louise. I want to know if Avery Cockersham ever named the killers. I know the money won't go far, but I want to contribute everything I have. If that means forgoing this winter's Florida vacation, then so be it."

But before they could begin their investigation, Rubin and the Canadians needed more documents. Among other things, they wanted to re-examine, in the light of the Caruso revelations, the original police reports that had been turned over in discovery at both trials. Rubin had requested so many documents from Beldock that Beldock had said it would take ages to find and photocopy them all. "Discovery alone is two file drawers deep," he said.

Rubin suggested he send a couple of friends over to do the work. Myron could dig out the files; they could photocopy them. Myron readily agreed. Rubin told him that the people he was sending were familiar with the case. They would be his legs, and to please give them anything they requested, as though the request had come directly from him.

The lobby of the building at 565 Fifth Avenue was quiet, except for an attendant sitting outside the elevators, tapping his foot to a portable radio. The Canadians were impressed that Beldock, a $250-an-hour lawyer, would take the time to come into the office on a Saturday and have the patience to pull files for an indigent client who wanted to reinvestigate his case. Rubin had sent Beldock the money he had won in the lawsuit, and Beldock—disregarding how much he and his firm had put out over the years, by now into the millions of dollars in expenses and lost fees—agreed to use the money to pay for a new investigator.

Terry and Sam got off the elevator on the sixth floor. To their left, they saw a wide door covered in black suede—the law firm's reception entrance. But before they reached it, a beret-clad head poked out of another door down the hall.

"Terence and Sam—Rubin's legs, right? This way! Hi, I'm Myron Beldock." Beldock spoke with a cultured New York accent. He was short and was casually dressed in a jogging suit, tennis shoes and his trademark beret (a holdover from his days in Paris at the Sorbonne in the fifties). They told Beldock that they were honoured to meet him, and praised his dedication. They had read his impressive briefs.

Beldock led them through the empty offices to two huge boxes full of discovery which were sitting next to an enormous photocopier. They spent the entire afternoon going through files and photocopying, and what they didn't have time to copy, Myron promised he would do himself and send off first thing in the week. He unearthed all the ballistics reports, as well as photo exhibits from the trial*—black-and-

---

*Beldock also found Pat Valentine's 1979 deposition concerning her suit against Bob Dylan and Columbia Records for a "fair and equitable share" of the monies earned by the song "Hurricane." Valentine claimed that the song presented her "in an unfavorable light," but then had to admit that everything Dylan had said about her was true. Her suit was thrown out before it reached trial.

white pictures of the Lafayette Bar inside and out, of the victims, of Rubin's 1966 Dodge Polara.

Just before they left, Terry asked Beldock where Rubin's case stood in the courts. Beldock told them there was to be a hearing on the Caruso evidence the following Friday in front of Judge Leopizzi. They were hoping it would lead to an overturning of the conviction on the basis of suppression of evidence.

"Leopizzi again? Isn't that rather futile?" asked Terry. "What happened to federal court?"

Myron explained that because the Caruso material was considered new evidence, the defence had to present it to the trial judge (namely Leopizzi), who, being the most familiar with the case, theoretically would be best able to evaluate its import.

"It's the law. We have to exhaust our state remedies first."

"From what we know of the case, that doesn't sound like much of a remedy," offered Terry. He was thinking not only of the 1981 Bello lie-detector hearing, but of the 1979 jury misconduct hearing, the record of which he had studied.

After the retrial in 1976, one of the jurors, John Adamo, suffered a crisis of conscience and voluntarily came forward to reveal to Judge Leopizzi his serious doubts as to the impartiality of some of the deliberating jurors (as an alternate, Adamo himself never voted on the question of guilt or innocence). Adamo named three jurors he had heard make remarks that showed racial prejudice, including derogatory comments about black people as *"melanzana"*—Italian for "eggplant" but used colloquially as an equivalent for "nigger." There were two jurors who had their minds made up near the beginning of the trial and had told Adamo they didn't need to listen to any more evidence. Another juror had come to the trial prejudicially tainted because his wife had told him she had read in the paper that Carter had failed his lie-detector test. (This false information had been planted in the papers by the prosecution to its intended effect.)

But Adamo's testimony was rewarded with nothing but hostility and suspicion from the judge. Leopizzi accused him of being "extremely pompous," "reckless," "unfair" and simply out to gain notoriety for himself in a nationally publicized case. After a severely limited hearing, Leopizzi rejected Adamo's evidence, prohibited the defence from approaching any other jurors and upheld the validity of the jury's verdict.

"Yes," agreed Myron, "it has been said: going back to Leopizzi is a remedy that can only aggravate the ailment."

"Besides," asked Sam, "hasn't Leopizzi already refused to hear the Caruso evidence?"

"Not technically," said Beldock, explaining that they were now presenting it to him as a formal motion to throw out the conviction on the grounds of suppressed evidence. Sure, they expected Leopizzi to deny their motion, then they hoped to bypass the next level of courts, the Appellate Division, and appeal directly to the New Jersey Supreme Court, which, having just spent three years reviewing the case, would most likely refuse to look at it again and thereby send them packing to federal court, which was where they wanted to be anyway.

"But what about the issues the Supreme Court has already ruled on, like the Bello lie-detector? Can't those be taken federal while this is going on?"

"No. Not according to the rules of appellate procedure. We can't splinter the appeal and have one part of the case being heard in the state while the rest of the case goes on to federal court. That's considered an abuse of process."

"An abuse of process? You mean an *abusive* process?"

Myron took off his glasses, sighed heavily and massaged his eyes. "That's the history of this case, *mes amis,* and I can show you the battle wounds. But we have to keep fighting."

Beldock figured the appeal through the state courts would only take a few months, and they should be filing a "habeas corpus petition" and have their arguments, including the suppressed Caruso evidence, heard in federal court by the summer. The summer seemed a long way off, but as the Canadians were learning, legal cases move at their own speed.

"Discovery" was the perfect word to describe the papers that Rubin and the Canadians now reviewed. The documents the State turned over to the defence prior to the first trial consisted of a combination of typed police reports (most unsigned) and Vincent DeSimone's notes of interviews with various witnesses. Because he was in charge of the

Lafayette Bar investigation, DeSimone had the opportunity to filter everything through his hands. As he admitted under oath, he often rewrote and combined notes and reports, discarding the originals. DeSimone's presence could be felt everywhere among these pages, and his handwriting became instantly recognizable to the Canadians.

There was one typed report from a Paterson police detective, Howard Kline, that immediately caught their attention. It was dated July 1, 1966—two weeks after the Lafayette murders. The report said that shortly after midnight, a call had gone out for a detective to come to the Lafayette Bar and Grill, where there had been an altercation. When Detective Kline arrived at the scene, he was met by two policemen, who told him that there was a woman who might have some knowledge about the Lafayette Bar murders. Kline wrote:

> I walked around the corner . . . where I spoke with a short medium built Negro woman, dark skinned, and asked her if she would tell me her name, she . . . stated that her name was Louise . . . and that she lives at 257 Lafayette St; standing along side her during the questioning was a man she identified as Avery Cockersham . . . her husband.

Louise told the detective that she and Avery and another black man had been standing by the pool table when an argument broke out with a white man. Then the police came and put the white man out of the tavern.

Rubin and the Canadians were stunned again. They had assumed that Avery and Louise were white; finding out they were black was mind-boggling for a number of reasons. A main link in the State's motive argument at the 1976 trial was that the Lafayette Bar and its bartender had been a "natural" or "perfect" target for a racial revenge killing because Jim Oliver, the bartender/ victim, was a bigot and refused to serve blacks. But Louise Cockersham, who they now discovered was a black woman, had been in the Lafayette Bar on the night of the shooting and had been served by Oliver when she bought a bottle of whisky for her party! Louise, moreover, told Detective Kline that Jim Oliver "was a nice man, and that even on Sunday he would let her have whisky, even though she had no money . . ." So not only did blacks live in the neighbourhood, blacks were regular customers in the supposed all-white bar, the bartender served them and even extended them credit.

Perhaps most significant about the fact of Louise being black was that it supported Bello's in-the-bar story, which was *not* the story he gave at trial, when he denied being in the bar any time that night. According to Bello's in-the-bar story, he saw a black woman come into the bar and purchase "a package" (a bottle of liquor) from the bartender, and it was shortly after that the shooting started. Bello's presence in the bar is also consistent with Louise's statement to investigator Thompson that she saw two white men she didn't recognize in the bar; the other one was presumably Bradley, Bello's cohort.

Detective Kline, according to his report, also interviewed Pat Valentine, who had been drinking with Louise and Avery on this later date (July 1st) as well. Valentine told Kline that Louise had said to her, "If they sweat Rubin Carter, he'll crack and tell the truth."

Valentine and Louise and Avery were all then brought into the detective bureau for questioning. At five o'clock that morning DeSimone "confronted" Valentine and Louise with each other. DeSimone's handwritten notes state: "All Bullshit." It wasn't clear what this referred to, but Rubin and the Canadians suspected it was Louise denying having made the remark about "sweating" Rubin Carter.

DeSimone's notes were deliberately misleading, uninformative and unintelligible. When they were turned over to the defence prior to trial, they served only to confuse matters and steered the defence away from potentially fruitful inquiry. Only in hindsight and with the keys provided by the Caruso file did the notes reveal something different. DeSimone, unlike Rubin, was very much aware of the existence of Avery and Louise as eyewitnesses. Under the heading of "Avery Cockerham [sic]," DeSimone wrote: "I never saw Reuben [sic] Carter." In the context of his notes, DeSimone makes it appear as if Avery had not found out about the Lafayette shooting until after returning home from work the next day, and had therefore never seen *anyone*, let alone Rubin Carter. Given the Thompson revelations that Avery *was* at home and *did* see two men running from the bar, "I never saw Reuben Carter" means something far more definitive and momentous: Avery did see the two men, and neither of them was Rubin Carter.

. . .

At the Caruso evidence hearing in Paterson on Friday January 20, 1984, in the middle of a routine request by Myron Beldock for the court to accept an exhibit, Judge Leopizzi stormed off the bench, ranting: "I am sick and tired of your nonsense. That's it." He slammed his office door as punctuation behind him.

He had accused defence attorneys Beldock and Steel of deliberately abusing the judicial system, had accused *them* of lacking diligence and of deliberately holding back the Caruso issue "as a means of triggering the appellate process all over again." Ignoring the fact that the defence had been systematically prevented from developing the Caruso information—first, by the prosecution that had suppressed the evidence and denied its existence; second, by Leopizzi himself, who had refused to consider the evidence and sealed it at the remand hearing three years before; and third, by the State Supreme Court who ignored the defence's repeated requests to have the evidence unsealed—Leopizzi nonetheless accused the defence of waiting until they lost the Bello lie-detector issue in the Supreme Court before proceeding with this new issue.

"This case must come to a close," he said. "That's my humble opinion. . . . It makes the system look pretty sad when a case can go on for eighteen years. . . . This has gone on long enough."

After the hearing, Beldock told Rubin that Leopizzi's vehement denial of their request for a third trial worried him. He was afraid Leopizzi was "going to bury us." But Rubin wasn't worried. He was too dug up now to be reburied.

19

After reviewing the discovery documents, Rubin and the Canadians had to agree with investigator Caruso's conclusion that, at best, "the original [Lafayette Bar murder] investigation was bungled." No weapons were ever recovered, no fingerprinting was ever done (at least none that was ever disclosed), no paraffin tests for gunpowder residue were given, which would have conclusively shown that Carter and Artis had not fired weapons. Because nothing was concrete, Rubin was snared in an inextricable web of ever-shifting and impossible-to-combat confusion.

The ballistics evidence was a case in point. According to police reports, an exhaustive search of the area surrounding the Lafayette Bar was carried out by ten named police officers and "possibly a couple of others" after dawn on June 17, 1966. The search ended at 7:30 A.M., "fruitless." Yet a bus driver named John Opperly, right at the time the search concluded, was able to spot a shotgun shell lying in the roadway in plain view as he drove his bus along the street near the bar. Opperly stopped, retrieved the shell and turned it over to the police. This story intrigued the Canadians, but trying to track the elusive bullet proved an exercise in the absurd.

Although the Canadians didn't know a thing about ballistics, it didn't require expertise to notice that, in different parts of the record, the shell was described in three different ways (all mutually exclusive), was allegedly found in three (possibly four) different locations and had three different chains of possession, albeit all beginning with bus driver Opperly. There were so many discrepancies, inconsistencies and contradictions in the official logging of this shell that the Canadians were driven to make another chart.

The "Opperly shell," in and of itself, was not significant. It was, however, a typical example of the unreliability of *any* of the evidence in the case. Rubin sent the chart and the analysis of the evidence to Beldock, including a map of Paterson highlighting the assorted locations of the shell. Beldock found it as fascinating as he had found Rubin and the Canadians' penetrating analyses of the Caruso information. He was convinced that their probing was heading in the right direction.

"Damn good job!" he told Rubin on the phone. "You're right on the money!"

Working on his case every day, Rubin was now on "outside" time— real time, taking care of business as it arose—as opposed to prison time, in which tasks are drawn out and procrastination is a virtue that fills calendars. Real time meant not staying up nights and sleeping during the day, which had been Rubin's routine before Lesra and the Canadians had come along. It meant keeping office hours so that calls to lawyers could be made, window visits received and letters readied for posting when the guard came around in the morning to pick up outgoing mail.

Rubin exhibited a sudden interest in acquiring memos, addenda to the *Inmate Handbook,* circulating from the warden to the "Inmate Population." Prisoners who had absorbed or, more likely, couldn't follow the incomprehensible jargon in these notices of rule changes would gladly hand theirs over to Rubin. He would stack them neatly and staple them together. Not that these were for his edification or to preserve as artifacts—the blank sides served as notepads. He had run out of the few legal pads the prison allowed to be sent in.

When not studying documents in his cell or hammering out letters to his lawyers on his typewriter, Rubin would be on the phone with

Terry, Lisa and Sam, talking about his case, dissecting the evidence, analysing the issues, writing notes on his makeshift pads. Calls still had to be made collect, even though they were in the same city. There were two pay phones to share among the hundred prisoners in 6-Left. A phone list was posted daily; every prisoner who signed up got access to one ten-minute call. Generally, the prisoners were able to police themselves; some would cede their scheduled calls to others, thus those who for some reason needed more phone time could sometimes get it. Everyone in the wing could see, and everyone in the prison knew, that all of Rubin's actions were geared to freeing himself, so most prisoners, and many of the guards, were especially generous with him. Whenever a phone became free, it was his.

There were some guards, however, who refused to let Rubin out of his cell except at his appointed telephone time. And there was the odd prisoner who was so "whacked out" that he'd hog the phones for no purpose, causing trouble for whomever he could, Rubin included. Consequently, Rubin could never count on consistent telephone access.

Rubin, anxious to get to the phone to call his lawyer one day, was prevented by the antics of one prisoner who was making crank calls, trying numbers at random to see if anyone would accept the charges. Rubin paced the flats—something he never did—and made his displeasure known to another prisoner who happened to be standing near the phones, a friendly guy Rubin and the Canadians called "Sweet Al."

That evening, the "whacked out" prisoner's cell was burned out. Luckily, he wasn't home at the time. Not only was his cell now uninhabitable, but the authorities said his safety was in jeopardy. They concluded that the fire had been deliberate, and moved him to another wing.

As Rubin came down the stairs from the fourth tier the next day, he was hailed by Sweet Al, who was grinning from ear to ear.

"Hey, Rubin! I guess that 'whack out' won't be giving you any more trouble with the phones, huh Rube?"

When Al burst out laughing, Rubin remembered his comment to Al about the phones the day before. "Oh, Lord!" thought Rubin. He had to remind himself to watch what he said.

A newly hired guard named Cooper, a white man about Rubin's

age, was assigned to Rubin's wing. After observing Cooper for a few days, Rubin asked if he'd noticed how hostile the prisoners seemed to be toward him. Cooper was aware of the animosity but had no idea what was causing it. Rubin asked if he'd mind if he made a suggestion. He explained that he understood the guards' handbook stated that after releasing the brake and opening the cell door, a corrections officer must wait for the prisoner to leave his cell, then follow *directly* behind the prisoner all the way to his destination, be it the shower or the phone or whatever.

"That's right."

"But consider how a man feels after being locked down, sometimes for twenty-three hours at a time, to finally get out of his cell and find a guard literally on his heels. It's just too much." Rubin's suggestion to Cooper was to open the door and step back. "Give the man the only space he's got for that short moment and let *him* pick the pace at which he's going to walk to wherever he's going. A small consideration like that means a lot to a prisoner. And it could be even more important to a guard. It would be a shame if the man he'd let out of his cell had just found out his mother had passed away or that his appeal had been denied. It could well mean that the guard, pressing that closely, might be putting his life on the line."

A few days later, Cooper came by Rubin's cell. He said this wasn't the first time he'd worked in a prison; in fact, he'd just come from Raiford State Prison in Florida, having worked there for some nineteen years. He told Rubin that he had thought Raiford, which had a terrible reputation, was the worst hell-hole on earth, but Trenton made Raiford look like a kindergarten. And he wanted to thank Rubin for his advice.

Rubin said that it meant a lot to him just to have someone respond to his suggestions in the spirit in which they were given.

"You know," said Cooper, "I've been watching you move around the wing. Everything about you—and I've observed countless prisoners over the years—tells me that you don't belong here. I told my wife about you. I told her I'd seen a man at Trenton State Prison who I know in my heart of hearts is innocent. Rubin—that *is* your name, right? I want you to know that me and my wife are praying for you."

A week later, the Canadians were in the visiting hall with Rubin.

It was Cooper's first time on duty there. Indicating Rubin, he asked one of the regular guards about him.

"Rubin 'Hurricane' Carter?"

"No," said Cooper, "the little guy sitting over there."

"Yeah, him. That's Rubin 'Hurricane' Carter."

Cooper almost ran over to Rubin. "Are you 'Hurricane' Carter? Are you? You never told me!"

"You knew my name was Rubin," Rubin said, smiling.

"I can't wait to get home and tell my wife who we've been praying for!"

Rubin and the Canadians were determined that 1984 would live up, not to its Orwellian renown, but to its promise as a leap year, an over-the-wall catapulting kind of year.

With the lawsuit money, they retained Herb Bell, the private investigator from Plainfield, New Jersey that they'd used in The Rose's case. The Canadians gave him background material, including relevant Caruso documents and their copy of the large chart summarizing Rubin's case. Herb met and consulted with Rubin at Trenton and travelled to New York to talk to Beldock. Because the case was so complicated, an extraordinary amount of preparation was required.

Bell's first assignment was to travel to the Charlotte, North Carolina area to find out any information about Avery Cockersham. Rubin had given Bell a list of questions that they wanted answered.

Dr Boween, who had attended Avery at the Davis Community Hospital in Statesville, was very polite to Bell and happy to open his files. Avery had been a patient there from January until March of 1976, the month when Rubin's first trial verdict was overturned. He was then moved to a Veteran's Administration hospital, where he died in July of that year. The doctor could find no notation in the files of visits by police or investigators, but he did have records showing that Avery had suffered a seizure on January 26, which was two days before investigator Thompson had gone to see him.

Bell's interview of the nurse who attended Avery was unproductive, and he could not find Avery's second wife, Fanida Cockersham, in North Carolina. He returned to New Jersey empty-handed.

This was the first time Rubin had been actively involved in an investigation of his case, and he remained undaunted. According to Thompson's reports, Louise Cockersham was still living in Paterson in 1976. Rubin decided to look there. He would call his cousin Ed, who also lived in Paterson and had his finger on the pulse of the black community; Ed knew everybody.

Edward Carter was fifty-one, five years older than Rubin. Although the cousins hadn't communicated in a long time, they had been close during the 1960s, the "war on poverty" and civil rights activism days. Ed had been at Rubin's side during the first trial and later, after Rubin had been released on bail in 1976, Ed had accompanied him everywhere and stood by him during the second trial. Ed was "a long, tall drink of water" as Rubin described him, lanky and six-foot five. They made a comical pair, reminding the Canadians of a picture they took of William and Lesra in Toronto.

It was a month before Easter when Rubin called Ed. Before Rubin had a chance to ask him if he knew a Louise Cockersham, Ed said he was glad Rubin called because he had something important to tell him. He had recently taken a cab and got to talking to the cabdriver, a white man originally from the South but who had been living and working in Paterson for some years. The cabby knew that Ed was Rubin "Hurricane" Carter's cousin, and commented on how Rubin had been framed.

"I know your cousin's innocent," he had said.

"How do you know that? Or are you just trying to be nice to me?" Ed had asked, almost tongue-in-cheek.

"I know it."

"Well two juries didn't know it."

"I know it because I saw him at the Nite Spot when the shooting at the Lafayette Bar was going down."

The cabby explained. On the morning of June 17, 1966, he was driving a fare on East 18th Street and found himself blocked from getting onto one-way Governor Street. Obstructing the way was a white Dodge that was parked out from the curb. He got out of his taxi and saw that the keys were in the Dodge's ignition. He was about to move the car when someone outside the Nite Spot told him that if he didn't want to get "fucked up," he better not touch that car. "Don't you know whose car that is? That's the Hurricane's car." So the man asked where Hurricane Carter was, and was told, "In the Nite Spot."

The cabby then went inside the Nite Spot, which was busy. He found Carter and asked him to move his car. Carter was talking to some people and told him to "move the damn thing" himself. Which the man said he did, then went back inside and handed the keys to a bartender to give to Rubin, because he couldn't get close to him, the place was now even more crowded.

When the cabby got back into his cab, he heard over a police band on his radio that there was "trouble" at the Lafayette Bar. After driving on with his fare, he heard sirens.

All along it had been clear to him that Rubin could not have been in two places at the same time. But he was too scared of reprisals from the cops to come forward, so he had said nothing.

"I met with him another time, Rube, to get him to talk some more. But he checked me for a wire, a microphone. He wouldn't say any more. He's scared, Rube."

"Ed," said Rubin, "listen to me carefully. This is very important. I have to be getting off this phone but I want you to repeat exactly what you've just told me to some friends of mine who are down in Trenton helping me out, Terry and Sam. Treat them like family and answer any of their questions."

When Rubin hung up, he noted on the back of "Inmate Handbook Addendum No. 011-83" that they needed to get Beldock and Bell to go with Ed and get an official statement from this witness.

Terry and Sam were so excited by Ed's information that, even though it was late in the evening, they decided to call Beldock and Bell without delay and pass the news along. Its significance was immediately clear. This was the alibi of iron-clad alibis.

Significant to the Canadians, who by now knew the record cold, was that the call the cabby overheard was the *first* call that had been broadcast over the police radio, just after the shooting. The first call had said there was "trouble" at the Lafayette—not shooting or murder, but trouble. Upon receiving that call, police responded immediately and, on their way to the scene, spotted the white getaway car and gave chase, losing the car several minutes later somewhere near the bridge on the highway to New York. How could that have been Rubin's car, or Rubin in it when he was at the Nite Spot? Also, that Rubin had been in the habit of leaving his keys in his car was a well-known fact. And that he would have left his car parked in such a way as to block access to the street was consistent with his arrogance as a sports "star" and, moreover, with the fact that having just returned to the Nite Spot from driving Cathy McGuire and her mother home, he was intending to leave again with "Wild Bill" Hardney and drive to his house to pick up some money. That the Nite Spot was more crowded when the cabby went back in to return the keys was consistent with the time that the band stopped playing and the back room was clearing out, the crowd now moving toward the bar area in the front. This was precisely when Rubin, unsuccessful at getting Hardney to accompany him home, had asked John Artis along. Finally, that Rubin had tossed John the keys would be consistent with the keys no longer being in his car, but with his having been given them by the bartender. It all hung together.

The only troubling point was why Rubin hadn't remembered the incident himself. But what would have motivated the cabby to make up such a story if it weren't true, and how could he have fabricated one with so many aspects fitting precise details of the case if it had not actually happened that way?

Beldock, whose temperament as a lawyer was cautious, agreed that if the man came forward and talked, it would potentially give Rubin an incontrovertible alibi. "But before we even think of bringing it to court," he told Rubin, "we have to check it out for ourselves." As "newly discovered" evidence, it would have to be presented to Leopizzi. So not only did the cabby have to be willing to take the stand, he had to be clean and he had to be strong, because the prosecution and the judge would cut him to ribbons.

The Canadians asked Rubin why he hadn't remembered the cabby episode. He said he didn't know. He said it would not have been a particularly memorable or important event, the kind of thing he would pay much attention to. But since Ed had brought it to mind, he had thought about it carefully, trying to reconstruct the scene in his mind. And he thought he could remember seeing a white man, wearing a big plaid shirt with lightish brown tones and brown pants, come into the

Nite Spot shortly before closing time, but he couldn't remember getting keys from him or from a bartender or anything like that.

Over the following days, Ed Carter made two attempts at setting up a meeting between the cabby and Beldock and Bell. The first attempt was aborted by a freak storm—of all things, a hurricane—that battered New Jersey's coast on March 29, causing extensive flooding in the Passaic River basin. On the second attempt, two days later, they were to meet at the Meadowlands Hilton. The cabby failed to show. There was no question that he did not want to talk. A new strategy had to be devised.

At 4:30 P.M. on Wednesday April 4, Ed Carter, having staked out the cab company, watched and waited for the cabby to come on duty, then got into his cab. Ed asked him to drive to East 18th and Governor Street. It wasn't a long ride. The cabby was nervous. They stopped at the corner where the Nite Spot used to be, and before he knew it, Myron Beldock and Herb Bell had jumped into his cab. They told him not to be afraid.

They said they understood that he didn't want to talk, but perhaps he could just show them what he had done with Rubin's car on that June night in 1966—where it had been parked, where he had moved it. He repeatedly stated that he was afraid he would lose his job, afraid of what the Paterson Police Department might do to him or his family. He was sure they would come after him.

Ed Carter ran through the incident, as the cabby had related it to him. The cabby did not deny it. He said that because of what he had seen he wanted to help Rubin Carter, but he was afraid that no one could give him the protection he and his family would need if he were going to continue living in Paterson. Ed, Myron and Herb each pleaded with him to come forward—an innocent man was in prison. He said he was sorry he could not talk but he had a wife, children and a mortgage to think of. He was genuinely tormented. They suggested that he speak to a clergyman or someone he trusted and get back to them if he changed his mind. Beldock left him his card.

"Rubin, it was just like in the movies!" said Myron over the phone that evening, exhilarated. "Our timing was great. We were a real team."

Although Beldock was far from certain that the cabby would

come forward, he was convinced that the cabby had indeed seen Rubin and his car, just as Ed had reported. Beldock was sure the cabby had not said it for publicity or for his own glorification. He was clearly frightened of police retaliation, a not uncommon thread running through this case.

"And we really can't do a thing to protect him. The State has all the power—we have none. But this is very exciting, Rubin. I'm not discouraged."

20

Lesra and Marty were making strong impressions at the University of Toronto where they were both majoring in anthropology. In a course they took together, they collaborated on a major research project on racial prejudice. Their oral presentation of the history and sociology of the cycle of racism against blacks in Canada and the United States was a real eye-opener for many of the students. Few of their classmates realized how the legacy of slavery still affects attitudes and opportunities today.

Lesra was also taking courses in philosophy. In one of his papers, an essay on principles of justice for a second-year political philosophy course, he received an A-plus. His tutorial leader, a PhD student, wrote this comment: "Look, this is just superb . . . you might think about publishing it *immediately*. . . . You are working at a level which approaches *my* limitations and I feel uncomfortable advising you on my own."

Lesra's work also came to the attention of anthropologist Richard Lee, a former Harvard University professor and world-renowned specialist in the hunter-gathering !Kung people (the "Bushmen") of Southern Africa. The !Kung's traditional egalitarian way of life, with its priorities of co-operation and sharing, held a particular interest for Lesra. It wasn't long before he became Lee's protégé at U of T.

In Trenton, Sam, Terry and Lisa were involved in academic pursuits as well. When they weren't busy with Rubin's case, they were busy with Dorothy, their friend Isabell's oldest daughter. Dorothy was in grade two at school. She was very bright, and the Canadians couldn't understand why she had been held back a year. They had her read for them, which she was able to do, although not well. She needed some remedial work, especially in phonics, but most of all she needed encouragement. She was not doing well in school because her teachers did not expect her to do well, and we all have a habit of living *down* to other people's expectations.

The Canadians were delighted to be able to spend time with Dorothy, one of the most sensitive and appealing children they had ever met. She provided a welcome respite from the miasma of Rubin's predicament and the peculiar claustrophobia they felt living in New Jersey. Three or four times a week, Isabell would drop Dorothy at their apartment after school. They would teach her by reading aloud and playing games. In one game they would play "store" with real coins; Dorothy would have to be able to give and receive the correct change, having to be on her toes at all times because her tutors, it seemed, were either not too good at arithmetic themselves or were always trying to cheat her. And she had to watch out for Terry who took a devilish delight in untying her shoelaces when she least expected it.

Sam spoke to Dorothy's teacher one evening at an open house held at her school. Her teacher was African-American, very light-skinned, almost yellow, with freckles. Dorothy was very dark-skinned. Her teacher had a low opinion of Dorothy's scholastic ability and had placed her in the second-slowest reading group in the class. Sam told her teacher that he'd been tutoring Dorothy and thought she was an unusually intelligent and capable student. He said there was no reason Dorothy shouldn't be in the most advanced reading group. Such comments, delivered with conviction, impressed the teacher.

Sometimes, at their apartment, Dorothy would get on the phone and say hi to Rubin. She knew all about him. Isabell had told her who he was and why he was in prison. She had looked at pictures of him in his book.

One time when Dorothy was over, the TV was on, showing reruns of old "Saturday Night Live" shows. "Look!" she shouted. "Rubin's on television!"

She was almost right. It was a show from 1976, around the time Rubin's first trial verdict had been overturned. A bald Hurricane lookalike is seen behind bars. Suddenly the door to his cell swings open and he is released. A voice says, "Don't leave home without it!" and letters are then hammered onto a blank American Express Card: "Rubin Hurricane Carter."

Dorothy finished the school year in the top reading group in her class and received awards for being the pupil who had made the greatest progress, and read the most, over the year. She was to go on, in the third grade, to score in the top 10 percent on a nationwide scholastic test.

Rubin and the Canadians never doubted that Rubin's freedom would become a reality. It was a premise that informed and sustained all their actions.

The only time there was any disharmony was when the Canadians brought up the idea of moving to Rahway State Prison.

"Why would we want to do that?" Rubin had said, contemptuously.

"For one thing, the conditions there aren't quite so horrible," they answered.

"Prison is prison. They're all the same."

Rubin didn't really want to talk about it, but knew that since it was on the table he was going to have to. They discussed the various reasons why going to Rahway might be a good idea. There were the practical ones: it was closer to New York, providing greater access to the lawyers and to the investigator, visiting hours were longer and, from what they had heard, telephones were more accessible. This move would facilitate Rubin's ability to co-ordinate and participate in the investigation and in his appeal. Cousin Ed was trying to find Louise Cockersham; Herb Bell was sniffing around for the cabby's fare or anyone who had seen him at the Nite Spot at the crucial time; and Rubin, in addition to talking to Beldock regularly, was also having legal strategy discussions with Professor Friedman.

Possibly more important, moving was a critical step toward de-institutionalization. If Rubin could not move now, when the prison doors finally opened, he might not be able to move then either. The outside, after nearly twenty years, would be a whole lot more destabilizing. To be thrust now into an unfamiliar environment would be good practice. A move would enable him to adjust to changing circumstances, to less restrictive conditions. In Rahway, visits were held outside in the warm weather, and prisoners and visitors weren't confined to chairs but could walk around, drink coffee, eat together. It was a marginally more humane environment, but that margin was important.

Rubin said that there were other factors to consider, like safety and danger. In Trenton, Rubin was well known by the guards and the prisoners. They knew his style of dealing with the penitentiary and, for the most part, kept away from him. They knew he didn't participate in prison programs, go to work, to parole hearings, to social workers or psychologists for evaluation or advice. In a new prison, he would have to establish his position all over again. Then, too, there was the "young gun" syndrome. "Someone might want to make his own rep by trying to fuck with me." No, Rubin concluded, it was safer for him to stay in Trenton State Prison.

It took a lot of discussing and more difficulty and frustration gaining access to the phones at Trenton before Rubin grew to like the idea of moving. He put in a request for a transfer. Soon he was glad he did. The atmosphere in Trenton State Prison was to become very tense.

"War zone," wrote Rubin on the third volume of his makeshift pads. "Moving away from here . . ."

It was May 15, eight days since the Canadians had thrown a surprise party for Rubin in his wing to celebrate his forty-seventh birthday. For this unprecedented social event, they had conspired with the prisoners they knew in the wing—with The Rose and Brownie and Rockfish—had circulated invitations to Rubin's friends around the prison (to Cap'n Dick and A.J. and Zig and Smalls and Zeke and Glen and Ray and Brother Franklin and Gamu and Nick and the Greek and Saifuddin and Misra and "Four Fives and a Nine" and Top Choice and "Swamp Man" Smitty), had sent in a huge birthday cake (it had to be cut into four smaller cakes before being allowed in) and had arranged with the "store man," Sam Jennings, to have ice cream and soda pop for the guests. It had required some tricky manoeuvering, The Rose getting Rubin to go out to the yard with him while the men inside put a tablecloth (a sheet) on a table on the flats, where they spread out all the goodies, and over which they hung Lenny's large sign: "Birthday party for Rubin today for everyone. 6-Left. 4:00 PM.

The surprise was a surprise. Despite the restriction on movement, many of the invitees from other wings in the prison managed to get there. The guys loved to be able to trick Rubin, who hadn't suspected a thing. And double-chocolate cake with chocolate fudge frosting topped by a dollop of vanilla ice cream? What a treat!

But now a different atmosphere pervaded the wing. A few days before, a new prisoner had come into the wing, and he should never have been put there. He was in prison because he had raped and killed his own baby; having committed the unspeakable, he was the object of everyone's wrath. He should have been placed in segregation and under psychiatric care, although even that would not have guaranteed him protection. One of the regular officers on 6-Left, Willis, had been "laying in the cut" with two other guards, waiting for this prisoner to go to the showers. They had bided their time until he took off his clothes. Then they attacked. They moved in swiftly and beat him unconscious. They kicked and pummelled him and tossed him naked back into his cell.

A high-pitched screech coming from the wing-officer during the attack sounded familiar to Rubin. He was certain he had heard it before. In the Vroom Building. It was the sound one of the anonymous marauders had made in revving the others up into a frenzy of sadistic glee. Now Rubin was sure that Willis was one of the goon squad, and Rubin was disgusted. Willis was the son of an old-time line-officer that Rubin had known for years and had respected.

Rubin now watched Willis carefully.

That Tuesday, Rubin watched him leave the wing early, before his second shift was over, and Rubin suspected the "punk" guard was up to no good. When the lights in the wing failed to go off at their usual time that night, Rubin knew for certain that something untoward was going on somewhere in the penitentiary. The next day he found out what. He got the news from a "runner," a prisoner who worked as a kind of messenger and delivery man.

A group of fifteen young prisoners had been shipped in from Southern State Correctional Facility in Cumberland County, New Jersey. Someone apparently had complained about the liver served for dinner and refused to eat it. The authorities later claimed that several inmates had tried to encourage others to join in a protest, and the inmates were transferred for "engaging in or encouraging a group demonstration." They were handcuffed and shackled, put into vans and transported to Trenton, where they were beaten and terrorized unmercifully.

Rubin told the runner to get statements from these guys, so that something could be done.

Later that day, ten handwritten, signed statements were delivered to Rubin's cell. What he read in these accounts infuriated him.

> Ken:
>
> *On May 15, 1984, I was brought to Trenton State Prison. To begin with none of us knew what charges we were being brought here on. . . . As soon as we got inside the complex, that is, out of the receiving area, we were made to strip down. We were given 30 seconds to do that. . . . I wasn't finished stripping in 30 sec's. so the officers started beating me with their nightsticks in the back and sides of my body. After I finished stripping I was given another 30 sec's. to redress. I wasn't finished in 30 sec's. so I started getting beat again with the nightsticks. After I finished dressing I was turned around and the officers started yelling obscenities at me and I was handcuffed again. They started beating me again with both fists and nightsticks. I was then pulled down the hallway by the handcuffs which had started cutting into my wrists. We got to a doorway and I was thrown into the wall next to it. After we went through the door I was made to start screaming in a way which was humiliating to myself. There was a line of officers on both sides of the hall and I was pushed, shoved and beat through these officers, sergeants, lieutenants and captains standing around observing this. I was then taken*

down another hall forcefully and when we turned a corner I was tripped up and when I fell to the floor the officers started kicking me around . . . I was picked up by the handcuffs and the officer started dragging me toward some stairs. My left boot fell off on the way and the officer dragging me picked it up. On the way up the stairs I was repeatedly being beaten by the officer's fists and nightsticks. The officer had me by the handcuffs and was running up the stairs. When I couldn't keep up with him I was hit in the head with my boot. This continued up 4 (four) flights of stairs. At each landing I was shoved, hit and beaten on the way to the next flight of stairs. When we reached the cell I was told to put my hand through the food port in the door. While the officer was taking my handcuffs off another officer was hitting my hands with a nightstick. This same treatment was issued to all 15 inmates that came up from Southern State. . . . One inmate had to be taken to the hospital and he hasn't returned even today. No doctor was brought to attend our wounds. A nurse did come by but was only giving out aspirin. . . .

Joseph:
 . . . We were pulled from the van and told to keep our heads down and not to say a word or else. . . . Then they took us in to the hallway and threw us up against the wall and told to kiss the wall, then I felt a sharp pain in my back some-one was punching me in my back and they said for the three of us [who were shackled and handcuffed together] to start dancing and don't stop till they tell us to stop. While they hit us with there billyclubs. . . . My head was slammed up against the wall and I was told to dance somemore and they told us to say that we were Trenton State faggots while they hit us with the clubs. . . . And then a Sgt. . . . from Southern State asked me . . . who started the food strike, I told him I don't know anything about a food strike I told him I don't eat liver and then he punched me in the face and grabbed me by the hair and slammed my head against the wall. . . . Then some guy a C.O. grabbed me by the hair . . . and pulled me into a

room an told to strip then they said I was too slow and they kicked me and punched me some more, and then they told me to get dressed fast and they said I was too slow then they started to beat me and slam my head against the wall again. Then one of them told me to leave my clothes and then another C.O. told me to pick up my clothes and run and then another one said why are you running and he would hit me for running and then they took me down the hall punching and beating me all the way. Then I was grabbed by the neck and drug and beat up by another guard. Then one of them told me to start saying that I was a Trenton State pussy and this other one told me to say I was a Trenton State homo. . . . I did nothing to deserve the beating that I got and also no other inmate or human being for that matter deserved the beating we got last night. I still haven't seen a doctor and I am hurt real bad!

James:
*   . . . They broke one inmate's arm. . . . I don't remember the [guards'] names but the faces I will never forget. There name tag and badges had tape on them so they could not be known . . . they said don't look at me motherfuckers keep your head down they said let me see if your asshole is big enough to take this stick bitch. . . .*

Rubin slid these statements unobtrusively into a large bundle of briefs and legal documents which he then left at the mailroom on the way to a window visit. The Canadians picked up the parcel after the visit. They sent the statements to the New Jersey attorney that had handled Rubin's successful suit following his 1974 Vroom Building confinement, Jeff Fogel, now head of the New Jersey American Civil Liberties Union.

When Willis next came on duty, Rubin called him over to his cell. He had always been friendly toward Rubin. Rubin said, "I know who you are, punk, and I know what you've been up to. Your father would be ashamed."

Willis feigned ignorance.

Rubin looked him straight in the eye and continued: "Some day this is gonna come back on you. Because some day you're gonna run up on someone like me, someone who won't dance for you. When I tell you I can do a fuck of a lot of damage in handcuffs and leg irons—believe it! Next time you try to hurt somebody—watch out. It could be somebody like me you'll find yourself fucking with."

Within days, the story of the prison beatings hit the newspapers. The headline in the Newark *Star-Ledger* read: "Liver refusal led to abuse." Three superior officers were suspended immediately without pay; Willis was to follow; others later not only lost their jobs, but were brought up on criminal charges, tried, convicted and themselves sent to prison; and the warden was reassigned to the central office for other duties.

Rubin had to ask himself: Were things at Trenton getting worse or were they always that bad? Were these events a signal that it was right to make a move? He was getting the message.

During a contact visit, Lisa and Rubin talked about the upcoming move to Rahway. Rubin was surprised Rahway had accepted him, after having so unceremoniously kicked him out in the middle of that night in 1974 when they'd dumped him in the Vroom. But the administration had long since changed.

While Rubin and Lisa were talking, a new white guard stared at them intently, with disgust. He'd already warned Rubin to remove his arm from the back of Lisa's chair. Rubin ignored him. When the guard came around the second time, this time from behind, he touched Rubin's arm; it was a terrible mistake. The guard could scarcely get out the words—"Get your arm off this chair!"—when Rubin spun around, his fist cocked.

Suddenly there were no male voices audible in the room. The women continued talking, not recognizing the danger.

Lisa leaned close to him. "Read my lips," she said. "If you hit him, I'll knock you out."

"Say what?" demanded Rubin, so loud the whole room became rigid.

"I said if you hit him, I'll knock you out," she repeated in earnest, but quietly so only Rubin could hear.

Rubin was now half standing, fist still cocked, his pinky not extended as it would have been in play—from him, the worst kind of threat. All eyes in the room now focused on him. The prisoners and the regular guards knew no one touched Rubin with impunity.

So what did the Hurricane do? A smile broke across his face, then he started to roar with laughter. He was laughing so hard he slumped down into his seat, almost bent over double. Tears came to his eyes. He could hardly speak.

"I can see it," he spluttered to Lisa. "I can just see it. You knocking me down! Can you imagine how quickly the word would spread? 'Rubin got knocked out by a woman! No shit? Word up—I saw it with my own eyes!' Then I'd *have* to leave this joint. My life wouldn't be worth shit. The only sound I'd hear would be 'Punk!'"

Lisa laughed too at the absurdity of the picture. She was under no delusion that she could have done anything to stop him: if Rubin had really meant to hit the guard, it would have been done before anybody could react. In years past he would have taken that line of least resistance; he wouldn't have hesitated. Now, in hesitating, he had allowed her to catch his attention, and he had been disposed to listen. He was manoeuvring the man-eating monster; it was no longer taking him to *its* destination. Where before he'd seen only fury, now he saw humour.

The tension in the room dissipated, the new guard was told by the regular guards to back off and everyone resumed their conversations. The guard later sent his apologies through a prisoner friend of Rubin's, Johnny D'Amico, as well as through another guard. He was too scared to come face-to-face with Rubin himself until the apologies had been rendered and accepted. From that day forward, he called Rubin "Mr Carter."

Mr Carter was ready to move to Rahway.

21

Rubin didn't have to send out any change of address notices. His move to Rahway on June 29 was sent out over the wire services and announced in articles in all the New Jersey papers. Said James Stabile, a spokesman for the state's Department of Corrections: "He's getting older. He's done a lot of time, and he doesn't need the security of a Trenton. . . . His behavior merited the move." Stabile also said that Carter would be eligible for parole around the year 2000.

The day that Rubin was moved was the same day the Canadians rented an apartment in Rahway. They were glad to be leaving Trenton and the iciness of their neighbours. The farther north the Canadians went, the more comfortable they felt. Rahway was just twenty-two miles by car from the Lincoln Tunnel and Manhattan. The apartment they rented, in the more congenial black section of town, had a balcony with a view of the rotunda of Rahway State Prison, not exactly the scenery one would normally seek out, but it suited them for as long as Rubin was there.*

---

*The Canadians, who were familiar with Rahway State Prison from the TV show "Scared Straight" about RSP's "aversion therapy" program to keep young people out of prison, couldn't believe that RSP, whose horrific conditions were enough to frighten anybody, was a step up from Trenton.

At the prison, Rubin hadn't yet been removed from the Department of Corrections van when he heard a voice outside shouting, "Where's Carter? Where's the Hurricane at? Lemme see him. He saved my life!"

When Rubin emerged into the daylight, the guard that belonged to the voice hugged him heartily, and Rubin was almost embarrassed. Rubin remembered him—Piscatelli. He had been a guard in 3-wing in Rahway when the Thanksgiving Day riots Rubin described in *The Sixteenth Round* had broken out. That was in 1971. Rubin had locked Piscatelli in the toilet area so that he'd be safe, and Piscatelli had stayed there through one long night and well into the next day. Even when the rioting stopped, he was too scared to come out and face the prisoners. The administration had had to get a crane and a wrecking ball to smash through the exterior wall and remove him that way. Since then, he never hesitated to tell everyone that Rubin "Hurricane" Carter had saved his life.

Being "new" to Rahway, Rubin was temporarily housed, as all new inmates ("fish") were, in a wing called "the ghetto." The head of the Lifers Club immediately had a runner bring him a "care package" of soap, toothpaste, deodorant, and cigarettes. (As all prisoners knew, personal belongings always took a while catching up.) A steady stream of people came by to say hello.

One young prisoner, no more than nineteen years old, who had been in the ghetto for months now, watched all the activity in fascination. He'd never seen anything like it. It was as if Rubin had checked into a hotel and the room service was non-stop. Seldom would high-ranking corrections officers come to that area, but with each shift change, more arrived—sergeants, lieutenants, and even captains—a virtual parade of them, all welcoming the new inmate. The young prisoner concluded that if Rubin was a fish, then Mona Lisa was a man!

When Rubin came out of his cell to use the telephone, the youth could no longer contain his curiosity. "Who *are* you, man?" he asked, stumped. But he had to wait for someone else to give him an answer because the Chief Deputy Keeper had just arrived to pay his respects too.

Despite the unexpectedly convivial reception, it took Rubin weeks to get over the disorientation of the move. Everything was so different.

He had to attune himself to different sounds, different warning signals, movements, people. There were so many new inputs to sort out, he was constantly watchful, on edge.

After three days in the ghetto, he was moved to a cell in One-Up. It was a quiet wing, and his tier of about twenty men was separated from the tiers below. Unlike at Trenton, Rubin did not have to descend four flights of stairs to get to the only phones in the wing. Here there were two phones on the tier itself. Rubin would be able to continue his work of freeing himself with a minimum of interference.

First he got his cell in order. Before settling in, he scrubbed and painted it. Then he unpacked his stuff. Among his belongings was some food that he'd been storing in his cell in Trenton: boxes of pre-cooked, vacuum-packed dinners, cans of nuts and tuna and salmon. He also found one old onion that delighted him. It had sprouted long green shoots, and he couldn't wait to tell Terry, an avid gardener, about it.

"You won't believe this, Typh," said Rubin, using the affectionate abbreviation for a brother storm, the Typhoon, with which he'd christened Terry.* "This onion is growing, Typh! How can that be? How can it grow when it doesn't even have any dirt?"

"Not 'dirt,' Rube," laughed Terry. "In horticultural circles, we call it 'soil.' You know, I bet you could get that onion to flower."

"I could?"

"Sure. An onion is a bulb, and it has everything latent in it. If you plant it and see that it gets enough light and some water, the green shoots will continue to grow into tall stems and you'll eventually get tiny flowers on top. Onion flowers aren't much to look at, but they're flowers."

Had the prisoners in the yard been privy to this conversation, they wouldn't have wondered why Rubin was earnestly scooping "soil" into a little plastic bag and smuggling it back to his cell.

---

*On visits Rubin would introduce Terry to fellow prisoners as "Typhoon, the prizefighter from Canada" because Terry looked a bit like a boxer, having broken his nose in a youthful accident in the somewhat more genteel surroundings of Upper Canada College (Canada's Establishment prep school). Rubin told Terry, though, never to make a fist or feign throwing a punch—he'd blow his cover.

Every morning on the phone Rubin would issue to the Canadians a state-of-the-plant report. It appeared to be a fast grower.

In Rahway, Rubin started to get in touch with the world. Telephone access perhaps made the greatest difference. In their Rahway apartment, the Canadians had a new three-way calling system installed on their phone line, which meant that once Rubin called them collect, they were able to connect him with a third party by phone. Even when the Canadians used it for simple tasks, like calling a library to locate a particular law book, Rubin would come along "just for the ride."

At Rahway State Prison, the Canadians were able to send in two twenty-five-pound food packages per month. On the phone Rubin would listen to them prepare meals for him in their apartment kitchen: breakfasts of bacon and eggs and pancakes and maple syrup; lunches of fish and chips; exotic gourmet dinners like Beef Wellington and crab with béchamel sauce; and treats of angel food cake, chocolate mousse pie, handmade eclairs and *millefeuilles*. Rubin would stay with the Canadians as they cooked, and they would give him a colour commentary, a blow-by-blow description of what they were doing, including sound effects. They would hold the receiver over the pan of frying bacon, for example, and the sizzling was music to his ears.

After listening to them pack everything up, he would look out the window in his wing and wait for them to drive up the long, horseshoe-shaped driveway, past the pond with the Canada geese and up to the mailroom, which was in a separate outbuilding outside the wall, at the rear. From his tier, one of the few in the prison high enough to provide a view over the wall, he could catch a glimpse of the pond and the geese and a portion of the driveway and the mailroom. Interestingly, it hadn't even occurred to Rubin to watch for them from the window until the Canadians suggested it; having access to a window to the outside was so removed from the realm of what he had been used to that windows may as well have been walls. In order for Rubin to get the best view, they would park just past the curve of the horseshoe. He could actually see their car, see them get out of it and carry the carton of food and disappear into the mailroom. Being a part of the process from start to finish was wonderful.

When Rubin received the food, he would spend hours staring at it.

Everything was neatly wrapped; the dinners were laid out in plastic containers, garnished on beds of lettuce with parsley and cherry tomatoes and baby carrots; and the cakes, pastries and pies were ravishingly decorated. A feast for the eyes no less than the palate. He would share the food with others in his wing, and save the rest (to last two weeks, if possible) in the styrofoam cooler that the prison allowed in.

The Canadians also sent a small Persian rug for his floor, art prints for his walls (impressionist works by Gauguin, Monet and Cezanne; Rubens's "Head of a Negro"), "RHC"-monogramed hand towels, a stereo radio-tape-deck system. They sent in cassette tapes of music Rubin liked: Otis Redding, Wilson Pickett, Merle Haggard, Sam and Dave, James Brown, Aretha Franklin, Johnny Paycheck, Johnny Cash, Buffy Sainte-Marie, Bob Dylan (the song "Hurricane" and the album *Highway 61 Revisited*), Elmore James, Gil Scott Heron, The Staple Singers, Percy Sledge, Memphis Minnie, Sweet Honey in the Rock, Lightnin' Hopkins, Willie Dixon, the Rolling Stones.

A barren cell was thus transformed into a home, and Rubin's senses were constantly being stimulated. Quite a contrast from the Rubin who had refused the television set for fear of getting too comfortable inside. But the more "comfortable" his surroundings now became, and the closer he felt to the outside, the more unbearable was his confinement.

In the meantime, the investigation into Rubin's case continued, and what they were uncovering was nothing short of dynamite.

One avenue they explored was suggested by Caruso's file. Caruso seemed to be very concerned with pin-pointing the "timing of the action," suspecting that the actual time of the crime was earlier than the 2:30 AM version espoused by the prosecution. The timing was critical because even the prosecution accepted the fact that Rubin was in the Nite Spot from some time before 2:00 until 2:15 that morning.

Notes in Caruso's file stated: "Scrap-book: time noted as shortly after 2:AM. Article says 2:30." This scrap-book apparently belonged to the second Pat (not Valentine) who was alleged to have been in the vicinity of the Lafayette Bar when the crime took place. Furthermore, Caruso noted as "IMP," the following from surviving victim William Marins's June 22, 1966 statement to the police:

2:00 AM looked at clock—decided to stay. "Suddenly" [Caruso's emphasis] two colored men [the gunmen] were standing behind Bob —

In addition, Caruso emphasized that:

Jean Wall operator—received call at 2:28 AM re: shooting— called police who said cop [sic] are already on way. (TIME??)

If the police were already on their way before 2:28, then the shooting obviously must have occurred earlier. But the prosecution claimed the shootings occurred at 2:30 A.M. and the police supposedly did not get the initial radio alert until 2:34.

The Canadians found another interesting piece of evidence that contradicted the State's claims. This was the testimony of a taxi driver (not the recently discovered cabby) from an August 1966 grand jury, before Rubin and John had been set up:

The only time I learned about the shooting was when I picked up Willie Marins' father at [his house address]. It was about 2:25, 2:30 in the morning and he was going to the hospital.

How was it possible for the shooting, to have been over; for the police to have already been notified and to have had the time to get to the scene; for the ambulance to have been summoned and arrived and have transported Marins to the hospital; for somebody to have called Marins's father and given him the news; and for him to have then called for and been picked up by a taxi by 2:25 or 2:30 A.M., unless the shooting occurred much earlier than the police later claimed? According to discovery evidence, the police retrieved from the manager of the cab company the records that would have shown the time of Marins's father's call, but this information was never disclosed.

So how was the time established at trial? Pat Valentine testified that, after being awakened by the shots, she surmised from the test pattern on her TV that it must have been around 2:30 A.M. and she called the police minutes later. And a number of police officers testified from memory—not from their original notes, which were never produced—that the radio alert for trouble at the Lafayette Bar went out at 2:34 A.M. But there was no hard, primary evidence pin-pointing the time, such as tape recordings, contemporaneous police logs or ambulance company records. The prosecution claimed that the machine that tape recorded all emergency calls into police headquarters as well as all outgoing radio dispatches had "malfunctioned" that night.*

There was, however, one document brought out at both trials, a Record of Customer Contact from the phone company, that appeared to be a bona fide contemporary notation of an emergency call for the Paterson police, the one to operator Jean Wall that Caruso referred to in his notes. The time noted at the top of the record was 2:35 A.M. But in Caruso's notes and in other police reports, including one from a Paterson detective named Edward Callahan, who purportedly examined the original call ticket at the phone company, the time was marked as 2:28 A.M. Only the document with the later time was entered as an exhibit at trial.

Needless to say, the Canadians were puzzled by the contradictory evidence and kept coming back to the Record of Customer Contact for clues. According to the transcripts, the memo was written not by Jean Wall but by her supervisor, who did not testify at trial and whose initials, "LH," appeared at the top. This was not Wall's original ticket stub, which was at the phone company, but a rewritten record. Why, the Canadians asked, didn't they bring the original into court, and why wasn't "LH" brought in to identify her own memo? But then, the more they looked at it, the more familiar the handwriting seemed. In fact, they suddenly realized that it looked identical to Vincent DeSimone's script, of which they had countless samples. Could this memo be a forgery?

The Canadians in Rahway sent the group in Toronto four documents that unquestionably were written by DeSimone, plus a copy of the suspect memo. Armed with these, Gus went to one of the top handwriting experts in Canada, Linda G. Pitney, founder of the first

---

*This seemed to be a common occurrence when it suited police purposes. In the official investigation into the Paterson police riot of 1968, according to Christopher Norwood's book, *About Paterson: The Making and Unmaking of an American City,* "the tape recorder at headquarters which automatically recorded orders to the men in the field had mysteriously broken down that night."

school in Canada dedicated to the teaching and study of handwriting analysis, the Canadian College of Kinesiography. Pitney also acted as an expert witness for law enforcement agencies in the area of forged documents. Gus did not tell her what the case was about or who had written the documents. The Record of Customer Contact was treated as the "Questioned Document" (QD) and its handwriting was to be compared to that of the four "Standard Documents" (SDs).

Meanwhile, the Canadians in Rahway were trying to track down the original phone company records. They found that the records for New Jersey Bell were normally kept in Newark for up to five to ten years, and that the likelihood of being able to retrieve records close to twenty years old was just about nil. They ran into the same problem with the cab company, which had gone into receivership and changed hands in 1981; no records were available from before then. Too much time had passed.

Linda Pitney, after many hours of careful examination of the documents, concluded that all the documents were written by the same person. She wrote two reports, totalling five pages, listing the many reasons for arriving at her conclusion, including matching letter formation, the presence in all of horizontal connective strokes, strong initial strokes and "t"s with crossbars to the left. But she also said that whoever did the forgery had some knowledge of forensic handwriting techniques, which made patterns difficult, but not impossible, to discern. (She had no idea that the author was a detective.) Transparencies were able to reveal, among other things, that the rhythm of groups of letters, as in the word "for" was always in the same proportion; that the small "f," for example, was always identical in height and depth.

She also ventured a description of the character of the forger based on graphoanalysis, a technique increasingly used by corporations for assessing potential employees. Rubin found her personality portrait of DeSimone uncannily accurate. She said he had been hurt as a child and now (now was 1966, when all the documents were written) felt vengeful. He loved organization and power, but feared his power being usurped by younger people. He was quick with sarcastic or mean remarks and held strong ideological beliefs. He would never forget any slight.

"Wow!" was Myron Beldock's response when Rubin apprised

him of the handwriting expert's conclusion. Although he could see the similarity between DeSimone's hand and the writing in the QD, Beldock had been sceptical. "I would think that DeSimone was too smart to make such an error," he had told Rubin, "so I'm not letting my hopes fly in that direction too far."

Now he was excited. "This is explosive. What do we do with it? And where?" He was thinking out loud.

"Here we have a key document that we can prove has been forged by the architect of the State's case. It was all part of the cover-up of the real time of the crime, which was earlier than they claimed. We're talking about the prosecution suppressing exculpatory evidence and falsifying documents. I can see it clearly, Rubin. But it's one expert's opinion. We're going to need corroboration, and it would help if we had a sample of LH's handwriting in order to definitively determine that she did not write the memo."

"Done!"

Because Herb Bell was often busy, Rubin and the Canadians had enlisted the assistance of another private investigator, Mims Hackett, also African-American, also from New Jersey. Rubin had met Mims in Trenton State Prison. Mims had been convicted in 1976 of kidnapping and given the minimum sentence of thirty to thirty-one years, despite the fact that he had two witnesses (not family members) who were with him in his house at the time of the crime. Because of a technicality, the trial judge refused to allow Mims to call his alibi witnesses, but after the trial, two State witnesses recanted their testimony against Mims, saying that it had been a frame-up by a local police detective. After an evidentiary hearing, the trial judge ruled that the "ring of truth is totally absent" in the recantation of both witnesses. (Shades of Bello's and Bradley's recantations!) Mims was sent to Trenton State Prison.

One day in the yard, Mims approached Rubin and asked him how to go about getting some publicity. Rubin put him in touch with people at CBS-TV, and his story was ultimately aired on "60 Minutes." In 1980, a federal judge issued a writ of habeas corpus and nullified Hackett's conviction because his constitutional right to call witnesses in his own defence had been violated. In comparison to Rubin, Mims had served only a short time, but it had been enough to throw his life into ruin, and he was only now picking up the pieces. Luckily he had been able to go back to his regular day job as a high school biology teacher, and his wife, Bernice, and their children had had the strength and the wherewithal to survive the tribulation. They were barely able to hang on to their home in Orange, however, and years later, Mims was still paying off outstanding legal fees.

On July 31, 1984, Mims delivered a lovely plant from a florist in Paterson to the apartment of one Lenore Harkinson. She was an elderly woman, in her seventies, and not physically well. She was happy to be receiving flowers, even though there was no note saying who they were from. All she had to do was sign the receipt next to the words "Received by" and note the date and her initials at the bottom.

Upon examining this receipt and re-examining the Record of Customer Contact, the QD, using spectrograms and photo blow-ups, Linda Pitney was even more convinced that the QD was a forgery. While she thought that Lenore Harkinson herself may have signed her initials at the top of the QD, it was not her handwriting in the rest of the document, which showed patching throughout, as well as blobs and corrections—"a trademark of forgers unable to keep up the flow of the pen." Three independent handwriting experts reviewed and confirmed in writing Pitney's analysis and conclusion.

Beldock now thought that to nail this evidence down, it was necessary for a lawyer to question Harkinson directly. He and New Jersey attorney Lou Raveson arrived at her apartment building at 3:30 P.M. one Wednesday afternoon. They buzzed her apartment, but there was no answer. Entering the building, they went up to her apartment and knocked on the door. No answer, but they heard someone inside. They went back outside and phoned. Busy. They went back inside and the superintendent said that if the woman didn't answer her buzzer, then he couldn't let them in either. They phoned again and she answered and hung up. They went back again and buzzed. No answer. They called again—busy signal. At six o'clock, they left.

The following Saturday, Sam and an attorney, William Perkins arrived in Paterson at 9:15 A.M. Bill was driving, playing Nat King Cole on his car tape-deck and trying to make Sam feel at ease. Sam was horrified to be in Paterson. He knew too much about its history, and the sight and feel of the decayed industrial city fulfilled his dread imaginings. He had come along because no one else was available to brief Bill on the facts they were trying to ascertain.

Rubin had always felt a special affection for Bill Perkins, a brilliant and affable attorney who at the drop of a hat would take time out from his busy schedule to help in any way he could. He had been educated at the University of Iowa, was fluent in Spanish and Russian and could get by in Portuguese and Polish, and had been a professional football player with the Minnesota Vikings. In the late seventies, he had been chairman of the New Jersey State Assembly Judiciary Committee and successfully blocked the reinstatement of the death penalty in the state until the early eighties. Now he was a lawyer with his own thriving practice on Journal Square in Jersey City. And he loved to cook. Bill was something of a Renaissance Man.

Bill came prepared. Before they entered Lenore Harkinson's building, he made sure the tiny tape recorder in his suit jacket pocket was working and ready to go. He turned it on as they walked in. The lobby door was open and they walked nonchalantly to the elevator, went up eight storeys, walked down the hall and knocked on her apartment door. Someone looked through the peephole and asked, in a high, shrill voice, "What do you want?"

"Mrs Lenore Harkinson? My name is William Perkins, ma'am. I'm a New Jersey attorney. I'd just like to ask you some questions."

"No! I will answer no questions at all!"

"Mrs. Harkinson, we'd just like to talk with you for a moment. Couldn't you please open the door, ma'am?"

"I don't open the door for no one!"

"All right, Mrs Harkinson. You don't have to open the door. If we just slide a memo under the door for you to look at, will you look at it?"

"Only if you promise to go away afterwards."

Perkins agreed. He then took a copy of the Record of Customer Contact from Sam and slid it under the crack at the bottom of her door, leaving a corner of the paper exposed so that they could see if and when she pulled it in. She did, then they heard her fumbling and mumbling about getting her reading glasses.

"Do you recognize this memo?"

"Yes, I recognize it."

"Is that your handwriting?"

She was silent. "These are my initials."

"How about the rest of it? Is it yours? Did you write the whole thing?"

At this point, her voice rose and she started screaming. "I won't answer any more questions. Go away! Go away!" She refused even to return the document until Bill and Sam promised they would go away if she slipped the paper back under the door to them, which she finally did.

As they left the building, straight ahead, parked on the other side of the street, was a Paterson police car. An officer was just getting out of the vehicle, his gun prominently on display.

"Oh, shit!" mumbled Sam. The ground seemed to sway underneath him and his heart was in his mouth. He was certain that the old woman had called the cops and that they were about to be arrested. He was glad that he was with an attorney, although the fact that Bill was black did not at that moment fill him with confidence. He remembered what Malcolm X used to say: "What does a redneck call a black man with a PhD?—'Nigger!' " And he remembered what the Paterson police had done to Rubin.

Visions of the Passaic County jail danced like sugarplums in his head. "Oh shit!" he mumbled again, as they continued their deliberate pace down the steps and past the cop to Bill's car. They left unmolested, but it took Sam hours to come down from the adrenalin rush.

They later interviewed a neighbour of Harkinson's who told them that Harkinson had worked for the phone company for forty-seven years until she retired in 1971 at age sixty-five. Harkinson told her neighbour that she remembered the murder case vividly: "I told them I wouldn't be no witness, no nothing. I wouldn't go to court. . . . I put my initials on [the memo], what more do they want from me? It's eighteen years ago it all happened."

"I love it, Rube, but it's hearsay," said Beldock, having to play the legal wet-blanket. "If Harkinson won't talk to us, we can't use it in court."

22

Despite the passage of eighteen years and the clouding of memories, in New Jersey the general fear of getting involved in the case remained fresh. Rubin and the Canadians were nonetheless able to come up with an impressive array of evidence and a number of significant witnesses.

Although the cabby himself was too scared to come forward, in the course of their search for witnesses who were at the Nite Spot at the key time that night, they came across two who recalled and would corroborate the incident of the cabby and Rubin's car. Mims Hackett got notarized sworn statements from them.

Witness One:
My brother and I went to the Nite Spot in Paterson, New Jersey late in the evening of June 16, 1966. When I walked in the door, Rubin Hurricane Carter was the first person I saw that I knew. He was standing at the far end of the bar talking to some women sitting at the bar. I don't remember exactly what time it was when I left the Nite Spot but I do know that I left Rubin Carter there.

I remember that when I left . . . just as I was opening the passenger door to the car we were driving in, I heard someone on the sidewalk say, "You lookin to get fucked up?" I turned around and saw Rubin's white car was blocking a cab on the street. The cab driver, a white man, was outside his cab near Rubin's car. I knew it was Rubin's car because I had seen it around many times. There were quite a few people leaving the Nite Spot then, and I remember people standing on the steps.

I don't remember exact times but I do remember reading the newspaper the next morning and saying . . . that Rubin couldn't have done those shootings because I was with him at the Nite Spot. . . .

Witness Two:

On the night of June 16 going into the 17th, 1966, I arrived at the Nite Spot on Governor and E. 18th St. in Paterson, New Jersey on my way home from work at about 12 or 12:30 AM. . . . When it was getting close to 2:00 AM, I asked Rubin Carter to take me home. Rubin said he would take me in a few minutes. I went into the back room where the band was playing and people were dancing. I remember seeing that this young fellow by the name of John, who danced real good, was dancing; in other words he had the floor.

I went into the bar area of the Nite Spot at around 2:15 AM. The back room was closing. I saw Rubin . . . I was tired of waiting on Rubin and I was glad when I saw my friends, K. and H., coming in the front door.

While I was standing by the front door, I remember a cabby coming right into the bar and hollering, "Who's [sic] car is blocking the street?" "Can I move that car so I can get by?" The cabby was white about 5' 9" tall about 155 to 160 pounds, had dark brown hair and spoke with a southern accent. Rubin was standing in the middle of the bar at the time.

. . . Later . . . we all started out the door. I told Rubin I was going with my friends. He said "As long as you got a ride." He got in his car with Bucks and John. John was driving. . . .

When I found out that Rubin and John were charged with the three homicides that happened that night, I knew they had the wrong men because I had seen Rubin and John at the Nite Spot when the shooting was supposed to have happened somewhere else. . . .

What I just stated is all true. I never forgot. It's just like it happened yesterday. I told this same story many times. I guess why I never could forget is because if Rubin had taken me home that night, I would have been locked up a long time ago for something I didn't do—just like Rubin and John.

This witness had gone to see Rubin's lawyer, Ray Brown, before the first trial. Brown had told him that he already had over 150 witnesses. (This was before DeSimone went to work on them.) Witness One had not come forward because he had heard that Rubin, after questioning, had been let go. Then the witness moved to Boston and "the next thing I heard was . . . that Rubin had been convicted. I never even knew he had been arrested!"

Mims obtained from a third witness, a sergeant at Trenton State Prison, a statement, not about the cabby, but supportive of Rubin's Nite Spot alibi. The guard had met William "Wild Bill" Hardney (Rubin's sparring partner in 1966) at the Muhammad Ali–Jimmy Young fight in the spring of 1976. Hardney told him that he hadn't testified at Carter's first trial because DeSimone had threatened to arrest him, but that he intended to testify at the upcoming retrial even though he was afraid of further police harassment.*

In late summer 1984, Lesra was in Toronto, preparing for another year of university. He finally had the opportunity to bring up one of his brothers for a visit, and Leland had been the most eager to come.

Leland was a curious blend of adult and child, hard and soft, jaded and yet totally unexposed. At thirteen years old, he thought that he was in his "prime" and that Lesra, at twenty, was over the hill. His

---

*Hardney did testify at Rubin's retrial, but he testified for the State. After being hounded with middle-of-the-night visits from the prosecution and the police at his home in Washington, D.C., after being threatened with jail and charges of obstructing justice, after being arrested by no less than fifteen policemen and members of the Passaic County prosecutor's office, after being shipped back to Paterson and held in custody, he finally succumbed to police pressure and testified that his story about being in the Nite Spot with Rubin Carter was a lie.

deep voice, which he exaggerated to sound low and menacing, contrasted with his small frame. "Man," he said, as he walked with his brother to the car in the deafeningly noisy parking lot at Pearson International Airport, "dis place is quiet!" And he meant it.

Leland stayed for a few weeks, fitting comfortably into the household and happily participating in everything that everyone was doing. He was full of energy and raring to go. He even went to work with the group, who were renovating a Victorian house downtown. He loved sanding doors, and knocking down walls. He earned enough money to buy himself a pair of "'Didas" high-top running shoes, the "innest" thing, with laces that had to be tied just so, loose and flat, and he wore a baseball cap, twisted sideways and with the visor flipped up. The latest styles, in clothes and dance, came from the very streets in Brooklyn where Lesra grew up and where Leland lived.

Toronto brought new experiences for Leland. One day while bicycling down the street, he passed another kid on a bike and just about fell over when the kid he passed smiled and waved at him. Leland thought to himself that in Brooklyn, if you wanted to keep your self-respect and your rep, you could never let anyone pass you, no matter what. Somehow the stakes in Canada were not the same.

At Lesra's house Leland discovered he could sing. Incredibly, he had never sung before. He liked to "rap" and he was good at it, but that was more like talking than singing. No one had ever asked him to sing—not even in school.

Gus and Lesra used to love going at it on the guitar. Gus had taught Lesra some basic chords and they used to sing old blues and folk songs, like "Shorty George," "The Midnight Special" and Leadbelly's "Bourgeois Blues." They encouraged Leland to join in. He had a beautiful, rich singing voice that surprised and thrilled him. They would stay up late at night, Gus strumming the guitar, Lesra and Leland wailing their hearts out. They taught Leland the song, "The Tramp on the Street" and they tried to sing it loud and fervently, the way Ramblin' Jack Elliott did:

> *Only a tramp was/ Laz'rus that day*
> *He lay down by/ the rich man's gate,*
> *He begged for some crumbs from*

The rich man to eat,
But they left him to die like
A tramp on the street.

He was some mother's darlin',
He was some mother's son,
Once he was fair and
Once he was young,
Then some mother rocked him,
Little darlin' to sleep,
And they left him to die like
A tramp on the street.

The group in Toronto at the time—Lesra, Marty, Kathy, Michael, Gus, Mary and Terry—told Leland all about Rubin. He wasn't too impressed. He looked at *The Sixteenth Round* and he still wasn't impressed. "Aw, dat ain't nuttin'!" he harumphed. But his interest was piqued when he looked at the pictures inside, particularly the one from 1962 of Rubin, muscles bulging, left fist at the ready, glowering over a horizontal Florentino Fernandez, who he had just knocked out. And when Lesra read the book's first six "rounds" out loud to Leland, he was moved. It was the first time they had seen him subdued. The part that really shook him was Rubin's time in the Jamesburg Home for Boys and how Rubin had to fight to survive. Leland could relate to that.

Rubin made a point of calling Toronto when Leland was there and speaking to him. Leland didn't believe that it was the Hurricane on the phone or that he had called especially to talk to him. It took a moment for it to sink in. Then Leland didn't know what to say.

Knowing Rubin so well earned Lesra a lot of respect in his brother's eyes.

Continuing their investigation, Rubin and the Canadians next turned their attention to the question of the car identification. They had found, among the discovery materials, a copy of a statement from Pat Valentine to Detective DeSimone. In the centre of the page was a line-drawing that looked like the wings of a bow-tie with a blank space in-

stead of a knot in the centre. This, Lisa realized, was an outline drawing of the shape of the illuminated tail-lights Valentine said she saw on
the getaway car. And sure enough, another review of the transcripts revealed that Valentine, upon questioning by Artis's attorney, Lew Steel,
had identified this sketch (Exhibit D-508) as such.

Bello and Valentine described the distinctive design of the getaway
car's tail-lights as having "lit up like butterflies" across the back of the
car, like elongated triangles, wider at the outside and tapering in to a
squared-off edge near the centre of the trunk, with only a foot-and-a-
half space in between that did not light up. As Steel forcefully brought
out at trial, this is an exact description of the illuminated tail-lights of
a 1966 Dodge Monaco, and indeed Pat Valentine had originally testified that the getaway car was a Monaco. The '66 Dodge Polara, on the
other hand, the car that Rubin was driving, had a similar-looking rear-
end configuration when not lit, but when lit, as the witnesses had seen
it, the Polara looked totally different: the lights did *not* extend in
towards the centre; only the very extremities lit up, creating nothing
remotely like an elongated butterfly effect, or anything like the drawing that Valentine had made.

Unfortunately, at trial, only black-and-white daytime pictures of
Rubin's Polara were in evidence. There were no colour photographs of
his car taken in darkness with the rear lights on, or equivalent photographs of a Dodge Monaco, that would have conclusively demonstrated for a jury the impossibility of mistaking Rubin's car for the car
that had sped off into the night.

Well, thought the Canadians, mindful of the worth of one picture,
perhaps it was not too late to get a federal judge to see the difference.
So they set about trying to find 1966 Dodges with working tail-lights
to photograph. They called auto yards and wreckers in New Jersey,
New York and Pennsylvania, and encountered laughter when they
said what they were looking for. In the States, when cars are junked
they are usually crushed; unless they're classics, nothing hangs around
intact for that many years. One man suggested they would have an
easier time tracking them down in Canada. So Lesra was given an assignment.

· · ·

About this time, Rubin agreed to an interview, his first in years, with David Gates of *Newsweek* magazine. Gates did his own review of the evidence in Rubin's case, and privately concluded that Rubin should not be in prison. He was even more convinced after meeting Rubin face to face, and Rubin very excitedly showed him the wealth of new material that he had been uncovering.

"You sell yourself very well," the reporter told Rubin, "but then you've got something to sell."

In his full-page article in *Newsweek*'s October 8, 1984, issue, Gates described Rubin as "a warm, articulate man who never seems to lose track of the sentence structure of his long, cadenced speeches." The reporter noted that Carter, although still as trim and muscular as he was in the ring, "with his neatly sculpted Afro—which hasn't a trace of gray—and without his beard . . . looks almost nothing like the way he did in the 1970s." But unchanged was his perseverance. Too "ornery" to give up, Gates wrote, Carter continues to protest his innocence, spending most of his time working on his tortuous and protracted case; his lawyers may have found a witness who could provide an airtight alibi. "But," ended Gates, "if the history of his case is any indication, [Rubin Carter] won't be walking through that door anytime soon."

Rubin and the Canadians liked the tone of the article as a whole, but they had to take exception to the pessimism of its conclusion. There was a tide-turning force in operation and the winds of history had been known to change.

Lesra and Gus, after much telephone work, managed to locate a 1966 Dodge Monaco that someone who knew someone in the Kingston area, about 175 miles east of Toronto, was restoring. A day's excursion resulted in some night-time photos of the tail-lights of the Monaco, shot at various distances. There was some minor difficulty due to the cool, drizzly autumn weather, which made the exhaust from the car visible. But nothing could obscure the unmistakable shape of lights so startlingly butterflyish, as their colour photos revealed.

They were equally successful in finding a 1966 Dodge Polara, at Archie's Wrecking, on Highway 124, between Burks Falls and Sundridge. Lesra was happy for the opportunity of a trip to northern Ontario. Archie McCabe, the owner of the yard, had never seen a black person before—at least, so Lesra thought—and didn't know quite how to react to him. But as soon as Lesra started giving him a hand putting a new battery into the junked Polara so they could get the lights working, Archie warmed up instantly.

When Lesra told Archie that they needed pictures for a famous murder case in America, Archie enthusiastically offered to tow the car out of the yard so they could get good, clear pictures.

The Canadians were now trying to pin down the time of the crime through Metzler Ambulance Service, the ambulance company that had taken the victims to the hospital. But Metzler's had been sold in 1978 and now operated under the name of Eagle Ambulance. Sam called them and was told they had no records before 1978, but Mr Metzler might. Eagle Ambulance didn't have Mr Metzler's phone number but said he was living in a town outside Paterson and to try telephone information. Sam was sceptical about being able to obtain Metzler's number—so far, in keeping with the air of paranoia, everyone they had tried to reach in Paterson had an unlisted phone number. People did not want their numbers known and, above all, they did not want to talk about this murder case. For the most part, the Canadians had had to rely on the phone numbers that had been listed in various discovery reports, some eight, others eighteen years old.

But a number for Mr Metzler was listed, and when Sam spoke to him, he was very friendly. No, he didn't have records from that far back, but he did remember the night of the Lafayette Bar shooting. His company never got paid by the city for taking the victims to the hospital. His son, William, might remember more about it; he was working that night as an ambulance attendant. He gave Sam his son's unlisted phone number and told him to call in the evening.

The Canadians could hardly contain themselves. They were about to talk to someone who had actually been there at the Lafayette Bar, minutes after the shooting, someone who had actually seen the victims and taken the survivors to the hospital. They no longer believed a thing they read about the case, and were even beginning to wonder whether any crime had actually occurred at the Lafayette Bar!

At six-thirty that evening, Sam called William Metzler and told him he was researching the Carter case and asked him if he could remember anything about what happened on that night of June 17, 1966. His memory was crystal clear, not about specifics of the time, but about the horror of what his young eyes had seen. Yes, he was ready to talk about it, he wanted to talk about it, he had kept it bottled inside for so many years. He would never forget.

In 1966 he was just seventeen years old and had gone to work for his father for the summer. He was fresh on the job as an ambulance attendant, working the midnight to 8:00 A.M. shift. After getting to work, the first thing the employees did was sit around with coffee and donuts, chit-chatting. Then they would take turns staying awake for two hours at a time. But it wasn't too long into the shift when radio messages started coming fast and furious over the police band. It was "in the early morning hours, before 4 A.M. It could very well have been two or two-fifteen." The police, he said, kept logs of when ambulances were called and when they arrived at the scene. The ambulance company kept call sheets that they cross-referenced with the police dispatcher. (Like so many other documents, these were not now, nor had they ever been, available to the defence.)

Metzler remembered the calls to police units coming in rapid succession, and the escalating panic. The first alert was directed to one unit, something vague about "trouble." A short time later, the call said "shooting" or maybe "hold-up." The final call was that shots had been fired. He remembered the first police car at the scene sending out a "Code One for ambulances" which meant "emergency—come as fast as possible."

His older brother, Walt, was working that night too; he was the driver. When they arrived at the Lafayette Bar, twelve blocks away, they saw one police car and two officers. Inside was "a wild west scene." There was one man sitting on a stool at the bar; his head was slumped over on the bar; his shot-glass was completely full and he had money in front of him, to pay for the fresh drink. His head was in a pool of blood. There was money strewn behind the bar, money out of the register, and the bartender was lying back there, dead. The female victim, Hazel Tanis, was in bad shape but alive. The fourth victim, William Marins, was "amazing. He was still walking around. He was very coherent. He said two people came in and said, 'This is a hold-up' and when the bartender went to get money, they started shooting."

"Are you sure he said that?" asked Sam.

"Yes. I remember it as clear as day. I was so surprised at how coherent he was. It was amazing for someone who was shot."

Sam's mind was reeling. This revelation destroyed another of the State's contentions. The prosecution had always tried to discount Marins's non-identification of Rubin and John at the hospital (within an hour of Metzler having seen him) because Marins, they claimed, was totally *in*coherent. Even more shattering, if the shooting was the result of a hold-up, then it was not a racial revenge killing by crazed racist militants who, as the prosecution claimed, walked into the bar and without saying a word, opened fire. That it was a hold-up was also what the police told the newspapers the day after the shootings, and it was only later that the prosecution claimed that there was no evidence of robbery as a motive. Well here it was!

William Metzler said the police helped him and his brother load the stretchers with the surviving victims into the ambulance. First they went to Paterson General, about three minutes away, where they dropped off the woman (the hospital couldn't handle two gunshot victims), and then they drove about five minutes more, taking Marins to St Joseph's Hospital.

"It all happened so fast," he said. "It was gruesome. I'll never forget walking through the side door into the bar. I-I-I slid on the blood, there was so much of it, and almost fell. . . . It's very difficult talking about it. . . . I can't add anything more."

After months of searching, the Canadians managed to find Avery Cockersham's first wife, Louise, who had remarried (and divorced) and had a different last name. She was about fifty, lived in a well-kept house with her daughter, JoAnn, and was still working at the same job she had in 1976, as a nurse's aide in a hospital. She received two visits: the first from Mims Hackett and Ed Carter; the second from Ed and attorneys Myron Beldock and Bill Perkins.

Louise confirmed that Pat Valentine and Sandy had indeed been drinking at her house on the night of the shooting. She said she had gone into the Lafayette Bar twice that night to buy bottles of liquor.

She categorically denied ever telling anybody she saw Rubin Carter in the bar or anywhere else. She saw the regulars in the bar, four white people, and they all waved at her and said hello. But there were two other white men there, sitting on the short end of the L-shaped bar, next to the woman (Mrs Tanis). They were whispering to each other and drinking whisky with a beer chaser (Alfred Bello's usual drink, known as a "boilermaker"). In retrospect she was sure that these two had had something to do with the shooting.

Around one in the morning, Valentine's boyfriend came over to Louise's; he was a veteran who had been injured in Vietnam. Valentine and her boyfriend had an argument about her always being out drinking and him staying home and babysitting all the time. He wanted her to come home and look after the kid. She left after a little while; Sandy stayed for another hour or so.

Louise's daughter, JoAnn, now thirty-one, was present that night and corroborated this story in every respect.

Louise said she was asleep when the shooting happened. JoAnn said she remembered hearing the shots and Avery telling her mother it was a car backfiring and to go back to sleep. Avery told them both afterwards he had seen the men running from the bar. He said he recognized them, and it was not Rubin Carter and John Artis, but he never told his wife or daughter who they were.

Louise said the next night, the night after the shooting, there was an altercation at the Lafayette Bar. She and her daughter were certain it wasn't July the first, as Detective Kline's report had indicated, and the row was not between Avery and anyone else, as was misleadingly reported in discovery; Louise herself was at the centre of it. She had got into an argument with Valentine outside the bar, saying that what Valentine had told the police she had seen was a lie, because Valentine had told Louise a different story. (So that was what the "all bullshit" in DeSimone's notes meant!) Shortly after the murders, Valentine had told Louise she had seen only one man, not two, running to a white car, a Cadillac parked in the gas station across the street. (Bello owned a Cadillac in 1966.) Louise told her: "If you tell the truth, ain't nobody gonna be mad at you."

A detective (Howard Kline) overheard them and took them all down to police headquarters for questioning: Avery, Louise and Valentine. According to Louise, Avery told the cops "It wasn't no Rubin Carter."

Louise said she and Avery "were split up four years later by a woman named Mae."

"Did you ever meet Avery's second wife, Fanida?" asked Mims.

"That's who I'm talkin' about. Fanada Mae. Fanada Mae Blackwell. They moved down to North Carolina together."

Luckily, people in North Carolina were not as paranoid as those in Paterson and, the next day, after some calls to long-distance information and some wrong numbers, they managed to get Fanada. Mims, then Rubin himself, spoke to her on the telephone. She had recognized Rubin's picture in the recent issue of *Newsweek* magazine and so somehow the calls did not come as a total surprise. She remembered Rubin well from years ago in Paterson. Yes, Avery had told her he had seen two men running from the bar and he had said they were not Carter and Artis. Yes, he had told that to an investigator before he died in 1976.

"Did he ever identify who he saw?"

"No, he was never able to because his condition got worse. Avery acted like he really knew who they were, but he never talked about it."

That secret now rested with him.

23

On Wednesday, November 14, 1984, at 8:00 P.M., a strategy meeting took place at Rahway State Prison. Myron Beldock was the first to arrive, and Rubin gave him the Polara and Monaco photos and the latest reports from the handwriting experts. Then Lew Steel and Leon Friedman came in. Professor Friedman brought with him a copy of a seventy-four-page paper he had prepared for his Hofstra University Law School students, entitled "The New Federal Habeas Corpus." That was the subject of the meeting. Going federal.

Beldock began the discussion by bringing Lew and Leon up to date on the results of their investigation, and Rubin listened and beamed.

"Rubin's been doing some amazing work," he said. "Things we're uncovering would stagger the imagination!" He told them about the cab driver, about Avery and Louise and Valentine, about the earlier time of the crime; he showed them the handwriting experts' analysis of the DeSimone forgery and the colour pictures of the Dodge models' tail-lights.

Lew and Leon were suitably impressed.

"But Myron," said Lew, "what are we doing? We're not trying the case again. It's like starting all over."

"If it comes to a third trial, we'll be ready for them, Lew."

"We *have* to start all over," joined in Rubin, "because what we've been led to believe was nothing but bullshit!"

"But Rubin, you're jumping ahead of the game. We haven't been granted a new trial. We're trying to get a hearing on the Caruso evidence and you're out there digging up new evidence."

"But we're not talking about *new* evidence, Lew, we're talking about *suppression* of evidence. All this we uncovered directly as a result of Caruso's investigation and notes that were not turned over to us prior to the '76 trial."

"That's right," said Myron. "Caruso was the springboard. If we had had the information then, which we were entitled to under the *Brady* rule, we wouldn't be meeting here with Rubin in this prison today."

Beldock went on to explain how they'd been duped by DeSimone, how he'd steered the defence away from exculpatory witnesses like Louise. "We were tricked. Any statements damaging to Rubin that were attributed to Louise we now find out were not true, never happened. They inserted incriminating remarks into the discovery reports, and that was very effective. It kept us away from her, and God knows how many other exonerating witnesses."

"And we found this out," continued Rubin, "only because we finally got Caruso's file."

"Well," said Lew, "we always figured the Caruso material was a bombshell, or was it 'a pot of gold'? But let me play the devil's advocate. The matter of the cab driver—that didn't come out of Caruso and it can't be considered *Brady* evidence, known to the prosecution but unknown to the defence. It's newly discovered evidence pure and simple. We'll have to take it back to Leopizzi."

Rubin would not hear of such a Sisyphean prospect. "Fuck that!"

"But we would have to, Rubin. This stuff is dynamite. Evidence of your innocence you can't sneeze at."

"No, but Leopizzi will. Just think of what he'd do to a witness that is so reluctant to talk we'll have to subpoena him."

"Rubin's thinking is that once we get a hearing in a federal court," explained Myron, "we can bring all the fruits of our investigation in under the Caruso umbrella."

"That's right," continued Rubin. "We have to do something different. We can't go back! The problem we've always faced is that the State wants to keep a stranglehold on this thing, and never let it go. No, we have to move ahead, and without further delay. Look, I'll be frank with you. This place is intolerable. I won't stay here—now that's that!"

Leon now spoke. "Rubin, I've always been apprehensive about the Caruso business delaying the appeal as a whole. I've been urging that we go federal ever since the 4-3 decision in the State Supreme Court and the strong dissenting opinion. The Caruso information, I must say, is a benefit and a curse at the same time. It's good because we want a federal judge to know this is really a guilt and innocence issue and we're not talking about legal technicalities. But, really folks, we don't need one more issue. If it means years more in the state courts, is it worth that? The Bello lie-detector and the racial revenge are absolutely solid issues. They alone are strong enough for us to prevail federally. We can move on them now. The quicker we get them to the federal court the better."

"I'm glad to hear you say that, Leon, because that's exactly the way I feel. Here we are still messin' around with state courts when we know we can't get shit from them. We know our only chance lies in getting this thing out of the hands of the state and to a federal judge. So what the hell are we waiting for? Reagan to finish packing the federal courts with his right-wing friends?"

"You know, Rubin," said Myron, "we can't bring the Caruso issue with us until we exhaust all our state remedies. And we can't give it up, it's too important. We can't qualify for habeas corpus with an unexhausted claim."

"We *have* no state remedy, Myron. It's been years now since we've tried to get this thing heard in the state. I know you and Lew haven't forgotten that Leopizzi stormed off the bench while you were still trying to reason with him. Myron, you talked about putting the Caruso appeal on a fast track and kicking it up to the Supreme Court. What happened? Ask Ed Graves. He'll tell you! It's bogged down . . ."

"Ed Graves," interrupted Myron for Leon's benefit, "is the new lawyer in our office. He's been through a baptism of fire with Rubin's case. He's been handling all the paperwork in the Caruso appeal."

"And they've been running his ass ragged!" continued Rubin. "We file our first notice of appeal at the beginning of February this year. The court clerk tells Ed they lost or misplaced it. We file another one; they say it got lost in the mail. Then months go by while they send us on a wild goose chase for docket sheets that don't exist. They deliberately keep us spinning in circles. We finally file our appeal brief in the Appellate Division in May; the prosecutor fails to respond on time in June and he doesn't even have the courtesy to request an extension. Then we make a motion to suppress the prosecution's response for inexcusable delays and their brief is accepted anyway, in August, two months late. Then we apply directly to the Supreme Court for certification so that we can expedite the appeal; the prosecutor opposes the motion, and we are denied. So where are we now? It's November 14 and we're still in the Appellate Division, still waiting!

"And you know what would be even worse? What if the Appellate Division or later the Supreme Court grants our request and calls for an evidentiary hearing? Then we win this battle, but we lose the war. Then we're really stuck in the state because then they'll remand it back to Leopizzi—and the last time we had a hearing with him, it took five and a half years between our request for the hearing and its final adjudication—and we lost to boot. No, we gotta get outta there and fast! We want an evidentiary hearing, but we want it in an impartial federal court."

"I must say, I agree with Rubin," said Leon. "We should submit the habeas corpus petition now. These things always take a couple of months to process. By the time a federal court is ready to hear our petition, we'll either have been technically exhausted on the Caruso issue because they'll have denied us in the state, or we'll argue that we *are* exhausted because we have no real state court remedy, that the corrective process in the state is so deficient as to render futile any further effort to obtain relief."

"Go ahead, Professor! I hear you!"

Lew and Myron nodded. "All right, Rubin. I think we all agree," said Myron.

The meeting lasted until 9:40 P.M., and as Beldock was leaving, he smiled back at Rubin and told one of the officers: "We're getting out soon."

Habeas corpus is Latin for "you should have the body." Although the phrase is bandied about in Hollywood movies, few people are familiar with its workings.

The "Great Writ," as the writ of habeas corpus is known, occupies a singular and exalted position in the world of jurisprudence. Originating in common law and the Magna Carta of England, it has long been recognized as "the best and only sufficient defence of personal freedom," and was central to the concepts of liberal individualism that transplanted easily to the British colonies. In the words of the U.S. Supreme Court:

> The writ of habeas corpus is a procedural device for subjecting executive, judicial, or private restraints on liberty to judicial scrutiny. Where it is available, it assures among other things that a prisoner may require his jailer to justify the detention under the law. In England . . . and in the United States, this high purpose has made the writ both the symbol and guardian of individual liberty.

Be that as it may, because of the peculiarities of the state/federal division of powers in the United States, access to the writ by state prisoners is severely circumscribed by the principle of "comity" (or deference to state courts out of a polite non-interference), by legal statute and by increasingly restrictive precedent. Federal courts are empowered to intervene in state convictions only if the convictions are the result of a violation of a right guaranteed under the federal constitution, and only if that claim has been presented first to all the state courts. So habeas corpus is no quick fix for illegal detention; you have to be able to survive in prison for years while your appeal wends its way through the state system first. And even then, on average, only 3 percent of habeas corpus petitions are successful, and many of these are overturned on appeal.

Furthermore, if hearings have been held in the state, then what is subject to independent federal review is not the state court "findings of fact," which must be "presumed" to be correct, but only the application of constitutional law to those facts. In plain English, this means that if a state court says it's a fact, it's a fact, even if it's a fiction. So, for example, if Judge Leopizzi says that Bello was standing in the hedge outside the Lafayette Bar, then Bello was standing in that hedge outside the Lafayette Bar, regardless of the fact that there was no hedge outside the Lafayette Bar. This "presumption of correctness," a sort of doctrine of infallibility that can be overridden only under the most extraordinary circumstances, gives the state courts powers usually reserved for popes.

The initial petition for a writ is supposed to be very brief. There's a form to fill out, with spaces for the answers to seventeen questions, including a history of the case, the grounds on which the petitioner claims he is being unlawfully held and so on. The idea is to provide the court with an overview of the case, procedurally and substantively, for a quick determination (usually by a magistrate) on whether the petition meets the criteria for meriting further consideration.

Rubin's case was so lengthy and complicated that, despite the November 1984 decision to file a petition immediately, a draft was not circulated among the various lawyers and Rubin until two months later. Rubin by this point was beside himself with frustration, and the Canadians were beside themselves too. But there was no quick way to review the literally dozens of lengthy briefs that had been filed in the state and to cull from them the most important issues to proceed with federally.

There was some discussion of the principle of "judicial economy"— that judges generally decide issues only when absolutely necessary and that if many are presented, usually only one or two are looked at. Although the Bello *Brady* violation and the racial revenge motive were the strongest grounds for habeas corpus relief, the team decided that they could not afford to omit the many other due process violations that might ultimately be successful (like the "jury misconduct" issue) and, at any rate, needed to be raised in order to give a judge the full flavour and scope of the travesty of justice presented by this case. They had to write for the benefit of someone who was coming into this mess fresh.

When they finally received Beldock's draft of the petition, Rubin and Terry and Sam, of the phantom law firm of Carter and Partners, went to work. They had carefully studied all the appeal briefs the lawyers had filed in the state. They knew the issues. Emboldened by the results of their investigation, they decided they had nothing to lose by using the strongest possible language in the federal papers. Nothing could be more outrageous than what the prosecution had done to Rubin, and they wanted that outrage to jump off the page.

Rubin had a new attitude. No longer a defendant but a prosecutor, he was about to put the State on trial. The prosecution, in having to defend the legality of his continued incarceration, was going to have to defend itself.

Carter and Partners' additions to the draft of the petition were well-received by the lawyers in New York. Ed Graves had assumed the changes had come from Lew Steel, he thought they were so powerful. Leon also was infected by the punchy spirit of the document, and wove his own magic into its fabric. "The conviction which is under attack here has been in the New Jersey courts for over 18 years," he wrote in an introduction enumerating "the two full trials, the four appeals to the New Jersey Supreme Court, the many extensive hearings . . . and the numerous rulings on the dozens of issues raised in the state." Leon went on: "It is safe to say that among twentieth century criminal proceedings in which serious injustice has occurred only the Sacco-Vanzetti and Scottsboro cases rival the present action in terms of notoriety and world-wide attention."

The petition ended up being a tad longer than the usual three or four pages. It was fifty-seven pages and delineated twelve separate grounds for habeas corpus relief. Ground twelve was the Caruso issue that was technically still pending in the state, but which they argued should be considered exhausted because of the inordinate delays and futility.*

After much revision, Rubin's petition was finally ready on February 11, 1985. Before it could be filed, Rubin himself had to sign it. So Ed Graves trekked across the Hudson River, and down to Rahway State Prison with the papers to get Rubin's signature.

Ed Graves was a product of the sixties generation. Close in age to the Canadians and like them in many ways, he did not become a

---

*John Artis, being on parole, was still therefore in state custody. His separate petition of seventeen pages incorporated all the grounds listed in Rubin's and added three others that concerned him alone.

lawyer until his mid-thirties. Before that, he had been a musician with a rock band and before that a psychologist. An Irish-American with an affinity for Caribbean music, he was also a big fan of Bob Dylan. Being assigned to work on Rubin's case could not have made Ed happier. He was impressed with Rubin's legal ability, his forceful arguments, the clarity and objectivity of his thinking. He had spoken to Rubin many times over the phone, and Rubin had always been enthusiastic and full of energy. "How're you doin', Rubin?" he would ask, and the answer would invariably be "Oh, I'm perfect, brother!" And although the words jolted Ed with what he would normally consider hubris, he didn't doubt that Rubin meant exactly what he said.

Ed was apprehensive about meeting the legend in person. And what happened when they did meet did nothing to diminish Ed's awe. Rubin greeted Ed warmly. The strength of his hug belied the trimness of Rubin's physique. They were shown into the office of a prison psychologist, and as Ed sat down, so did the psychologist.

"I'm sorry, but you'll have to leave," said Rubin, still standing, holding the door open.

"This is my office. I'd like to hear what you have to say."

"Well this is my attorney, and our meeting is confidential."

"I'll just sit here and do some paperwork. Go ahead."

Rubin pointed the way out. The psychologist was getting angry, and Ed was getting nervous and lit a cigarette. The psychologist finally got up and left the room. Rubin closed the door behind him and sat down. Ed was amazed that an innocuous situation could, without warning, become so charged and that Rubin, a prisoner, was handling the reins, was in control. Or so Ed fervently hoped.

Suddenly the door flew open. There was the psychologist again, his nose twitching, his face flushed red.

"Leave this goddamn door open! I can write you up on charges! You don't make the rules in this zoo!"

"Zoo? You better watch who you're calling 'animals,' mister," warned Rubin, up on his feet again.

"I'm telling you to leave this door open. This place stinks!" (This is a psychologist? Ed asked himself.)

Rubin closed the door in his face with a calm "Go fuck yourself."

He turned to Ed, apologized for the intrusion. "You see why I need to get out of here? Now where do I sign?"

Rubin's petition was filed in Federal District Court in Newark, New Jersey on February 13, 1985. There were eleven judges sitting in the district at that time, and cases were assigned to them at random. (Lawyers called it "going on the wheel.") The most senior judge on the court was Clarkson Fisher, who was appointed by President Richard Nixon in 1970. Rubin prayed that his case would come before Judge Fisher, because he knew that Fisher, who had conducted hearings into Rubin's unlawful confinement in the Vroom in 1974, was a fair judge. He had not been afraid of Rubin, or put off by his dishevelled appearance after three months in the hole. He had been willing to listen to what Rubin had to say, and they spoke eye to eye.

On February 14, Ed Graves called the court and found out that the petition had been accepted and assigned to Judge H. Lee Sarokin. Rubin had not heard of this judge, and his heart sank.

Because Judge Sarokin was an unknown quantity to Carter and Partners, they set about doing some research, consulting *Who's Who in America* and various other sources. They found out that Sarokin was born and raised in New Jersey, where his father had been editor and publisher of the *Perth Amboy Record*. He attended Dartmouth College and then Harvard Law School, where he graduated in 1953, and then practised civil litigation in Newark for the next twenty-five years. He was the finance chairman for Bill Bradley's successful 1978 bid for a seat in the United States Senate. A year later, Sarokin was appointed to the bench by President Jimmy Carter. So far so good, they thought.

Rubin asked Lou Raveson at Rutgers for a compilation of all of Judge Sarokin's decisions, and was sent a computer printout with an up-to-date list, numbering a staggering ninety-six. He was a prolific writer. Carter & Partners then scoured the list, eliminating cases that appeared purely business-oriented, and highlighting criminal cases and ones that appeared to concern civil rights issues directly. Then Terry and Sam went to the nearest law library, where they became familiar with the hardbound *Federal Supplement* volumes in which district court opinions are published. They photocopied the most interesting and relevant of Sarokin's decisions and studied them with Rubin.

They were impressed. Here was a judge that could reason. Here was a judge with a heart. Here was a judge that loved not only the law, but justice.

In a 1983 case, Judge Sarokin chastised Reagan's small Business Administration for seeking to collect a $300,000 loan from a penniless, mentally disturbed widow. "Better to have no government at all than a government devoid of compassion and basic human decency," he wrote. In another case, he compared city officials who balked at abiding by consent decrees on hiring minority firefighters to "hooded nightriders." He did not mince his words; his language was forceful and colourful, his logic solid.

But by no means was he anti-prosecution. As he said in an interview with *The National Law Journal,* published in May 1985, "If I'm concerned about protecting the rights of a defendant, that isn't anti-government. That's exactly what I'm supposed to do." He wanted everyone to leave his courtroom "with a feeling that the result was just and fair." Such noble sentiments were not mere rhetoric. In reviewing a lengthy criminal trial over which Sarokin presided and in which government officials were convicted of extortion, the Third Circuit Court of Appeals went out of its way to compliment Sarokin on his "scrupulous sense of fairness." In another criminal case, a black defendant who had been given a lengthy prison sentence by Judge Sarokin wrote the judge to say that he was proud to have been sentenced by him!

Judge Sarokin was all that Rubin had been looking for.

On February 20, Judge Sarokin issued an order to the State to file an answer to the petition by March 31, 1985, accompanied by copies of "all briefs, appendices, opinions, process, pleadings, transcripts and orders filed in the state proceedings . . . as may be material to the questions raised in the petition."

Within days, the state's Appellate Division, after delaying for over a year, happened to schedule oral arguments on the Caruso issue, thus providing the prosecution with fuel for an argument that the petitioners had not yet exhausted their state court remedies. But now that Rubin was firmly ensconced in federal court, nothing was going to budge him. Rubin told his lawyers to waive the oral argument. "I won't tolerate playing any more in the state—unless someone is willing to trade places with me while we diddle."

Leon told Rubin to be prepared for a huge battle over the exhaustion issue in federal court before the judge could even get to the substance of his case.

"Well put on your thinking cap Professor. You're the expert on federal law. Think of how we can short-circuit the system."

Not a day went by when Rubin was not on the phone to at least one of his New York attorneys if not all three—Leon, Myron, Ed—planning strategy, always trying to be several steps ahead of the State. It got to the point where Myron would come on the phone half-singing, "A day without Rubin is a day without sunshine." Or Leon would greet him excitedly: "RUBIN! We were worried. We didn't hear from you in two days!"

Carter and Partners, with a zeal more commonly found in a prosecutor's office, were busily assembling mini-briefs on various aspects of the case. They were researching the exhaustion issue, dissecting factual errors in the State Supreme Court's majority opinion, putting together proposed appendices of exhibits. There was a constant stream of "legal" mail arriving in New York from Rahway.

The Passaic County prosecutor's office was on unfamiliar ground now that they were out of their state cocoon. There were different rules in the federal ballpark, which was Professor Friedman's home turf, and the rules were taken seriously. The prosecution tried their usual tricks, but they could not withstand the juggernaut coming at them.

March 31, 1985, the prosecution's deadline for filing, arrived and nothing happened. They had ignored Judge Sarokin's order (later claiming they never received it) and submitted nothing: neither an answer to the petitions, nor the state court record. Rubin immediately had the lawyers file a Motion for Default Judgment in the district court. Leon told Rubin: "It won't end this simply. We can embarrass the prosecution a little, but there's no way the judge will decide in our favour on the basis of this motion."

"All we want to do, Leon, is make them play by the rules. We want to force them to answer. And we want to show the judge by our swiftness and our intensity that we mean business."

"Then this is a step in the right direction. It's not a knock-out punch, but it's a body blow. The major campaign is yet to come."

For the same reasons, and to assist the court in its consideration of the petition, they decided to take on the responsibility of filing with the district court all the relevant state court briefs (from both sides), appendices and opinions. Some of the lawyers were cool to the idea, thinking that no federal judge would look at, let alone review such a mountain of paper, but Rubin insisted. Carter and Partners, with the assistance of Ed Graves, took over the task, which required a solid week of collating and photocopying. ("Okay," Ed told Rubin, "we'll roll back the stone soon.")

On April 10, Terry personally delivered a box of documents to the clerk's office at the Federal District Court in Newark, and he was asked to take them directly into Judge Sarokin's chambers, where he left them with a clerk. The box weighed a good thirty-five pounds; its inventory alone was four pages long. They now had to wait for the prosecution's next move.

Rubin continued to be on the phone daily to New York, anticipating the State's response, weighing his options, picking his lawyers' brains. Sometimes tempers got frayed.

"If I'm pushy, Myron, forgive me. But this is our last chance."

"You're doing what you should be doing. You're not pushy."

"It's just that I can smell the end. . . ."

The Default Motion forced the prosecution to respond, which is exactly what was hoped for. But their answer addressed only the Caruso file exhaustion issue. They argued that the "petitioners have failed to exhaust available state remedies" and that there was "no . . . basis to excuse petitioners from compliance with exhaustion requirements." The prosecution wanted the court to rule on this so that they would never have to argue the merits, the substance of the case. But the request was not presented in the form of a motion, as it should have been, and thus left the court unable to act. So nothing was about to happen.

"What do we do now, Leon, to get things going?"

"Well, I've been thinking, Rube. We can make a Motion for Summary Judgment. That means we're saying to the judge, 'Look, we have issues that are so clear and so strong that they don't require going through the usual business of hearings. Go ahead and rule on these right away.' We'll still get to file briefs and make oral arguments. But that's it. We can't call any witnesses. We have to rely on the existing record. This is an unusual strategy for a habeas action and normally I wouldn't recommend it. But it would be fast and efficacious. With this route, Rube, come October tenth—you're out!"

"Leon, you're a genius."

"Rubin, the problem is Caruso. We're still going to have to deal with the issue they raised, whether they did it properly or not. As you know, the judge cannot consider a 'mixed petition,' a petition that has both exhausted and unexhausted claims. So we should write a separate brief giving our best arguments on why we consider the Caruso matter exhausted. But I warn you. The way the law currently stands, the chances of winning the argument are virtually nil. We may just have to cut Caruso loose and amend our petition to delete that one ground. There's a Supreme Court case, *Rose against Lundy,* which says we can do just that."

"Which means we lose the Caruso evidence forever?"

"I'm afraid so; it would be considered 'mooted'—unless by the time our Summary Judgment Motion is heard, the state will have disposed of the matter and you will then be technically exhausted."

"I *am* getting tired, Leon. I'm almost fifty years old."

"I got you, kid."

"Well, let's go!"

24

The U.S. Courthouse and Post Office building, located between Franklin and Walnut Streets in downtown Newark, is an imposing and dignified neo-classical structure. Its exterior is finished in a smooth, light-coloured limestone. Opened in 1936, the building houses Newark's main post office on the first floor, and on the third, the United States District Court, with the clerk's office and various courtrooms and chambers including those of Judge Sarokin.

As Terry and Sam exited the elevator onto the third floor, they felt a peacefulness they'd encountered nowhere else in their New Jersey sojourn, a refuge from the hubbub and smallness of the workaday world. The hallways were wide and high, adorned by decorative mouldings, marble pillars and statues of classical Greek design and proportion. Upholstered doors appeared at measured intervals. If the justice meted out here matches the grace of the surroundings, thought the Canadians, then it is a justice that is balanced, considered, elegant.

They had arrived early. It was nine o'clock Friday July 26, 1985, and oral argument on the Motion for Summary Judgment was scheduled for ten. Rubin, waiting in the penitentiary, was on the phone with the others back in the Rahway apartment, all of them patiently biding the four hours it would take for the call from Newark with a report on how it had gone. Sam and Terry had already scouted the building for pay phones. There were some near the elevators; some outside the washrooms in a jurors' lounge; others outside a press room, between the clerk's office and Judge Sarokin's chambers.

The lawyers arrived: Professor Friedman, Myron Beldock, Lew Steel, Ed Graves. Together they entered the wood-panelled courtroom, taking their places at the counsel table next to the empty jury box. Leon looked distinguished and authoritative in his dark navy suit, his face tanned, his eyes sparkling, his hair dipping professorially over his shirt collar at the back. In a khaki-coloured cotton suit, Myron was laid-back but ready. Lew, in a blue-striped seersucker suit, looked bold and confident. Ed blended into the group, as a junior lawyer was supposed to. They spread out their papers, briefs and notes on the table in front of them.

Terry and Sam sat in the first row of spectator seats behind a waist-high wooden partition, just behind Ed Graves. Terry had two briefs balanced on his knees; Sam had a briefcase open on his lap and a yellow legal pad ready on which to transcribe the proceedings so that Rubin would know as thoroughly as possible what happened.

And right behind them was Rubin's cousin, Ed Carter, looking dapper, dressed to the nines. He had come with Norman "Lush" (nicknamed for his abstinence) Brown, an old friend of Rubin's who had helped out with the investigation, and Barbara Samad, another old friend, also showed up to give moral support.

Sitting at the counsel table on the other side of the aisle was John P. Goceljak, then first assistant prosecutor for Passaic County. He was bald, average height and tending to plumpness. On his side of the courtroom sat an aging investigator and a couple of young zealots from the prosecutor's office.

There was no press present, no fanfare, no media circus to cloud the issues—just an atmosphere of quiet reasoning.

Judge Sarokin, in a full-length black robe, entered the courtroom. In a resonant voice, he apologized to those assembled for the Carter-Artis case: he first had to entertain an emergency application in another matter. The judge was patient but firm with the attorneys for the other case who had stepped forward and now stood before him, mumbling and rambling and having a hard time making themselves clear in what they considered intimidating surroundings. Sarokin had a gentle face, was slim, wore glasses and was almost bald. A youthful spark that countervailed his fifty-six years could be read in the wry smile that every now and then threatened to break over his lips.

While this application was being heard, Terry reviewed his copies of the two briefs they'd worked on with Rubin and his lawyers, briefs that had taken months of intense concentration and unremitting collective effort to prepare. The lawyers had been constantly prodded and prodding, questioned and questioning; every issue had been discussed, reviewed, dissected from various perspectives and put back together even more forcefully than before. It was as if everyone involved had caught a kind of contagion, an infectious energy, each one inspiring the best from the other. No stone had been left unturned, no argument unexplored. This was the final push and everything had to be perfect.

What was it, Terry asked himself, that had galvanized this kind of phenomenal dedication, commitment and care? Rubin's charisma? The strength of his character? A shared conviction that the right thing must not only be done, but be done right?

Terry looked down at the biggest brief first: "Petitioners' Joint Memorandum in Support of Motion for Summary Judgment." It was 253 pages long, excluding tables and exhibits. At close to two inches thick and neatly bound, it resembled a phone book. The table of contents required six pages; the table of cases cited was five pages. They'd had to request permission to file an overlength brief, because normally only a thirty-page submission was allowed. Rubin was confident that Judge Sarokin would understand the necessity for such length. This judge would welcome the opportunity for a complete overview of a case with such a complicated and protracted history. And it had to be told like a story, not like a dry recitation of disconnected facts.

Terry remembered how he and Sam had worked, day after day, with Rubin on the telephone, writing out factual sections on the ballistics evidence, on the police intimidation of William Hardney, on the misidentification of Rubin's car and so on. Kathy would type these out, and then night after night they would drive to New York to the offices of Beldock, Levine and Hoffman. There, they would give the product to Ed, who would add his input. Then Amanda George, using a word processor, would enter the material into the draft to be reviewed by all the lawyers. Sessions went well into the night, with Ed, Amanda, Sam, Terry and Kathy sometimes staying till five or six in the morning, consulting transcripts and proofreading.

Up until then, Leon and Lew had both been unaware of the involvement of the Canadians. One day, after Terry and Sam had picked up Leon at his East 78th Street office and ferried him down to Beldock's, Leon said to Rubin, "I can't believe it, Rubin. Who are these people? I get picked up, chauffeured around. What the hell is going on?"

He was to learn that the Canadians would do anything to speed the process, to save the lawyers' time and to stretch the value of their resources. For example, every statement the lawyers made in the briefs had to be supported by a citation, a specific reference to the transcripts, which had to be accurate as to the volume, page number and content. In Beldock's file room, Sam and Terry retrieved a complete set of transcripts—the forty-six volumes from trial, the twenty from motions and related proceedings and the fourteen from the Bello polygraph hearing—and piled them onto a double-decker shopping-cart-like contraption which they wheeled upstairs into Ed's office to search for and check all the citations. The lawyers had been surprised with Sam and Terry's familiarity with the record, that they seemed to know answers to the most obscure questions, or at least where the answers could be found. The Canadians had been exercising that Canadian tendency of keeping a low profile, and it was now apparent that their knowledge was the result of years of behind-the-scenes participation and study.

Yes, thought Terry, weighing the big brief in one hand, this has been a mammoth undertaking, and its size reflects that.

Then he looked at the slimmer "Memorandum Regarding Exhaustion of State Remedies" on the Caruso question. He flipped through the brief, his eyes lighting on the passages that he now had a moment to savour:

> . . . in its nineteenth year before the courts.
> There is one overriding reason why this case has been such a protracted and exhausting ordeal: namely, petitioners [Carter and Artis] have never enjoyed full, fair and unforced

disclosure of the facts to which they have been constitutionally entitled. For the prosecution to now claim a lack of exhaustion is insufferably galling. It is akin to plucking out a
man's eyes and then condemning him because he cannot see.
The petitioner has always sought swift and effective administration of justice. It has consistently been the misconduct of
the State, under the color of law, which has frustrated and
prolonged its realization.

They had written of "the suppression of exculpatory evidence and its
selective trickle-down disclosure." They had highlighted the enormous
significance of the Caruso material that:

> undercuts the very foundation of the State's case . . . and re-
> veals, from within the Prosecutor's office itself, a telling expo-
> sure of the machinations to which the prosecution resorted to
> advance its case, culminating in Caruso's resignation because
> of his conclusion that the reinvestigation was a farce and the
> prosecution was contrary to the evidence.

These were compelling, persuasive arguments. Thus it was hard to
believe that Professor Friedman, now on his feet, his voice reverberat-
ing, was about to announce the most agonizing decision Rubin had
had to make in his legal life. He was about to abandon the Caruso evidence, as invaluable as it was, because it was miring the appeal in
quicksand. Although the state's Appellate Division had denied them a
hearing into the matter, they still technically had a remedy left in the
State Supreme Court. There was no way Rubin was going to step back
onto the state treadmill and delay consideration of the other grounds
in federal court. And to complicate matters further, if Judge Sarokin
accepted their argument that technical exhaustion in the state was not
necessary, there was a danger that he would be overturned on appeal.
No, they had no choice but to cut Caruso loose.

Beldock had strongly recommended against it. As a good defence
lawyer, he had to advise against closing any doors, shutting off any av-
enues that might eventually be successful. And with Caruso, they were

not talking about run-of-the-mill cumulative evidence but evidence of innocence. Lew Steel was adamant: "We cannot afford to lose *any* opportunities!" But as Artis's attorney, Steel was arguing from a different position: with Artis free, out on the street, Lew *could* take the time necessary to technically exhaust Caruso; the stakes were not the same as they were for Rubin, for whom each day behind bars was a keenly felt day behind bars.

Rubin, well understanding the import of the Caruso material, was loath to give it up. But to hang on to it would be to act defensively. He compared his dilemma to his fifteen-round championship fight with Joey Giardello, in which he consciously held back so that he would have the stamina, the reserve strength, to go the full distance. He lasted all right, but he lost the decision. Why hold something back in anticipation of an extended fight when it was possible to go for the knock-out blow now?

Leon had agreed with Rubin. All along he had wanted a federal judge to be aware of the Caruso material, to have "the full flavour" of the corruption in the case. But, as the professor feared, the State was more than eager to get bogged down in procedural technicalities. It was necessary to resort to extraordinary measures.

They expected Judge Sarokin to have read the Caruso material in their exhaustion brief, because the State had requested a ruling on that issue first. So now Rubin could afford to let it go. Now Rubin knew the judge knew what he knew. Rubin figured that it was similar to the situation in trials where explosive evidence is presented to a jury and, for technical reasons, they are requested to "disregard" it—jurors never forget. Well, Rubin counted on Judge Sarokin to similarly "disregard" this evidence.

"Now," boomed Professor Friedman, "on the issue of exhaustion . . . we are amending our petition . . . to delete the one unexhausted claim, the Caruso file claim. We have twelve claims in our petition. The [prosecutor] says one of them is unexhausted, and for that reason he has a defence to the whole thing. We are deleting it."

"You do that formally?" asked the judge, aware of the significance of such a move.

"We are formally doing that." Friedman cited *Rose against Lundy,* wherein to ensure a "prisoner's principal interest . . . in obtaining speedy federal relief," he can delete an unexhausted claim from a "mixed petition."

"So as far as we're concerned—and I have to tell you this, Your Honour, that is on Rubin Carter's behalf, because Mr Artis is taking a different procedural stance on this—but as far as Rubin Carter is concerned . . . the exhaustion issue . . . is out of the case and we are now prepared to argue the merits."

With those few words from Professor Friedman, the Caruso material was lost to Rubin on any appeal, in the state or in federal court, now or ever.

Prosecutor Goceljak had to concede to the court that exhaustion was no longer an issue. He could no longer delay. He was prepared, he sighed, to argue the substance of the petition.

Professor Friedman was the first to speak. He began with a discussion of the State's racial revenge motive theory, which he said was presented at trial in violation of the defendants' Fourteenth Amendment right to equal protection under the law and to due process. As he explained to an attentive court:

"It was the State's theory in this case that the three killings in the Lafayette Bar were in revenge for a killing of a black man [Holloway] by a white man [Conforti] the night before. And they argued to the jury in very forceful terms that the reason the three people were killed in the Lafayette bar [was] not for robbery, but only because they were white. . . .

"Now, what is there in this case that would justify the prosecutor's effort to make this into a racial war murder? Was there any evidence that the [earlier] killing [was] because of race? Any evidence of that? None whatsoever. [The evidence showed, and the prosecution conceded it was a dispute over money between former business-partners.]

"Was there any evidence that the defendants knew the victim? Did they know Holloway? No evidence at all. The testimony was they didn't know the victim.

"Was there any evidence at all that Carter or Artis had hostility towards whites? No . . . and [the prosecutors] don't disagree. . . . So there was no showing of any hostility by these defendants toward whites.

"Why the Lafayette Bar? Was there any evidence that the Lafayette Bar [was racist]? There was third-hand hearsay evidence by
one of the policemen that this was in a racial border area . . . that the
bartender was anti-black, didn't serve blacks. There's other evidence . . .
that the bar did serve blacks. . . . But most important, there's absolutely no evidence that the defendants knew this bar was [allegedly]
anti-black. . . .

"So there's absolutely no link anywhere down the line to show
that these defendants had either anti-white attitudes, [or] that the
Lafayette Bar was an appropriate target as far as they were concerned,
[or] that they had any personal motive to get themselves involved in a
murder of any whites anywhere."

Nor, argued Professor Friedman, could it be termed simply a retaliation killing. Conforti, Holloway's murderer, was arrested instantly and put in jail. The alleged revenge was not sought against him
personally or against anyone connected to him. The only link between
this murder and the later one was that victim and murderer were of
different races.

"So what it comes down to . . . what the prosecutor was saying
was that, 'Ladies and gentlemen of the jury, these defendants killed
those victims because the defendants were black and the victims were
white.' That's what he said. And he said it in summation. He didn't
just drop it down as something you could forget about. He came back
to it again and again: 'We don't like to think about the fact there is
hate in the world.' Again and again. '*Hate.*' He used that word again
and again: 'People *hate* people because of their colour.'

"And he was telling that jury . . . and I just want to allude to the
fact that . . . anti-black statements were made by members of the jury.
And that one of the alternate jurors testified to that effect. So it is not
like these words fell on an unreceptive jury. . . . So on that kind of soil,
this kind of theory, and that kind of argument, and again and again
coming back to that—'This is a world where people do not judge by
character (but) by the colour of their skin. . . . It is a world filled with
people who *hate*.' And back again: 'None of us like to admit . . . race
prejudice and anger and hate for people because of the different colour
of their skin, exist in the world.'

"So it was . . . a main motif of the entire prosecution. And it was a motif that only concentrated on colour and race. And it was a motif that had absolutely no evidentiary basis for submitting to the jury."

Professor Friedman directed the judge's attention to a number of cases where habeas corpus was granted simply on the grounds of a prosecutor's tangential remark that appealed to racial prejudice and stereotypes. But here, in the Carter case, where racism was woven throughout the fabric of the State's case, the violation, he said, was far more egregious.

Professor Friedman then went on to a lengthy explanation of the Bello lie-detector *Brady* point: how the prosecutors' manipulation of Bello with false lie-detector results demolished the basis of his "identification" of the defendants, testimony that was crucial to the state's case. Next the professor touched on a few of the other grounds in the petition. He spoke for close to an hour and a half. His presentation had everyone in the courtroom mesmerized. He was eloquent and forceful, and, considering the scope of the issues, concise. Having lectured for years at Hofstra University, he was an old hand at simplifying complex legal questions to make them instantly understandable.

Next, Beldock, who had not intended to speak on this occasion, got up and made a couple of points that had been raised by questions from Judge Sarokin.

Then Lew Steel took the floor. He, too, was dynamite. Turning to the question of race, he stated:

"The [prosecutor] told the judge in arguing for the inclusion of the racial revenge theory that he didn't think he stood much of a possibility of winning without the theory. Well, why did he say that? In the first trial he had two eyewitnesses, he had Bello and Bradley. Now [for the second trial] he's got one. And he's in a position that if he doesn't come up with something to make up that loss, he's going to be in big trouble." So ten years after the events, argued Steel, they come up with this racial hatred business.

Steel explained that the prosecution accused the defendants of being motivated by racism, when the evidence showed it was the other way around. For example, "DeSimone says on the [October 1966] tape, to Bello: 'Well, Bello—' and he's trying to get Bello now to be his key witness—'Well, Bello, you know, these black people, they always hang together, they do all these bad things together, because they're black and different from us,' and so on and so forth.

"It seems to me," continued Steel, "that under any set of circumstances the defence was entitled to attack DeSimone . . . and argue to the jury that DeSimone was not the impartial investigator that he claimed to be, but came at this case from a racial animus, from a prejudicial understanding, and took all the evidence that he found as an investigator, and laid it from a prejudicial premise. And it seems to me if we wanted to make that attack we were entitled to do that. [But] for the prosecution to say that all black people will kill because they're black, they'll all kill whites—"

"Well, wait a minute," interrupted Judge Sarokin. "He didn't really say that. That might be inferred, but he didn't actually say that on summation."

"Oh, he did. When he starts talking about, 'Look at what Greeks and Turks and people do in Northern Ireland,'* he did say that, Judge."

"By inference."

"He talked about group guilt. And I can't think of anything in American law that we have held in disfavour more than that very concept. I go back thinking about . . . are all Germans guilty [of the Holocaust] or is there individual guilt in this world? And in America I don't think any, any sense of our community is held more dear than the sense that we're all entitled to be judged as individuals."

The prosecutor's arguments, Steel said, represented "a total breakdown of what we have been struggling and trying to build in this country for centuries, and certainly since 1954 in the *Brown v. Board of Education* decision. . . .

"Both Mr Beldock and I told the judge [Leopizzi], 'When this race issue comes in, what are we to do? Can't win. Because it overwhelms the process. And it leaves jurors with a whole different perspective of what it is they're supposed to decide. It pollutes the process, it destroys

---

*In summation to the jury, Prosecutor Humphreys compared racial animosity in America to religious violence in Ireland and to the historical hatred between Greeks and Turks. Was it mere chance that, out of all places on earth and all irrelevant examples of ethnic strife, the only "illustrations" which surfaced in the prosecutor's remarks coincided with the backgrounds of two of the jurors, one a Greek immigrant, the other an Irish-Catholic immigrant?

the process.' And I suggest to Your Honour that that's precisely what occurred here."

After a short recess, Assistant Prosecutor Goceljak rose to speak. He tried his best to downplay the racial aspect of the State's motive theory: "Our contention is that this is not so much a racial revenge theory as it is—I'd like to denominate it a revenge theory that has racial overtones as far as these two defendants were concerned. . . . These two individuals took it upon themselves to do their own thing. That's been our position."

But Judge Sarokin was not satisfied. He kept pressing Goceljak as to what motive evidence they had that was attributable to the defendants as *individuals*. And Goceljak, squirming uncomfortably, had to admit that there was nothing that "either Mr Carter or Mr Artis said that would support this motive."

Goceljak was happy to turn to the *Brady* issue, but his arguments were lacklustre. For the most part, he was content to urge the judge to read the state court opinions and to follow the way they ruled on all the issues.

Because of vacations, the prosecution was given until the end of the summer, August 30, a week longer than they had requested, to file their brief and the necessary transcripts. Petitioners were given to September 9 to file a Reply Brief. They would have to wait until sometime in the fall for the judge's decision.

The judge had barely adjourned the session and had not yet risen to leave when Ed Carter shattered the silence with his deep sonorous voice, "Have a nice vacation, Judge!" The remark was incongruous with the solemnity and decorum of the courtroom, but it was absolutely appropriate. Rubin's cousin then leaned forward to Terry and Sam, and whispered, "Damn! Hope nothin' happens to *him* over the summer!"

By the time the lawyers had packed up and walked to the elevators, Sam and Terry already had Rubin on the phone and had been briefing him for several minutes. As the lawyers approached, Sam held out the receiver. "Here. Your client would like a word with you." Rubin wanted to thank them. The attorneys chuckled at the efficiency of the communications network.

Rubin felt fortunate to have so many people who could give him their perspective on the day's events.

Leon was the first to speak: "Rubin, it went *very* well. The judge was really struggling with how this could have happened. How could the jury have reached this verdict and how could the state courts have upheld it on appeal? He was very sympathetic regarding our racial revenge arguments. If he decided today, Rubin, I'd say 'You're out!'"

Next it was Myron's turn: "If there's a bust out of everyone in Rahway tomorrow, Rube, don't leave! You'll be leaving legally. All of our strategy so far has paid off. I have a good feeling about it."

Ed Graves got on the phone: "I just think it couldn't've gone better, Rube. The judge didn't have any vibe of arrogance, obnoxiousness, or anything like that. The man really seems to have his ears open. I got a really good feeling from today. I feel like celebrating, but it's too early to celebrate."

Ed handed the phone to Lush Brown who was glad to talk to his old friend: "I enjoyed them defence lawyers, Rubin. They somethin' else. They was hoppin'! You got somethin' there. The one—Friedman—oh he bad, harpin' on prejudice, harpin' on the prejudice stuff for a long time. The prosecutor—he was stutterin'. All of us thought it looked very good."

Rubin's cousin Ed Carter took the phone to offer his own encouragement: "I was really amazed by Professor Friedman—a heck of an articulator. I was equally amazed that the judge is an intellectual; he posed several hypotheses; he was thinking ahead. I was really impressed. Your lawyers made it clear that the whole racial thing was painted in such a way as to cause the jury not to objectively evaluate the evidence.

"Something really interesting: Lewis Steel talked about class kind of guilt, as for example with Hitler and the Jews in Germany. He said, 'We can't have that situation in America. Today it's these defendants, tomorrow it'll be all those with blond hair,'—a classic argument . . . I found the judge fascinating as a human being. I felt, '*Well, now, go ahead, Judge!*'"

Under the heading of "Orals Federal Court," Rubin wrote on his pad the following simple word: "Wow!" The State now had thirty-five days to respond.

25

While waiting for some action from the court, Rubin took on a new
project. He started training a fellow prisoner, Art (Jeremiah) Tucker, a
light-heavyweight who was hoping to become a professional prizefighter. Because Rubin himself had had his first pro fight the day after
leaving the penitentiary in 1961, he was aware of how disadvantaged
prison fighters are. Although Rubin had won that fight, he had been
overwhelmed by the enormous expenditure of energy required to go
just four rounds. Contrary to popular belief, fighters coming out of
prison may be tough, but they are rarely strong. They have not had access to the trainers, to the proper facilities and, most important, to the
high-protein diet necessary to make a serious fighter. But prisoners
themselves do not realize how handicapped they are. (Similarly,
Lesra's brother Leland had been certain that he was much tougher
than Lesra when he visited Lesra in Canada. Figuring that Lesra had
got soft, Leland challenged him to a race, and was stunned when he
found that Lesra could beat him. Lesra, while no longer hardened by
Brooklyn streets, was now well rested, well nourished and strong, and
his energy was focused.)

When Rubin started to put Tucker through some paces in the

gym, Tucker quickly ran out of steam. Regardless, Rubin would then send him out to the yard to run laps.

"Mr Carter, you kiddin', right? Jumpin' rope, workin' the heavy bag, the speed bag, shadow boxin'—that's enough for one day, man. I'm tired!"

"Good! But not tired enough. If you got the energy to protest, you don't know the meaning of the word," said Rubin. And he kept pushing. He was trying to protect Tucker, not wanting to see him get hurt on account of not being prepared.

After this had gone on for a few weeks, Rubin thought what Tucker needed was some decent sparring, but there was no one in the prison who could provide it. Rubin was not about to put gloves on himself. Instead, he picked up the telephone and called down to Philadelphia, a city legendary for having the toughest fighters around. He was calling on his old friend, "Smokin'" Joe Frazier, who had his own gym and his own stable of fighters. Joe loved to hear from the Hurricane. Sure, he'd be happy to bring his "demolition squad" up to Rahway, if Rubin could arrange it.

"My boys need a good workout, and maybe while I'm up there," laughed Joe, "I might just whup your puny middleweight butt."

"Yeah? Just bring your slow-movin' heavyweight self up here and *I'll* send you to your Jesus!" retorted Rubin. Joe and Rubin (like Rubin and Muhammad Ali) took great pleasure in "selling wooftickets"—playfully threatening each other with grievous bodily harm.

Joe arrived at the prison sporting hot-pink boxing boots. With him was a carload of fighters, including his son Marvis and "Smokin'" Bert Cooper. They caused quite a stir in and out of the ring, and made all the prizefighting hopefuls behind the wall re-evaluate their high opinions of themselves. No one was able to go more than a couple of rounds with any of Joe's fighters, although Rubin and Joe's verbal sparring lasted the whole evening.

A guard at Rahway's mailroom one day was searching through a food package, while the visitor who delivered it was waiting for it to be okayed. The guard lifted the lid off one of the plastic containers and pulled out something round and dark-coloured, about the size of a Spanish onion, and which, like an onion, had a papery skin.

"What's this?" he asked.

"A vegetable."

"I never seen nuttin' like dat. What kind of vegetable?"

"It's a Jamaican root vegetable."

"Oh yeah?

"Yeah. It's called an *obeah*."

"What're ya supposed to do wid it?"

"You boil it."

"Oh yeah? Don't look too appetizin'," he said, placing it back into the container. "But *I* don't have to eat it, so that's okay by me."

It really wasn't okay, and it really wasn't an *obeah,* which is the Jamaican word for "voodoo." Arbitrary prison rules had forced the Canadians to live outside the law (or were they being led astray by the criminal element with whom they had been fraternizing?). Because Rubin had got such a kick out of growing his onion, the Canadians had decided to throw caution to the wind and smuggle. When Rubin's food package was delivered to his wing that afternoon, they knew they had pulled off the perfect crime. It was a heady victory. Flowers were contraband, and they had just sneaked in an amaryllis bulb.

But what happens when you break the law? It's often said that one crime leads to another. One smuggle had led to a lie, and it would lead to more smuggling. They were to progress to daffodils next. And it wouldn't end there.

Rubin, after surreptitiously scooping dirt, or rather soil, and collecting pebbles from the prison yard, planted the bulbs in the plastic pots that had come in as food containers. He kept some of the plants for himself and gave the rest away to a couple of the hardest men in the prison. One went to Watasi Leroi Gadsen, who was about five feet, five inches tall and five feet, five inches wide, without an inch of fat on a muscle-bound, square block of a body. Despite his lack of height, he was considered by most other inmates a rather imposing kind of person. He was taken seriously by all who knew him, including Rubin. Watasi couldn't have been prouder as he lovingly tended his plant. Prisoners walking by his cell were awed by the exotic spectacle.

"Where d'you cop the flowers, man? They sure is beautiful!"

"Watasi, how d'you get them flowers in here, man?"

Watasi, no big talker at the best of times, would harumph, turn his back and smile a big smile to himself.

Rubin gave another plant to a white Vietnam vet, who was considered extremely violent and having real trouble keeping himself together. The plant had a calming effect on him as it sprouted and grew. He told Rubin he loved it: he hadn't killed it; instead he helped it to live.

As for Rubin's amaryllis, it shot up tall, green stems that exploded into five huge blossoms, each close to eight inches across—vibrant red trumpets that blasted out their cheery presence to all who passed by on the tier. Guards' ever-watchful eyes seemed to glide right past the thing. There was one guard, however, who happened to mention to Rubin that he had seen a plant with gorgeous red flowers somewhere and wanted to get one for his wife and was wondering if Rubin knew what such a plant might be called.

Over the years Rubin had met a number of decent guards in the penitentiary. Among the names at the top of Rubin's list was a tough white guard named Bobby Martin. He and Rubin were a mutual admiration society. They had come to know each other when Rubin was first at Rahway. When Rubin returned in 1984, Lieutenant Martin was one of the first of the high-ranking officers who came to see him. Without having to be asked, Lieutenant Martin did his best to see that Rubin was able to have as much phone time as possible so that he could continue to work on his case. Martin also made it his business to see that Rubin wasn't hassled.

For example, there was the trouble with Rubin's stereo system. On three separate occasions, the guards in the mailroom rejected it and sent it back, even though it met all the requirements (was new, was in its original packaging, had come from the source of sale and was paid for). The Canadians were at their wits' end dealing with an incompetent bureaucracy, and Rubin was angry. When Lieutenant Martin overheard rumours of Rubin's frustration, he walked out to the mailroom and told the sergeant in charge, "Give Rubin his fucking property!" He told him to stop giving trouble to people who didn't deserve it. He said to the sergeant, "You make a mistake when you judge everyone by their jacket [rap sheet]. If Rubin Carter wanted to have the fucking Philharmonic come to play in the joint, the Philharmonic would be in here playing. All he wants is a stereo. So quit fucking around!" Rubin was enjoying tape-recorded music that evening.

Bobby Martin was soon promoted to captain and transferred to Bordentown. Just before Captain Martin left Rahway, Rubin asked him to look out for the Canadian kid, Bruce Curtis. Rubin had read in the papers that Bruce had been spending his time at Bordentown teaching illiterate black prisoners how to read. "Just keep an eye on him, Bobby, okay?" Nothing more needed to be said.

The month of August 1985 was a busy month for the law firm of Carter and Partners (C & P) with preparations for the arrival of the prosecution's brief. They knew there would be very little time to write a reply. Professor Friedman had told Judge Sarokin that they could reply very quickly to any brief the prosecution submitted, and the judge had allotted ten days. Rubin was determined to not have to ask for an extension, if their request for speedy relief was to be taken seriously.

So C & P went to work. Figuring the prosecution was going to rely on all its old tired arguments, they pulled out the prosecution's main state court brief, full of half-truths, misstatements, omissions, etcetera, and they started writing their rebuttals in advance. By the time the prosecution filed its "Respondents' Brief in Opposition to Petitioners' Motion for Summary Judgment and Habeas Corpus Relief," which was 157 pages long, C & P had drafted the major factual portions of their reply, and Leon Friedman was able to concentrate solely on the legal issues. Not one of the prosecution's contentions would they leave standing. It required more all-night sessions in New York with the attorneys, and with Amanda on the computer, working at fever pitch, to put it all together. The final product was a hundred pages long (plus fifty pages of appendix exhibits); it was filed on time and it was perfect.

Myron took the unusual step of adding a footnote to the list of names of counsel on the brief. The note read: "Counsel acknowledge the substantial assistance of petitioner Carter in the preparation of the factual discussions in the brief." Beldock had wanted to include the

Canadians as well, but they declined. Crediting Rubin was crediting the whole team.

With the legal work over, it was time to wait again. Rubin and everyone else who had been involved in "The Big Push" were convinced the end was near and Rubin would be freed. Lesra was so certain of the outcome that he became concerned Rubin wouldn't have anything to wear when he got out. Lesra, Marty and Sam went shopping. Since it was fall, Lesra declared that Rubin would need a warm coat. He found the ideal one: a well-tailored sheepskin jacket. They also picked an olive-green sweater, a button-down cotton shirt, pleated wool slacks and brown leather boots. Because ties and sports jackets were not allowed into the prison, they opted for the casual, elegant look. With Lesra now five feet, eight inches tall, exactly the same height as Rubin, it was easy to see how Rubin would look in the clothes that Lesra modelled.

The clothes passed muster at the Rahway mailroom, all except the leather boots. The guard pulled out his trusty ruler and measured from the bottom of the heel to the top of the boot at the ankle. "No way. Can't let them in. Quarter of an inch too high," he pronounced, as he shoved the boots back across the counter.

Now that the Canadians had embarked on a career of smuggling, they were not to be daunted. On Sam's next contact visit with Rubin, Sam wore a fine pair of brown leather boots. As they sat in the visiting hall, Rubin casually removed his old shoes and just as casually Sam took off his new ones. Rubin had always maintained that, in the joint, if you looked like you were supposed to be doing whatever it was you were doing, nobody would pay any attention. "It's all in the attitude." So, after cooling their feet for a moment, they put their shoes back on. Rubin left the visit sporting a pair of fine, new brown boots; Sam left walking in well-worn black ones.

As the weeks dragged on, Rubin started clearing out his cell, giving his things to other prisoners, sorting through his old papers, throwing out useless stuff and sending what he wanted to keep to the Canadians, to be picked up from the mailroom after visits. It was unusual for a prisoner to give his belongings away. It was regarded as a warning signal for one of three things: the prisoner was "going over" (losing his grip), was about to "commit sideways" or was about to escape. In Rubin's case it meant something else. As Rubin put it, "There's an ancient philosophical principle that you must act like you already have that which you require, and it will be yours. So in acting like I'm free, I will be free."

By the beginning of November, no decision had come from the court. Rubin was tense, waiting, but the atmosphere in the prison was even more tense. There was a drug bust in 2-Middle, Rubin's current address. He had seen it coming while he was on the telephone. He even knew who the stoolie was. He alerted the others of the impending danger, but to no avail. Lieutenant Magee, the best drug watchdog in the joint, swooped down and found what he was looking for. To protect his source, Magee even made a show of finding contraband in the stoolie's cell—cash, marijuana and rolling papers.

Problem was, the administration left the stoolie and the man he had ratted on still locked on the same tier, and both of them had "shanks" (homemade knives). Anything could happen, anybody could get cut, get hurt, could die. Rubin hated stoolies and wasn't interested in protecting them, but the situation was threatening to get completely out of hand. Blood was sure to be spilled. Rubin spoke to an officer: "Put one of them in lock-up and save both their lives. Because of your stupidity, you're jeopardizing everyone's safety."

Hours went by before the administration moved one of the men to lock-up, and it wasn't the stoolie. But the tension didn't end there.

Later that night, Rubin and his friend Tayu were taking boxes of Rubin's papers to the garbage at the end of the tier, near the dormitory. They were tearing up and dumping papers into the bin as a squad of guards came up the stairs and entered the wing. The corrections officers had come to terrorize and shake everybody down, which was par for the course after a drug bust.

A lieutenant leading the pack barked at Rubin, "Hey, you! Tryin' to get rid of the dope? We'll find it! That's what we're here for."

"Who're you talkin' to?" asked Rubin, looking up disgustedly.

"You! I'm talkin' to you. What's your name? Who are you?"

"I know who *you* are," said Rubin, tearing his papers into tinier little bits.

"There's ways of taking care of punks like you."

"Mister," warned Rubin, looking up again. "Make sure your mouth don't write no cheque your ass can't cash."

"Not me! I don't mean just me! I got men in here ready and willin' to take care of you, punk!"

"You better bring enough, cause a lot won't be goin' back!" Rubin then spun on his heel and, without once looking back, strode the length of the tier to his cell. Tayu couldn't believe it. You don't talk like that to an officer and walk away. But Tayu, caught up in the courage, spun on his heel too and followed Rubin down the tier.

Another officer, standing on the stairs behind the lieutenant, was absolutely livid. He asked the lieutenant, "Do you know who that was?"

"Yeah, some jump-off punk."

"You better know who you're talkin' to in here before you start runnin' off at the mouth!" Turning to the men behind him, he said, "Come on! Let's get outta here. It's over."

The lieutenant, however, was not about to give up. He walked up to the wing officer who had been watching the episode from his desk and asked, "What's that jump-off's name? What's his cell number?"

"You want his name?"

"Yeah."

"That's Rubin 'Hurricane' Carter."

"That wasn't Carter. I know Carter. Carter's in Trenton."

"He's here now. And that was him."

Tayu watched from the drinking fountain, where he'd stopped to observe the action, as the lieutenant hurriedly went to Rubin's cell and knocked on his door. (The cells in that wing have solid doors.)

"Come in."

Rubin was sitting on his bed surrounded by papers, which he was continuing to sort. He appeared calm, but his adrenalin was pumping. Who knew what this guard might try?

"I didn't know who you were, Rubin."

"But, as I said, I knew who you were." Rubin exhaled imperceptibly. The officer had come to apologize.

Just then Lieutenant Magee knocked on Rubin's door. He had heard there was trouble in the wing; he didn't want to see anyone get hurt.

"Come on," said Magee to the other officer. "Everybody knows Rubin don't play with that shit."

"Lieutenant Magee, tell this man," stated Rubin quietly, "there's nothing in here that the prison wants. This is where a free man lives."

Judge Sarokin's clerk called the New York lawyers on Wednesday November 6. They were told the judge's opinion was to be delivered in his chambers at ten the following morning. The hour was finally near.

On Wednesday evening, Terry went for a contact visit with Rubin, in order to be able to pick up his last box of stuff. All of Rubin's possessions, except for a pair of pajamas and his going-away clothes had, by this point, been distributed.

"Rube," said Terry, as he was leaving the visit, "you got your hair cut. Did Carlos do it?"

"No, Typh. I didn't get it cut."

"But your hair looks shorter than when I last saw you."

"It is . . . it's been falling out . . . in clumps."

"From the tension?"

"This is my last shot, Typh. If we don't make it outta here now, we're never gonna make it. Ever."

26

It was Thursday November 7, 1985. The hallways at the federal courthouse were quiet. Kathy and Terry were by the phones. It was almost eleven o'clock now, and they had been waiting since nine-thirty. Ed Graves and Lew Steel had just gone into Judge Sarokin's chambers. There had been an unexpected delay: the opinions were late coming back from the printers. These last hours had been the longest. But when Kathy and Terry saw Ed Graves coming around the corner holding Judge Sarokin's decision above his head in both hands, the waiting meant nothing. Ed Graves was jubilant.

"We did it! We won! We won!"

Those words flew from Ed's mouth to Terry's mouth and into the receiver to Rubin's ears. He drank them in, in holy silence. It was miraculous, and he was speechless.

Now everyone was crying. From the halls of the Newark courthouse, to the prison, to the apartment in Rahway, to the legal offices in New York, to Lesra and the group back in Toronto. It had been a Herculean struggle and they had won.

Through the haze of euphoria came Rubin's voice: "Terry, Terry, what's it say? What's it say?"

"I don't know, Rube, it's seventy pages. I just got it. I don't know if I can even read right now. Here. Check this out, Rube," shouted Terry, now reading:

" 'The extensive record clearly demonstrates that petitioners' convictions were predicated upon an appeal to racism rather than reason, and concealment rather than disclosure.

" 'The jury was permitted to draw inferences of guilt based solely upon the race of the [defendants], but yet was denied information which may have supported their claims of innocence. To permit convictions to stand which have as their foundation appeals to racial prejudice and the withholding of evidence critical to the defense, is to commit a violation of the Constitution as heinous as the crimes for which these [defendants] were tried and convicted.' "

"He wrote *that?* You sure that's what it says, Typh? The judge wrote that?"

Without waiting for an answer, Rubin turned around and yelled to the air, "Great googamooga! I'm free!"

While Terry tried to read Rubin portions of the opinion as best he could, neither of them could concentrate, what with the jumping up and down at the excitement and the relief and the fabulous language of the decision and the interruptions by the shouting in the prison background, as the news almost instantly hit the radio waves and everybody in the prison went crazy.

"Listen to this, Rube: 'The evidence did not support the imputation of the racial revenge motive to Carter and Artis. There was no proof that Carter and Artis were black militants with an inclination to kill whites; nor that they had even the slightest hostility toward whites. . . . In fact, the only blatantly racial statement placed before the trial court was Bello's testimony that while he was being interviewed by a prosecutor's detective in October 1966, that detective referred to blacks as "niggers" and "animals." '

"And this: 'Even at its strongest links, the government's chain of evidence has been substantially called into question by petitioners.' And, Rube, the judge isn't even ruling on Caruso and he didn't get to see any of the evidence we found in our own investigation!"

"Typh, it's unbelievable!"

The judge had granted the writ on two issues: the racial revenge motive and the *Brady* ground involving the prosecution's tailoring of Bello's testimony with the false lie-detector test conclusion. It had been unnecessary to rule on the other grounds.

"Rube, Judge Sarokin, on the Bello *Brady* issue, agrees with the three dissenting State Supreme Court justices. He repeats a lot of quotes from that blistering opinion of Justice Clifford's: 'Bello was in all respects a complete unvarnished liar, utterly incapable of speaking the —' "

"Jump to the end, Terry. Get to the conclusion!"

Somehow in the excitement Terry managed to hold the receiver in one hand and flip through the decision with the other.

"Here, here it is: 'The court does not arrive at its conclusion lightly, recognizing that it is in conflict with a decision of the highly learned and respected New Jersey Supreme Court (albeit a 4-3 decision). However, this court is convinced that a conviction which rests upon racial stereotypes, fears and prejudices, violates rights too fundamental to permit deference to stand in the way of the relief sought.

" 'It would be naive not to recognize that some prejudice, bias and fear lurks in all of us. But to permit a conviction to be urged based upon such factors or to permit a conviction to stand having utilized such factors diminishes our fundamental constitutional rights.

" 'Furthermore, the prosecution has resources unavailable to the average criminal defendant. Therefore, it is imperative that information which is essential to the defense in the hands of the prosecution be made available to the accused. If trials are indeed searches for the truth rather than efforts to conceal it, full and fair disclosure is necessary to protect and preserve the rights of the accused against the awesome power of the accusor.

" 'Although extended appeals in criminal matters have been widely criticized, the need for review is amply demonstrated by this matter. There is a substantial danger that our society, concerned about the growth of crime, will retreat from the safeguards and rights accorded to the accused by the Constitution. The need to combat crime should never be utilized to justify an erosion of our fundamental guarantees. Indeed, the growing volume of criminal cases should make us even more vigilant; the greater the *quantity*—the greater the risk to the *quality* of justice.' "

"I hear you! So why am I still here? How do I get out of here? Which of the lawyers are there? Who's there?"

"Lew's here with Myron's partner, Larry Levine. Leon's chairing that international judicial conference and Myron had an emergency court appearance."

"Lemme speak to Lew."

"I don't know where he is, Rube. He and Larry are off somewhere reading the opinion. They want to be prepared to answer questions from the press. Here's Ed Graves."

"Rubin, we made it, Rube!"

"Ed, how can I ever thank you, brother. You're beautiful."

"I want to thank you too, Rube. I can't tell you how much it's meant to me to be part of this. It's the most worthwhile thing I've ever done. Rube, you're outta there!"

"That's it, Ed! How do I get outta here? What's the next step? What do we do now?"

"It's clear from what Judge Sarokin said in the section called 'Appropriate Relief' that what he would like to do is release you immediately with instructions to the State never to retry you again. But because of that state-federal 'comity' crap, he's obliged to let the state itself decide whether they want to retry the case or not. Nevertheless he said that a third trial would not 'serve the interests of justice.' Listen to his words, Rube: 'the court will grant the writ . . . , mindful that the state can seek a retrial, but hopeful that constitutional considerations, as well as justice and compassion, will prevail.' Rubin, I think we should make a motion to the court to get you released right now. Man, you're officially innocent! Let the prosecution argue why you should have to stay in prison now that the conviction has been thrown out. Who knows, maybe they'll just let it go."

There was a momentary silence on the phone. "Don't kid yourself, brother. If it's up to them, they won't quit. But you're right. We should make a motion immediately, while they're still off-balance. Push it. Push it, Ed. Now."

Ed contacted the other lawyers and was back on the phone with Rubin minutes later. "Everybody's ecstatic, Rube! But, Rubin, they felt that as a matter of professional courtesy, they have to allow the other side a few days to review the decision before proceeding. That means till Tuesday, cause Monday's a holiday."

"Courtesy? Courtesy? Did you say *courtesy*? Was what they did to me courteous? I got no reason to be courteous, Ed. You tell those bastard prosecutors that they've got until this afternoon to read the goddam thing and be in court."

"Rubin, I'll try. But the only way we can get a fast hearing is if they agree."

Terry took the receiver from Ed. "Look, Rube, no fucking way are you gonna get stuck in there over another weekend. Not after *that* decision!"

"Take care of business, Typh. I got to go. There's a goddamn count."

Ed Graves, with Kathy and Terry at his side, called the prosecutor's office and informed Goceljak that at two that afternoon they intended to make a motion to have Rubin released immediately.

"We haven't even read the judge's decision yet. We need a little time."

Ed pushed ahead. "All right, we'll schedule it for two o'clock tomorrow afternoon. That gives you an extra twenty-four hours."

Goceljak agreed.

Terry and Kathy, having expected the prosecutor to try to delay as long as possible, were elated that Ed had got him to agree to such a speedy hearing. The momentum had been irresistible. He had just been steamrolled.

By eleven-thirty, virtually every radio station in the United States was carrying the news that Rubin "Hurricane" Carter's conviction had been overturned, and bulletins had begun to interrupt regular television programming. By twelve, it was the lead item on the news around the country. Normally impassive television news reporters smiled and seemed to enjoy reporting this story, which they peppered with colourful quotations from Judge Sarokin's decision.

It had struck like a thunderbolt; Rubin had kept such a low profile that no one had any idea that the case had been about to explode. Soon the airwaves were full of Dylan's song, "Hurricane"; images of the Hurricane storming into the ring; Muhammad Ali leading marches; phrases like "former number-one middleweight contender"; "Carter's autobiography, *The Sixteenth Round,* focused attention . . ."; ". . . became a civil rights *cause célèbre* . . ."; "A federal judge citing 'grave constitutional violations'"; ". . . based on 'racism rather than reason, and concealment rather than disclosure'"; "Carter KO's State!"

The reversal was big news, nationally and internationally. The story was to be told at the top of the front page of the next day's *New York Times,* and Rubin's picture was to be on the front page of Canada's *Globe and Mail.*

After count cleared, Rubin was told by the wing officer that the Chief Deputy Keeper wanted to see him in his office. As Rubin started down the stairs, guards and prisoners alike shouted out their congratulations. It was lunch-time, and several wings' worth of prisoners were crossing the main traffic area on their way to the mess hall just as Rubin, too, was crossing the centre. When someone spotted Rubin, all normal movement ceased. He was mobbed. Hundreds of men surged forward trying to get close to him, to touch him, to hug him, to shake his hand, anything. There was a riot of joyous emotion. With great difficulty, one guard pushed through the crowd and reached Rubin.

"You can't stay here," he said. "And you can't get through. Maybe you better go back to the wing."

Before leaving the centre, Rubin did his best to acknowledge everyone and shake as many hands as he could. He was amazed at such an outpouring. He had not expected all these people to feel so strongly and to express their feelings so freely.

Slowly he made his way back to his cell, where dozens of request slips for media interviews had started to pile up. The networks—ABC, NBC, CBS—the New York TV and radio stations, the print media, everybody wanted interviews. Rubin put the requests aside. He and the Canadians had decided that he would not speak publicly until it was all over. He did not want to give the State any spark around which to blaze, any magnet they might use to polarize people the way they had done in 1976, for the more Rubin had appeared in the media in the mid-seventies, the more desperate the prosecution had become, and the more rigid their determination to reconvict him and never let him go.

Rubin's tier was soon flooded with visitors from all over the prison, and those who could not come, sent emissaries with messages. By mid-afternoon, the prison was besieged by reporters. The Canadians, from their Rahway apartment balcony, could see helicopters hovering over the penitentiary, getting aerial shots for the network evening news. They spoke to Rubin briefly over the phone to discuss their plans for the following day. Then Rubin had to go; he'd received a notice that his cousin Ed was waiting downstairs for a window visit.

Moments later, the Canadians were watching the news and heard the New York anchor say they were going live to Rahway State Prison, where reporter Gloria Rojas had more on the sensational "Hurricane" Carter story. They saw Ms Rojas excitedly speaking into a microphone.

"We're trying to get an interview . . ." She was handed a telephone. "One moment . . . I have him here on the line! He's here on the phone! It's Rick Rowe, a representative of the Lifers' Group. Mr Rowe, you have actually spoken to Mr Carter since the court's decision was handed down?"

"Miss Rojas, I can hardly hear you, the noise in here. I haven't been able to get near the man. He's being mobbed."

"Can you describe what is going on in there?"

"I've never seen anything like it. The whole prison is celebrating. I've been here over twelve years. I've never seen anything like it. The togetherness. It's incredible. Everyone is so thrilled. Black, white, Hispanic. Hugging and crying. Even the guards. Rubin is an exceptional man. He never gave up. He was always working to get out of here. He *never* gave up. And somebody finally heard him. He's given us all hope!"

27

Friday, November 8, 1985. As the motorcade of federal marshals escorting Rubin from Rahway State Prison pulled up to the Federal District Courthouse in Newark, Rubin, looking through sunglasses, saw a building surrounded by literally hundreds of newspaper reporters and television crews with cameras. There were helicopters circling overhead, curiosity-seeking spectators lining the streets, scrambling for a view, jostling one another, while a score of uniformed policemen attempted to instil a measure of order into the escalating chaos.

What everyone saw was a man in a sheepskin coat getting out of one of the three cars, with a formidable crew of a dozen armed marshals gathered around him to form an impregnable shield. With the front entrance to the building virtually inaccessible, the marshals had to take Rubin in through the back. And even there, reporters flanking the doorway with their cameras were lined up three deep on the sidewalks and four abreast at the backdoor stairs. Forcibly but politely, Rubin's escorts elbowed a wide swath through the inquisitive crowd; questions were shouted from every angle.

Rubin found it strange. It wasn't the fact that he was surrounded by a plethora of armed guards. He had been smothered in armed guards for the past twenty years. Nor was it the fact that his ability to move quickly or to keep up with his escorts was not hampered by the handcuffs pinching his wrist, or the restraining belt fastened tightly around his waist, or the chains running from the handcuffs to the restraining belt to the shackles locked firmly around his legs. He had grown accustomed to this kind of mistreatment and was able to move with surprising speed and grace. Indeed, he moved so naturally, it was hard for anyone to notice the hardware.

No, what struck him was the fact that nobody seemed to know who he was. All these people were there to interview, if they could, Rubin "Hurricane" Carter—the prizefighter, the bald and bearded former contender for the middleweight crown, the short, stocky, mean-looking guy whose picture that very morning was plastered over the front pages of newspapers and on television sets across the country. Only old file photos had been available to the media, and that person was not there.

"Where is he?" someone asked a federal marshal. "Isn't he coming to court?"

"Who's the guy in the sheepskin coat?" one reporter asked another.

"Is that 'Hurricane' Carter?" Someone finally asked the obvious.

"Is that really him?" someone else shouted rhetorically. "How do you feel today, Mr Carter?"

Good question, Rubin thought, his own mind full of questions. *What if the judge orders me released immediately? I've been locked into a fight that has lasted twenty years—what do I do now if the fight is over?*

Rubin had no time to articulate these thoughts.

When they reached the third floor, the marshals removed Rubin's restraints and walked him through a doorway. Suddenly he found himself standing at the front of a large room packed with people. They had just entered Judge Sarokin's courtroom, and the air was electric. Bodies were pressed everywhere—against the walls, in every seat, overflowing into the aisles and out into the halls, filling every cubic inch of sitting, or standing space. There was so much commotion in the room that few noticed Rubin as he was escorted to his lawyers' table by a marshal in civilian clothes. Myron Beldock grabbed Rubin and hugged him unreservedly. The other attorneys reached forward to shake his hand—present were Lew Steel, Ed Graves, New Jersey counsel Ron Busch, Jeff Fogel, Lou Raveson, Harold Cassidy. Rubin was sorry that Leon Friedman, who could not get away from the conference he was chairing, was not there to share this day.

As Rubin was about to take his seat, he glanced back over the crowd. He saw Terry and Kathy rise from their seats near the back and nod unobtrusively toward him. It was a signal that their plans were set. Rubin also saw Ed Carter and Ed's twenty-eight-year-old daughter, Charmaine, who was vibrating with energy. He noticed Mims Hackett sitting with a young friend. And he was happy to see Amanda George from Beldock's office there. His eyes lighted on John Artis and Dolly, John's wife, standing at the back. John, who he had not seen in years, looked positively radiant. Rubin smiled at *New York Times* reporters Selwyn Raab and Dave Anderson, who were sitting close behind him.

"All rise!"

As Judge H. Lee Sarokin took his place on the bench, Rubin found himself looking directly into his eyes. Rubin thought: *The judge is wondering, 'What are you like? How have these twenty years affected you?'*

The judge asked, "What is the application that anyone wishes to make?"

Beldock rose. "I wish to apply that Your Honour release Mr Carter . . . and that you do so unconditionally under Rule 23(c). Your Honour knows . . . there is a presumptive entitlement for release pending appeal if the writ is granted. We are in that posture . . . I trust Your Honour will not require there be any bail in the sense of security posted."

"Why don't I hear from the prosecution as to what, if anything, they suggest that I do, and then we will decide what we are going to do."

John Goceljak, first assistant prosecutor of Passaic County, rose wearily to his feet. Perspiration gleamed from a forehead that extended back and down almost to the nape of his neck. He looked like a well-fed dormouse that had been rudely awakened from a long and pleasant sleep. It was plain to see that he was agitated. Losing publicly did not sit well with him.

"Judge, we are here," he said, motioning to his partner who was perched on the edge of his sanity, fairly bursting for an opportunity to speak, "to come before this court to show why the petitioner, Carter, should not be released. We are here to oppose that . . . release. Now, let me represent that there will be an appeal. . . . We are prepared as early as this afternoon, to file a notice of appeal to the Third Circuit Court of Appeals."

"What does that mean happens in the interim?" the judge asked.

"That means that we now have the right . . . to apply to this court that the existing incarceration be continued during the . . . appeal. We know that Your Honour has the discretion to set terms for release, including bail. We are prepared to argue that this court should, at the least, give respondents a further opportunity to present . . . whatever we have that touches upon the question of threat to the community. Chief Assistant Prosecutor Marmo is prepared to discuss that aspect of our application. . . ."

"The risk to the community . . ." interrupted Judge Sarokin with raised eyebrows, "that has arisen subsequent to these charges?"

The spectators in the courtroom gasped as it became clear what the prosecutors were trying to do. Their mission was to keep Rubin in jail, to continue to victimize the victim! Rubin couldn't believe their audacity. *They've been caught red-handed manipulating and suppressing evidence, appealing to racism, sending innocent people to jail for life. And now they're begging the court to keep me in prison because I'm the one who's dangerous!*

"Yes," answered Goceljak. "I will not go into that, but Mr Marmo is prepared to do so." Rubin had always thought Goceljak was more of a just-doing-his-job type and that he had some vague concept of lawyerly truth; he could twist the facts only so far and that's as far as he was willing to go. But if someone else on his team picked up the ball and ran with it, so be it . . .

"Well," Judge Sarokin replied, turning from Goceljak to his chief ball-carrier, "I will certainly hear from Mr Marmo."

"Thank you, Your Honour," blurted Ronald G. Marmo, jumping to his feet, his face hot with indignation. He had actively participated in every stage of this prosecution since 1976 and, since DeSimone's death, had assumed his mentor's mantle. It fell upon his shoulders now to redeem the good name of the Passaic County prosecutor's office, which had been sullied by the court's decision. And he had more than a passing personal interest in continuing Rubin's imprisonment. As Rubin would say, even a dumb prosecutor can manage to bring about a guilty verdict against a guilty person, but it's a real achievement to convict an innocent man. Getting Rubin convicted had been the high point of Marmo's career, and he wasn't about to let it all slip away, peaceably. *As far as Marmo is concerned, they've still got me and possession is nine-tenths of the law.*

"I suggest to Your Honour that [there] is information that you, in all likelihood, don't know about and didn't have with the papers that you studied in the course of rendering your decision in this case. We suggest to you, sir, that if you look at the defendant Carter's background, every aspect of his background, Your Honour, suggests a man who is a risk to the community, a man who is dangerous, who is violent and who is a legitimate threat to the community.

"If you look at his juvenile record, if you look at his adult criminal record, . . . if you look at his psychiatric record, I suggest to you, you will find the most frightening statements you have ever read in a psychiatric report. They were to me, and I have been a prosecutor eighteen years and I am accustomed to reading what psychiatrists say about people. . . .

"If you go back, sir, from the time that he was a juvenile, he has a juvenile record . . . that is not particularly substantial but it is a start of a career of a man who has never conformed to the rules of society. . . . You will find . . . he was sent to State Home for Boys, he escaped from State Home for Boys, he entered the military . . . [after which] he was institutionalized in the prison system in New Jersey . . . and after he was released, he was arrested for assault with intent to rob . . . and he admitted that he did these crimes. . . .

"What I am suggesting to Your Honour is that this is important and revealing information in his juvenile record, sir. This is important and revealing, I suggest, for a court that is going to decide whether this man should be at liberty. If history is any indication, if that means anything in the context of what we do and how we decide to deal with him today, then, the history here suggests that while this is an exceptional action that we are asking of the court, we think the court is justified in not setting the defendant at liberty because he is and has proven over the entire span of the time since he has been twelve years old, that he is a dangerous, violent person.

"What is startling here is the fact that the authorities in prison said, Your Honour, 'He continues to be assaultive, aggressive, hostile, negativistic, sadistic, he thinks he is superior, he has grandiose paranoid delusions, this individual is as dangerous to society now as the day he was incarcerated.'"

"What is the date of that?" the judge asked.

"Ah . . . 1959," Marmo mumbled and rushed on, hoping the court and the court reporter hadn't quite heard him, "and these same findings are adopted and continued into the 1970s. . . . If I may continue, Your Honour, 'This individual is as dangerous to society now as the day he was incarcerated —'"

"Again," interrupted Judge Sarokin, and this time more firmly, "I would appreciate it if you would give me dates."

"This is 1959, Your Honour," Marmo confessed, abandoning only for the moment his attempts to misdirect the court.

"I am interested," the judge reiterated patiently, "in evaluations that were made *since* this last incarceration."

"I am going to get to that, Judge," said Marmo with an edge to his voice. "This is by a Dr Farrell: 'He is an emotionally unstable, aggressive individual, embittered, hostile. When the time arrives that Rubin's ring aspirations do not exist, he will become more aggressive and I predict that a repetition of the present involvement will occur.' This is predicted before the Lafayette Bar murders occur. . . . These were examinations and diagnoses and impressions that were made in '59, '60, before these events [the Lafayette Bar shootings] occurred . . . and seem to sum up this man very well. So I suggest if you accept these findings, if you permit us to present you with information, you can find that these traits, that these characteristics, that these signs of being dangerous to the community existed far back in this man's past."

"What is the date of this psychiatric examination?" Judge Sarokin asked.

"This is 1970," Marmo shot back, positive now that he was on the right track.

"You mean there hasn't been one in fifteen years?" the judge probed.

"I don't know, Judge," answered Marmo, reluctantly. "I don't have the prison records from the last institution."

"Have there been any instances of violence in the last ten years?" queried the judge.

"In prison," Marmo said, trying to skirt the issue, "there was a prison record that shows all kinds of disciplinary violations well into the eighties. We don't have the benefit of getting the details of that. We have a summary sheet that was supplied to us from the institution when suit was filed against them in this matter. We don't have the details of that but they involve numerous citations of disciplinary actions, loss of time and credit."

Oh, Lord, thought Rubin and Kathy and Terry, as they realized that Marmo was talking about the two times that Rubin was sent to the Vroom Building. The first was the illegal transfer in 1974, for which Rubin had successfully sued the state and which the state was under federal court order never to use against him. Not that it bothered Marmo, but he had just violated that order. And the second was the not-standing-for-the-count put-your-dicks-on-the-bars non-episode in the early eighties.

"That may be," the judge said with some agitation, "but I am asking you about incidents of *violence.*"

"I don't have the documentation," Marmo fought back. He appeared to teeter in his elevator shoes, his auburn pompadour slipping suspiciously out of place.

"Well, that is why I keep asking you," the judge said pointedly, his chair swivelling from side to side. "What is the most recent psychiatric evaluation you have of this man?"

"I don't have the benefit of that," whined Marmo, "because we didn't have the opportunity, from yesterday to today, to go out and get this kind of information." In fact, as Marmo must have known, there were no psychiatric reports to get. Prison psychiatric interviews were connected with pre-parole hearings, which Rubin never attended. He had categorically refused to speak to psychiatrists, regarding them as educated stoolies, only more dangerous, because they were paid by the state to certify whether or not prisoners had been rehabilitated. And because Rubin steadfastly refused to acknowledge that he was *debili-*

tated, because of his insistence upon his innocence, to them he was unrepentant, delinquent, unmanageable and certifiably incorrigible.

"My question is," Judge Sarokin persisted, incapable of being steered from the point, "what is the most recent one you do have?"

"The most recent one, the psychiatric report, sir, I don't have the psychiatric report," Marmo said, giving up the bluff at last. "What I am reading from, Your Honour, is verbatim excerpts that were in an appeal that we filed back in the seventies. I don't even have those reports but I have them reproduced here word for word."

"What is the date of the most recent one?"

"The most recent one in this particular moving paper is 1970, I believe."

"All right. Thank you, Mr Marmo." And the judge turned his chair to face the petitioner's table.

The courtroom was stunned into silence by the virulence of Marmo's slanderous attack. The prosecution had done its best to inflame the passions of this judge in the same way as it had done in Passaic County with the jury. Terry and Kathy were appalled and outraged at what Marmo had said. His voice, his posture, his face—everything in his demeanour spoke of obsession. They had never heard anyone attack another human being with such apparent personal vindictiveness, and they were afraid of its effect upon the court.

Rubin, on the other hand, was able to be more reflective. He'd heard it all before. *Marmo's not talking about me! He's not discussing a man who's been railroaded into prison for something he didn't do. He's not talking about an innocent man who refused to co-operate with his captors. But Marmo's words don't surprise me. My refusing to work in prison was called "disrupting the orderly functioning of the institution"; refusing to shave off my moustache and beard equalled "disobeying an officer's direct order"; refusing to participate in rehabilitative prison programs labelled me "disruptive, hostile, aggressive, negativistic, having grandiose paranoid delusions."*

But I did the time the only way I could. Had I not—had I given up and given in—then perhaps the shit Marmo is heaping upon this court today might have been true. Perhaps then I could have been considered a danger. For then I would have been an accomplice to their crime. I would have had to have forgotten that I was innocent. I would have had to have been crazy. And for those reasons, I could have been considered dangerous.

"Mr Beldock," the judge said, offering him the floor.

Myron began slowly. "In 1966, when Mr Carter was arrested, he was a respected member of his community. . . . He was not only the prominent boxer who was about to fight for the middleweight title, but he was also a family man who lived in the community, which was a mixed white and black community, in a house that he owned, with his wife and his children. He mingled with that community freely and was accepted and respected."

"Do you know, Mr Beldock," asked Judge Sarokin, interrupting him as well, in order to penetrate to the heart of the matter, "and this may be against your client's interest, but I will pose the question to you nevertheless: Do you know of any instances in the last ten years of any acts of violence by Mr Carter?"

"I do not, Your Honour," Beldock stated emphatically. He pointed out that Rubin was a teenager when the psychiatric reports that Marmo was relying on were compiled, and that the so-called 1970 report was the 1959 report in a 1970 file. He explained that, in 1976, Marmo had tried to have Rubin's bail denied by using these same reports, and the judge, even then, ten years earlier, had considered them out of date and irrelevant.

"He is dredging up ancient history in an attempt to keep Mr Carter incarcerated. Beyond that, I know that Mr Carter was one of the prisoners most prominent in the Rahway Riots in 1971, which many people in New Jersey will still remember, in *protecting* guards and other prison personnel and the warden—there are citations in his file—when these people were subject to the potential of being maimed or killed by various prisoners who had lost control. . . . Mr Carter and Mr Artis . . . risk[ed] their lives . . . standing between what was an unruly and out-of-control populace at that time and the superintendent of the prison and others."

Myron's voice had now risen an octave higher than usual. His hands were not too steady. Marmo had upset him. After the excitement of yesterday's decision, no one had really been prepared for this.

Beldock wet his lips from a glass of water on the table. He turned and looked at Rubin.

"I know Mr Carter . . . I have had him in my house. He has been with my children. . . . All these things that we are hearing here are the spooks, literally, the spooks of the prejudice of Paterson. I am sorry to put it that way but . . . the view that Mr Marmo is pressing before you is a view that he will never relinquish, no matter what the facts are and no matter how many years of good life have been taken from Mr Carter. It is not fair. It is twenty years. Mr Carter should be released immediately."

On this impassioned note, Myron ended, emotionally drained, and sat back down beside his friend.

"Anyone else wish to be heard?" the judge asked. And wouldn't you know it, Marmo shot to his feet again.

"Judge," he cried, in a final fling of desperation, holding up a piece of paper in his hand with the same triumph as the Statue of Liberty holds her torch. "There is a reference to a 1982 date in the summary criminal sheet and it only says this, but I think perhaps it sheds some light on this, it is not specific enough but it says, 'January 13, 1982, due to the serious nature of the offence for which he received added time it is felt that reclassification at this time is inadequate for assuring non-dangerous behaviour.' "

Rubin sat there marvelling at Marmo.

"What is the document you are reading from?" asked Judge Sarokin.

"This is something from the Classification Department, State Prison, New Jersey Department of Corrections Assignment, Disciplinary and Transfer Process Report."

"Well, is that a general document that you have been referring to?"

"Yes, and it has much of this abbreviated type of citations with dates. It doesn't have the raw material. I can't interpret many of those symbols and the writings on here except that they reflect obviously that there are infractions of disciplinary process of some kind and there is some kind of process involved on a regular recurring basis that involves loss of some kind of credit or time at the prison institution.

What I am suggesting to Your Honour is maybe there is something for Your Honour to be concerned about here."

Oh, Lord, thought Rubin, *here it comes again, the same old not-standing-for-the-count infraction rearing its ugly head again. Marmo has definitely missed his calling in life. Rather than becoming a prosecutor he should have been a chemist: he has a great knack for turning soft shit into hard facts! I hope this Judge has a keen sense of smell.*

"Well," Judge Sarokin said, "what I will do right now is take a brief recess and look at anything that you want to show me, and then I will come back and rule on the pending application. I will take a fifteen-minute recess."

After Marmo handed the judge a thick stack of papers, court was adjourned.

The federal marshals appeared again and whisked Rubin away to a little room down the hall to await the judge's decision. Back in the courtroom the atmosphere was charged. Everyone was visibly tense. Marmo's words hung in the air like a toxic cloud.

Forty minutes later, the judge had still not returned. He was taking longer than expected. The tension in the courtroom mounted. People murmured nervously. Some paced the hallways, others didn't move at all. Having started out exultant with anticipation, Terry and Kathy just sat there, now frozen with fear.

Mercifully, court was reconvened.

"Ladies and gentlemen," the judge said impassively, as soon as everyone was seated. "I am about to render my opinion in this matter and I would very much appreciate it if everybody would remain silent until I conclude it. It is very brief.

"I have reviewed the materials submitted by the State and nothing in the proffer submitted by the State relates to any current evidence that Mr Carter poses a risk to society. I am reluctant to deny the State a full opportunity to be heard and that hearing can take place in the future if the State persists in its request for continued incarceration.

"In the interim, I cannot, in the face of the conclusions reached in my opinion and the injustices found, permit Mr Carter to spend another day or even an hour in prison, particularly considering that he has spent almost twenty years in confinement, based . . . upon a conviction which I have found to be so constitutionally faulty. To deny the relief sought would be inconsistent with my own ruling and render compassion meaningless. If my ruling is correct, Mr Carter's past imprisonment may have been a travesty. To continue it would even be a greater one. There is no evidence before me now which would permit me to conclude that society will be harmed by his immediate release. . . . Human decency mandates his immediate release. The historical purpose of a Writ of Habeas Corpus is served by Mr Carter's release. It is disserved by its denial.

"Therefore, petitioner shall be enlarged and released forthwith on his own recognizance without surety; the only condition being that he shall keep the State apprised of his residence."

The judge had not yet finished speaking before Charmaine Carter started clapping, leaped up and shouted a resounding "Yeah!" Thunderous applause then burst out everywhere. People were on their feet screaming. Ear-splitting whistles and shouts of jubilation erupted from the spectators and filled the room. In a half-hearted attempt to restore order, the judge rapped his gavel a few times. Above the din, he continued:

"I am confident that Mr Carter will not disappoint this court or all those persons who believe in him. Court is recessed."

The courtroom went wilder.

Everybody was crying and laughing and hugging. Rubin thanked and embraced his lawyers, and they all congratulated one another on their monumental victory. John Artis ran up and joined the group embrace. It was miraculous. David had slain Goliath.

Suddenly Rubin could walk out the door, no longer the dreaded murdering racist, but an innocent man who had been railroaded into prison. After facing the electric-chair and enduring twenty tortured years behind bars, the system was saying to him, *Never mind! You can go home now.* The irony of the situation was unreal.

As for facing the media, Rubin had made up his mind not to speak publicly until the war was completely over. "Completely" meant the State dismissing the 1966 murder indictment so that any further action, either an appeal or a third trial, would be impossible. Rubin and the Canadians were hoping that if he just disappeared quietly, then the prosecutors might have the good sense and the decency to let the case go. And if the Passaic County prosecutor's office couldn't, then they hoped the state attorney general's office would intervene and put an end to this madness. Rubin knew that if he was perceived to be glorying in his victory in the full glare of the media, further humiliating the prosecutors, then Marmo would sooner die than stop. There was no need to fuel Marmo's obsession, to give it any energy from which to feed. This time freedom had to last.

Rubin and the Canadians had set into motion a plan to facilitate his exit from the courthouse. They had hired a limousine, which investigator Mims Hackett had waiting at the back door.

As Rubin was being escorted out of the courtroom, Terry tried to approach him through the throng. Federal marshals barred the way until Myron looked up and said, "It's all right. He's with us." Terry leaned over and whispered to Rubin that everything was ready.

The marshals extricated Rubin from the mob and moved him out. Before he was officially out of custody, he had to sign for his release on his own recognizance. He was taken to an area behind the courtroom where the press were not allowed, although Mims, with his state-issued investigator's identification, was able to get back there with his friend, an African, he had brought along for the occasion. There Rubin handed Mim's friend the sheepskin coat and the sunglasses; the African gave Rubin his blue ski jacket. Nobody noticed.

The marshals began addressing the African, now wearing the sheepskin and glasses, as "Mr Carter." Was "Mr Carter" ready to go? Yes, he nodded, he was. The marshals walked "Mr Carter" downstairs to the back door where the limo was waiting. Rubin, in the blue ski jacket, became one of "Mr Carter's" escorts.

At the main entrance to the courthouse, in the rotunda area, a veritable sea of reporters, cameramen and onlookers was swelling, spilling out onto the wide front steps, down onto the sidewalks and out into the street, blocking traffic. John Artis, Lew Steel and Myron Beldock appeared on the top step, outside the front door, and were met by a bank of microphones. Myron, a beatific look on his face, gazed up at the cloudless sky. "New Jersey," he exclaimed, "has never looked so beautiful." He went on to say that the Carter–Artis case was "a case that should never have happened. It's a case of passion and prejudice that was wrong from the beginning. And the judge's decision said it loud and clear."

Beldock continued. "There is so much pressure on the police to arrest, and on prosecutors to prosecute and convict someone for a crime, that fairness and objectivity are swept aside, and all efforts are focused on making and often distorting evidence to fit the theory. . . . The defendant becomes the victim of this blind push to get a result . . . where there is public pressure to solve a particularly disturbing crime, to convict someone, to convince people the system is working when in fact it is not working at all—and you end up with people like Carter and Artis and many others who should never have been prosecuted. . . .

"I would like to dedicate this victory to all the people throughout the world who are serving time and shouldn't be."*

The media were eager to know where "Hurricane" Carter was. Beldock answered: "What Rubin wants right now is to find some peace and quiet—to paraphrase Voltaire, time to cultivate his garden."

Some of the reporters, surmising that Rubin would not be coming out the front door, broke away from the crowd and started running toward the back of the building. There they spotted the limousine and realized they had hit pay dirt when they caught a glimpse of the man in the sheepskin coat coming out of the courthouse, walking quickly toward the car. They swarmed around him, pushing and shoving. "Mr Carter! Mr Carter!" they shouted. Everyone wanted to be the reporter to capture Mr Carter's first words. They didn't notice the blue jeans and the sneakers and the fact that Mr Carter was now thirty years younger and had no moustache. All they could see was that sheepskin coat and those sunglasses getting into the limo. In their haste to get to Mr Carter, they knocked Rubin out of the way, almost trampling him. And there Rubin stood, pushed off to the side, watching them as they pursued the African and the sheepskin coat and then the limousine as it pulled away. The reporters gave chase on foot for about a half a block. One reporter jumped on a motorcycle and followed the limousine for miles.

Rubin walked through the crowd of disappointed reporters toward a nondescript car that had been parked directly behind the limo. He was free. For the first time in years, Rubin opened a car door himself.

---

*Much of this speech appeared in a New York *Daily News* article entitled "Justice Under Pressure" by columnist Earl Caldwell.

He slid into the back seat behind Ed Carter and Mims Hackett, who had been watching intently, hoping the pandemonium would enable them to pull the manoeuvre off.

"We did it, Rube! We did it!" and they relaxed with uproarious laughter.

"Come on, y'all!" said Rubin. "Let's not push our luck. Let's move!"

They drove for several blocks, making sure they weren't being followed by anybody. At a pre-arranged corner, Rubin got out, climbed into a waiting "Rent-a-wreck" vehicle and drove off into the proverbial sunset, with Kathy and Terry, ending up at their Rahway apartment with a view of the prison where he had started his odyssey that morning. Rahway State Prison was not even a mile away, but it might as well have been a million.

Dave Anderson, the noted *New York Times* sports columnist, caught the essence of the day's events in an article that brought tears to the eyes of Rubin and his friends.

Outside, in the dazzle of the sun on this steamy June day in 1974, the temperature sizzled in the 90's. Inside, two visitors were being screened by a correction officer at the Vroom Building, the maximum-security New Jersey state psychiatric prison in Trenton.

"We're here," one of the visitors explained, "to see Rubin Carter."

Slowly, one long steel door thunked open. The visitors stepped through, but another steel door loomed ahead. Behind them, the first steel door thunked closed. Then the other steel door opened and they stepped through.

Another correction officer waited.

"Rubin Carter?" he said. "Follow me."

Walking down a long empty corridor toward the cell blocks, one of the visitors heard a hissing sound. Looking around, he realized that it was coming from old radiators under a row of windows. Steam heat was hissing out of those radiators. With the temperature in the 90's outside, the prison had the heat on.

Moments later, Rubin (Hurricane) Carter appeared, glowering, a correction officer close on each side. Bearded but with his head shaved, the onetime middleweight boxer sentenced to life imprisonment for the 1966 murder of three patrons of a Paterson, N.J., bar, was brought into a small windowless room not much larger than a closet. He talked to his visitors there. As they spoke, perspiration glowed on their faces and soaked their shirts.

"Out of curiosity," one of the visitors finally said, "why do they have the heat on?"

"In the winter," Rubin Carter said, with a sneering smile, "they turn it off."

For anyone hoping to define what prison is like, let those words hiss like steam heat.

For most of 19 years, Rubin Carter was in prison for a crime that he always insisted he did not commit. And in Newark on Thursday, a Federal judge, H. Lee Sarokin, overturned his 1976 conviction at a retrial for the same points Rubin Carter had always asserted—the prosecution's suggestion of racial revenge and its withholding of evidence from the defense. Friday the same judge ordered that Rubin Carter be released in his own recognizance without bail, pending an appeal by the Passiac County prosecutors. . . . Rubin Carter's friends shrieked with joy. No longer a prisoner, he stood to embrace Myron Beldock, Lewis Steel and three other attorneys.

"He told me," Myron Beldock would say later, " 'Thank you, we did it.' "

But more than anyone else, Rubin Carter did it. Once a fighter, always a fighter. Once he went 15 rounds for the middleweight title; now he's gone 19 years with the New Jersey court system. And at age 48, he's surely not any softer, but he seems smoother. In earlier years, he strode defiantly, his eyes glaring through gold-rimmed glasses, his shaved head glistening. Friday he strolled into the courtroom with thick black hair and a mustache, but no beard. Holding a new beige sheepskin coat over his arm, he appeared to have stepped out of a men's shop window instead of his Rahway prison cell.

On his husky shoulders, he wore a heavy olive woolen sweater over a gray turtleneck shirt. His tan slacks had been pressed. His brown boots were polished.

But in prison, Rubin Carter had always been different. He didn't eat prison food; he used an electric coil in his cell to heat canned food mailed to him. He didn't wear the gray and blue clothes issued to prisoners; he wore his own clothes, sometimes a white high-collared tunic with white pants.

. . . [H]e kept fighting for his freedom. Jabbing, clinching, tricks Hurricane never used in the ring where he had always depended on the fury of his left hook. . . .

To understand how long Rubin Carter has been fighting for his innocence, consider that Muhammad Ali then had been the heavyweight champion for less than three years. Jose Torres then ruled the lightheavyweights, Emile Griffith the middleweights, Carlos Ortiz the lightweights.

All those champions stopped fighting long ago, but Rubin Carter didn't. Now he's ahead on points, perhaps to stay.

Whatever happens, Hurricane isn't talking yet. After his release on Friday, he was whisked out of the Newark court house through a back door. No questions, no cameras.

"He left," somebody said, "in a limousine."

28

The Canadians in Rahway were expecting to leave immediately with Rubin for Canada. As Rubin had packed up and shipped out his belongings, so had the Canadians packed up their Rahway apartment and were ready to go. Their Air Canada reservations had been confirmed. In Toronto, Lesra and the others were rushing about getting the house in order—cutting the grass, raking leaves, placing vases of flowers everywhere, preparing Rubin's favourite foods, making everything as perfect as possible for his homecoming. Given the short notice, Lesra and the others had been unable to be present at the release hearing. Having missed that excitement, Lesra had consoled himself with the anticipation of Rubin's imminent arrival in Toronto.

But it was not to be—not yet.

Rubin's recognizance bond stated (it was a standard term) that he must remain within the jurisdiction of the United States until all appeals were finished. He applied to have that restriction lifted. The prosecution—"magnanimous mother-fuckers to the end," as Rubin fondly referred to them—flatly refused. Lesra, Rubin and the Canadians were crushed.

Paulene was one of the group in Rahway at the time, and her nursing skills became very useful. Before that first day in freedom had ended, Rubin went blind. The vision in his right eye he had lost years earlier; his left eye now became infected to the point of being sealed tight. He couldn't see a thing. Every ounce of his energy had been focused on staying alive and getting out, and the extreme pressure and tension had taken their toll. He was completely and utterly exhausted. But he wasn't worried. He was free. Now he could afford the luxury of falling apart, and the blindness was only temporary. He had a home with friends who loved him and cared for him, who could give him the emotional and financial support so necessary to people who are abruptly released from an institution and are instantly bombarded by a million and one alien inputs, pressures and demands.

Within days, Rubin and his friends heard that Paterson cops were making it known that "if Carter so much as spits on a New Jersey sidewalk," he'll be locked up forever. The second time they heard the rumour, mindful of the old prison saying, they took it seriously. The third time they heard it, they left New Jersey and moved to Manhattan (although Rubin, to comply with the court order, still kept an official residence with relatives in New Jersey).

At Public School 296 in Brooklyn, Leland Martin woke up during a class on current events to hear his teacher say that one of the week's major news stories had to do with noted former middleweight boxer, Rubin "Hurricane" Carter, being freed from prison.

Leland jumped up out of his seat. "I know him! I talked to him! I talked to him on the phone up in Canada!"

Everyone in the class started to laugh. These kids had heard some stories, and they were too slick to buy this one.

"Honest!" said Leland. "I ain't lyin'." And he sat back down.

Rubin, when he learned of Leland's predicament, got hold of an old eight-by-ten glossy photo of himself knocking out Emile Griffith, wrote on it in his bold hand a personal message to Leland and sent it to him by courier. Rubin understood what it felt like not to be believed. Leland found himself very popular at school the next day when he turned up displaying a personally autographed photo of Rubin "Hurricane" Carter.

Better even than that, Lesra came down from Canada for Thanksgiving and brought the Hurricane from Manhattan to the Martins' home in Brooklyn with him. Bedford-Stuyvesant's Covert Street was abuzz. Along with Rubin and Lesra came a twenty-five pound turkey, stuffed, roasted with all the trimmings. Rubin was finally able to meet Lesra's family. Lesra proudly introduced his sister Loriel and her infant son, Kortrell; his oldest sister, Starlene, and her two daughters, Nakisha and Lashawn; his sister Nonie and her husband Turk; his nephew Shiquan, the son of his older brother Fru; and his younger brothers Elston, Leland and Damon. It really made Leland's day when Rubin took him and Elston and a few of their friends aside and showed them some boxing moves, including his famous left hook.

Rubin was particularly happy to meet Earl and Alma, and they were equally thrilled to have him in their home. Rubin said he had to let them know how important a role Lesra had played in his life. "So my first Thanksgiving in freedom," he told them, "is the perfect time to be here with you."

Rubin was out for six weeks without hearing a word from the prosecution. A seed of hope had begun to germinate, hope that the prosecutor's office or the state attorney general's office had found the grace to let this thing end. But, less than one week before Christmas, Rubin was served with notice that he had twenty-four hours in which to answer an over three-hundred-page submission from Marmo and Goceljak to the Third Circuit Court of Appeals in Philadelphia, alleging that Rubin was so dangerous to the community that he should be reincarcerated immediately, for the duration of the State's appeal on the merits—which could take years. The submission also sought that he be ordered to undergo a psychiatric examination. To bolster his arguments, Marmo had recycled the same garbage he had used to stink up Judge Sarokin's court, but if it remained unanswered, there was a very real possibility that Rubin would be back in prison for the holidays.

Rubin's lawyers applied for and received a ten-day extension to file a response. Rubin's first Christmas and New Year's after nineteen in prison was spent under the pall of having to answer three hundred pages of the most scurrilous and inflammatory character assassination imaginable. Ronald Marmo sought out the media and was unrestrained in the venom he spewed, exceeding even the elastic boundaries of normal prosecutorial ethics.

"Rubin Carter is a dangerous and violent assassin . . . always has been, always will be," he was quoted as saying in a nationally syndicated Chicago *Tribune* article. So much for peace on earth, good will toward men.

The lawyers and C & P did their usual masterful job in replying. They destroyed the foundation of every "fact" the prosecutors alleged and made it clear that there was no legal basis for the State's demands. Their four-hundred-page answering submission included letters of rebuttal and commendation from the likes of William Cahill, former Republican governor of New Jersey.

Two weeks later, after oral argument in Philadelphia, the State lost another round in federal court. Rubin remained free.

The prosecution was given until the end of March 1986 to file their appeal brief on the merits. Passaic County taxpayers' dollars now went to work to indulge their prosecutors' zeal. To proceed with the appeal, their office had to churn out massive amounts of paper, totalling some 150,000 pages. Each appellate judge was about to receive a five-foot-high stack of boxes containing one hundred volumes (20,000 pages) of material the prosecution wanted them to review, in addition to Marmo's two-hundred-page brief. To show the public they were protecting its interests, the prosecutors had a newspaper photographer take pictures of them using dollies to deliver this splendid mountain of paper to the Third Circuit Court of Appeals. The day before Good Friday, Passaic County Easter Bunnies also delivered to Rubin and John's lawyers the same Easter goodies.

C & P wasted no time reviewing these papers and, being so familiar with the record, spotted immediately where the prosecution sneaked in material that had been specifically barred from lower court proceedings, most because it was irrelevant, unreliable and prejudicial. As such, these materials were considered "*dehors* [outside] the record" and could not be brought before an appeals court.

Rubin knew the law well. Caruso, the DeSimone forgery, Louise and Avery's exonerating statements—all these were officially *dehors* the record and, for precisely that reason, had been lost to Rubin. He remembered the frustration and anger he felt when trying to convince his lawyers to allow him to submit at least the colour photos of the

Dodge tail-lights to Judge Sarokin. Rubin insisted that it was important for the judge to actually see the difference between the Polara and the Monaco. The lawyers maintained that, revealing as the photos were, they were not used at trial so they absolutely could not be used on appeal. Not wanting to taint his appeal in any way, Rubin had deferred to his lawyers' advice.

"Therefore," Rubin now argued, "since I've been forced to follow the rules, so will Marmo. If I'm not allowed to bring in new material that shows the *truth,* then he sure as hell can't bring in anything new to bolster his lies."

"But, Rube," said Professor Friedman, "maybe you should let them put in what they want. It doesn't matter. We don't want to look petty or like we're trying to hide something."

"Oh, I get it, Leon. If we submit the car photos, or use the Caruso evidence, we can be dismissed for violating the rules. But when *they* use manufactured documents or send in items that even Paterson judges have ruled improper, then *we'd* look bad if we object? No, Leon, I won't accept it. We're not acting like defendants any more. Let *them* defend what they've done!"

Leon agreed, and they filed a motion in the Third Circuit to limit the appendix on appeal to matters of record.

Thus began a series of court battles.

March 25, 1986: Carter's motion is granted by Circuit Judge John J. Gibbons on behalf of a three-judge panel.

March 28: The prosecutors, forgetting they're not in state court, ignore the federal court order and include non-record material in the appendix they file with the Third Circuit.

April 2: Carter makes a motion to strike the prosecutor's brief and appendix because of their violation of the court's order.

April 29: Circuit Judge Gibbons remands the matter back to Judge Sarokin to make sure that nothing off-the-record is included in the appeal appendix.

July 28: Judge Sarokin holds a hearing. Despite Professor Friedman's delineation of fourteen distinct items that are not of record in the State's appellate papers, Marmo refuses to concede. Judge Sarokin finds it "inconceivable" that there could be a dispute over something so concrete as to what is or is not on the record. He orders both parties to meet and to try to settle the matter. Professor Friedman and Ed Graves go to the prosecutor's office in Paterson, get nowhere.

August 20: Back in Sarokin's court. After another hearing, Judge Sarokin, calling Marmo's contentions "ludicrous," issues his opinion: "Notwithstanding the clear direction [of the Federal Rules of Appellate Procedure, of the order of the Third Circuit, and of the order of this Court], the State, choosing to ignore it, persists in its efforts to expand the record beyond what was presented to this court." Sarokin finds that the State has improperly included in its appeal papers fourteen items not of record.

September 8: Carter renews his motion in the Third Circuit to strike from the State's appeal papers the fourteen items.

September 11: The prosecutors file a motion to supplement the appendix on appeal to include the fourteen non-record items.

October 2: Circuit Judge Gibbons, writing for the panel, issues an order granting Carter's motion and denying the State's motion. The prosecutors retrieve their brief and the offending volumes of the appendix, rewrite the brief and extract the fourteen items from the appendix.

October 30: The prosecutors file an amended appendix and a revised (two-hundred-page) brief.

October 31: The clerk of the court issues an order refusing to accept a brief in excess of fifty pages and directs the prosecutors to file one in conformance with the rules, within ten days, adding: "The oversized brief previously submitted will be destroyed unless counsel retrieves it from the clerk's office within ten days."

November 5: The prosecutors appeal this order to a circuit judge.

November 12: Judge Aldisert denies their appeal.

November 17: The prosecutors appeal Judge Aldisert's decision to a circuit court panel.

December 11: The panel denies their appeal.

December 16: The prosecutors take the unheard-of step of appealing a procedural matter to the entire Third Circuit In Banc (meaning to all nine sitting judges).

January 5, 1987: The prosecutors are denied by the entire court and are ordered to file a fifty-page brief.

January 23: They file a brief of fifty pages—their "Revised Reduced" version. By this time the Third Circuit has before them an enormous file with example after example of how the Passaic County prosecutors intransigently flout court orders and steadfastly refuse to obey rules that lesser mortals must.

March 23: Professor Friedman files the Friedman-C & P fifty-page brief in answer, dubbed by them "the Red Zinger" because of its zinging nature and its requisite red cover.

June 22: Oral argument in Philadelphia, Marmo arguing for the State, Friedman representing Carter. The formidable judicial panel consists of Chief Judge Gibbons, former Chief Judge Ruggero J. Aldisert and Circuit Judge Joseph F. Weis.

August 21: The Third Circuit panel, in a unanimous decision written by Aldisert, upholds Judge Sarokin's ruling and his grant of the writ of habeas corpus.

Rubin had won another round, *a major round.* The score in the federal courts was now Carter, 14; State of New Jersey, 0. Incredibly, though, the fight was not yet over. Rubin now had to wait to see whether the prosecutors were crazed enough to continue on to the United States Supreme Court for their ultimate ass-kicking. Rubin had been out of prison for eighteen months without so much as a citation for jay-walking.

During this period, the phantom law firm of C & P, with their retirement plans put on indefinite hold, had taken up residence in the elegant old Delmonico's building at 59th and Park, above Regine's discotheque. They were now strategically located between Beldock's midtown office and Friedman's upper east side location, with the added advantage of being just two blocks from Central Park.

To escape from the blizzard of paper generated by the appeals in the Third Circuit, Rubin and his Canadian friends would take long strolls in the park to clear their heads. Near the children's zoo, they discovered a groundhog, who was known to the vendors and regulars in the park as "Fifth Avenue Phil." Rubin was intrigued by Phil and offered him a piece of chocolate. To everyone's great surprise, and to the delight of two park vendors, Hector and Benny, Phil came right up to Rubin, stood up on his hind legs and gently took the chocolate from Rubin's fingers, nibbling contentedly while Rubin stroked him. Feeding Phil (lettuce and other veggies) became a daily occurrence that Rubin, the Canadians and Phil all looked forward to. Some days dozens of little children would gather around this "dangerous and violent assassin" as he knelt beside them and showed them that they needn't be frightened of the little animal. Happy parents snapped pictures of their children with Phil and the nice black man. They had no idea who he was.

Rubin loved animals. He had once owned two horses and had been forced to give them up in 1966 when he was arrested for the Lafayette murders. In prison he had dreamed of the day he would be free to ride again. Now that he was out, Rubin and the Canadians wasted no time in finding a stable, with hundreds of acres of trails, in Van Cortlandt Park in the Bronx. The first time there, Rubin rode a stocky chestnut horse named "Mighty Mite"—part quarter horse, part Morgan—a show horse with a rich golden mane and tail. "Mighty Mite" had been brutalized by his previous owner. Rubin was warned that he was people-shy and very difficult to manage, often unseating his riders and returning to the stable alone. Rubin found him to be rough but of exceptional quality and decency, and they soon formed a strong attachment. As Rubin was later to say in a BBC-TV interview, "This is my friend. He came from an abused past. This is an extension of myself. My being released from prison and then finding this animal who mirrored me gave me and [him] an opportunity to acclimate ourselves into society."

Accompanying Rubin, Terry or Gus would ride on a spotted Appaloosa, creatively named "Apples," whose mulish appearance belied a high spirit and an independent nature. It wasn't long before they bought both horses. The owners were happy to see them go to people who appreciated them. The first thing Rubin and the Canadians did was give them new names. "Mighty Mite" became "Red Cloud," after the great Sioux warrior, and "Apples" became "Lakota," which means "the People," the name the Sioux prefer for themselves.

While Rubin was in New York working on his case, which was then still pending in the Third Circuit, he received a phone call from his cousin, Harriet, in south Jersey. She told him that several white men had come to her house and said they were friends of his and were looking for him. She was instantly suspicious because they called her Harriet, which was not the pet name that Rubin used for her. She insisted they show her some identification. They then had to admit they were investigators from the Passaic County prosecutor's office. They asked her if this was Rubin Carter's residence. She said it was and told them, if they didn't have a warrant, to leave. They left to return a few days later. This time they spoke to a number of Rubin's neighbours. An elderly man was grilled about Rubin's comings and goings. Harriet's fifteen-year-old son was followed, then stopped and questioned. Another neighbour was asked if she was aware that Rubin Carter, a triple-murderer, was living near her. She replied, "But he's been cleared of that!"

"Yeah, by one judge," came the retort. "Twenty-four jurors found him guilty!"

Rubin, who at this point was doing his best to keep a low profile and go about his business quietly, was fortunate to have been residing in a community where people understood what he had been through. Otherwise, the prosecution's poison might have made it impossible for him to live there when he wasn't in New York working on his case.

In the summer of 1986, Bob Dylan came to New York City to give a series of concerts in Madison Square Garden. Since getting out, Rubin had not yet had the chance to see Dylan. Dylan arranged to have tickets waiting for Rubin at the Garden, as well as special passes to go backstage after the show so they could talk.

At the July 17 concert, Dylan, from the stage, announced a warm welcome for "my good friend, Rubin 'Hurricane' Carter, who is somewhere out there tonight." After the show, Rubin and the Canadians went backstage, where Andy Warhol, Rolling Stone guitarist Ron Wood and Tom Petty were hanging out.

Rubin was ushered through a long, crowded, noisy hallway back into a small room where Dylan was sitting, talking quietly with a number of friends. At the doorway sat a giant dog, just slightly smaller than Rubin's horse. The guy who had ushered Rubin in went over to Dylan and whispered something. Rubin stood in the doorway, patting the dog. Bob looked up at Rubin and shook his head. "No, that's not him," he said. Then Bob took a longer look and slowly started to rise.

Rubin held out his arms and said, "Get over here, brother, and give me a hug!"

"It's you, Rubin! It really is! I didn't recognize you, brother!" Dylan exclaimed, as they joyfully embraced.

Dylan grabbed Rubin by the arm, took him over and introduced him to Jacques Levy, who co-wrote the lyrics to "Hurricane." Dylan commented on what a coincidence it was that Rubin and Jacques had both come that same night. Everyone there could feel the power of the energy that flowed between Rubin and Bob.

They arranged to meet the next day so they could continue to talk. Bob asked Rubin to join him on the tour. Rubin told Bob that he couldn't; he was still fighting, working on his case; the prosecutors were still after him. Dylan just shook his head.

Many times over the years, Lesra had asked both his parents to visit him up in Canada. But there was always something that seemed to prevent them from coming. Once they'd even got as far as the airport, but Earl suddenly became so ill they couldn't board their flight.

Lesra's mother's birthday was approaching, and Lesra made arrangements to have his parents come up to Toronto for a holiday. Lesra and Rubin conspired to make sure that nothing got in the way this time. As Rubin put it to Lesra, "If we can get me out of prison, we can get your parents out of Brooklyn."

So one summer day, a stretch limousine appeared outside the doorstep of the Martins' Brooklyn home. Rubin got out and went into their apartment, collected Earl, Alma and their suitcases, and walked them out to the waiting limousine. As Rubin had requested, the uniformed chauffeur, standing smartly at the door, greeted Mr and Mrs Martin formally by name, then took their bags and helped them into their seats. Through the tinted glass, Alma and Earl noticed there wasn't a soul on the street who wasn't glued to the action, not a window without at least one pair of eyes checking out the scene. As the car slowly moved off, Alma turned to Rubin and said "I was cool, you know, Rubin. I never been in no limo before. But with everybody watching, I stepped in like I been doing it all my life!" And they laughed.

Rubin saw them to the Air Canada departure lounge at La-

Guardia, and not until the flight was in the air did Rubin leave the airport. Lesra and Paulene were waiting at Pearson International to pick them up. Earl and Alma stayed in Toronto for several days and had a fabulous time. Lesra threw a huge surprise birthday celebration for Alma. In addition to the presents for her, there was something for Earl too. After months of searching, Lesra had found an old 45 rpm record of the Del Vikings singing "Come Go With Me." Tears came to Earl's eyes, as the familiar strains filled the room.

By the fall of 1986, it had become apparent to Rubin and the Canadians that his appeal could drag on for years. The Canadians decided they would try to find a place to rent in the country. They had the good luck to find a house with a small horse barn and pasture in Westchester County, only three-quarters of an hour north of Manhattan. It was a perfect place for them and the horses.

Rubin, thankful he was out of prison and able to give something back to his cousin Ed, invited him to Westchester, hopeful that the peace and quiet and clean air of the country might be of some benefit; Ed had just been diagnosed as having cancer. Ed stayed for a couple of peaceful weeks before Rubin took him to Sloane-Kettering Hospital in Manhattan to see a top specialist, who was running an experimental program for terminal patients. But it was too late for Ed. He died a few weeks later. Rubin felt this loss acutely, regretting the many years of companionship they had missed because of his imprisonment.

On November 12, 1987, the prosecution filed its "Petition for Certiorari" to have its appeal heard in the United States Supreme Court. Carter and Partners were called to the bar once again on the facts, and Professor Friedman wrote the legal portions of their Brief in Opposition that they filed with the U.S. Supreme Court on December 14. This brief, which was required to have an orange cover, they named the "Orange Squasher."

There was another Christmas spent with Rubin's future still uncertain. But everybody came down from Toronto—including Lesra and Marty and their friends—to be with Rubin, since he couldn't be up there with them. Many of Rubin's old friends also came to Westchester to visit him, among them Fred Hogan (who had obtained Bello's and Bradley's recantations) and his family, Dave Anderson,

Marvelous Marvin Hagler and Ed Carter's family. Being surrounded by people who cared for him, Rubin had a great Christmas.

The gift they all longed for came on January 11, 1988. The United States Supreme Court refused to hear the State's appeal. That meant that the highest court in the land had decided that Judge Sarokin's decision was correct and absolutely final. Carter, 15; State, 0.

But the prosecution still had the option of staging a third trial in Passaic County and, astoundingly, twenty-two years after the original events, Marmo was raring to go. The state attorney general's office at long last stepped in and persuaded Passaic County that enough was enough. On February 26, 1988, a Passaic County judge signed an order dismissing the indictments. The twenty-two year saga was finally over.

There would be no compensation for Rubin or John. No commission of inquiry to investigate what had gone wrong. Not so much as an apology. Nobody would have the decency to admit they had made a mistake.

That weekend, Myron Beldock and his wife, Karen, had a celebration for Rubin at their Greenwich Village loft. Forty-two people, including the Canadians and a good number of the many lawyers, investigators, paralegals, and support staff who, over the years, had devoted time and energy to Rubin's case, sat down to dinner together and celebrated the successful outcome of possibly the most litigated case in U.S. criminal history. It was staggering, even criminal, the resources that were needed to right this one wrong. Beldock's firm alone had put in over 11,000 hours and had put out $100,000 in direct out-of-pocket expenses. Fees for all the lawyers would have totalled between $4 and $5 million.

Everyone there was awed by the magnitude and the beauty of the victory, awed by what it was possible to achieve when people work together unselfishly. No one who had been involved was left untouched by the experience. And this feeling extended to Judge Sarokin as well. He has stated publicly on many occasions that freeing Rubin Carter was the most important and rewarding action he has taken in his tenure on the bench: "There is nothing greater a judge can do than free a person who has been wrongly imprisoned." (He has also said that the Carter briefs were the best he had ever seen in his legal career.)

Finally, Rubin Carter was free to speak publicly. A press conference was held on a rare twenty-ninth day of February. As Selwyn Raab described it in the next day's *New York Times*:

> Yesterday a recording of Bob Dylan's ballad "Hurricane," composed in honor of Mr Carter, boomed from a sound system as Mr Carter arrived to the applause of friends and supporters at the Baroque Room of the Plaza (Hotel).
>
> The setting was in sharp contrast to interviews Mr Carter had given in the 1970s in the bleak atmosphere of the former death row in Trenton State Prison with its gray walls, concrete floors and metal chairs.
>
> The pink-colored Baroque Room, overlooking Central Park, was bathed in light from crystal chandeliers. Waiters served croissants, danish, coffee and tea . . . Mr Carter [was] dressed in a tan suede jacket, white shirt, dark tie and navy-blue trousers.

In addition to Rubin's supporters, there were scores of media people and cameras present. After the lawyers—Myron, Lew, Leon and Ed—said a few words, Rubin addressed the audience:

"Ladies and gentlemen of the press:

"On June 16, 1966, twenty-two years ago, I left my home in Paterson, New Jersey, for a meeting with my business manager to discuss an upcoming prize-fight. But little did I know that the events of that night would sound the bell ending my career as a professional boxer, and mark the beginning of quite a different kind of fight, a fight in which the prize was life itself—and freedom.

"Well, we have just won that fight. The sixteenth round is finally over! It is over! *Yes.*

"The State of New Jersey has just now seen fit to dismiss the charges and the indictment—the same indictment that they used twenty-two years ago to try to take my life by seeking the death penalty. But they failed to get the death penalty, I am delighted to report. Instead, they sentenced me to a life of living death—and there is no other way to describe the nature of prison. Prison destroys everything that is valuable in a human being. It destroys families—it destroyed mine! It destroys one's dignity and self-respect in too many ways to even begin mentioning here—it got to me, and I knew I was innocent! It gets to everybody.

"I have seen people die in prison—needlessly—from the lack of medical attention and sheer neglect. And in that regard, I have always considered myself as being lucky because all I suffered was the loss of one eye, while John Artis, a mere teenager I barely knew in 1966, and who would not have gone to prison had he not asked for a ride home that [fateful June] night, was not so fortunate. He contracted, in prison, an incurable circulatory disease. To date, he's had several fingers and toes amputated and he can only expect more of the same in the future. Now, that's horrible! I mean, for what? For simply asking for a ride home. It's incredible.

"But you know I think what struck me most about being released from prison was that for twenty years, I was considered a danger to society. I was locked away in an iron cage for, not one, but three of my lifetimes. I was a prisoner, a number, a thing to be guarded with a maximum of security and a minimum of compassion. Not a person. Not a human being. But a body to be counted fifteen or twenty times a day. Even when I was brought to the Federal District Court to be released (and I think many of you were there to witness this) you saw me chained, you saw me shackled and you saw me handcuffed. I had to be escorted by three carloads of heavily armed guards. Man! I frightened myself, I appeared to be so dangerous!

"But, the very next moment, with the stroke of a judge's pen, I'm free! Completely and utterly free—with all of the rights and protections that everyone here takes for granted. Suddenly, I can walk out the door—as if the last twenty years had never happened. As if society was telling me 'Never mind!' One moment I'm a championship prizefighter. The next moment—and for twenty years thereafter—I'm reviled as a triple-murderer. Then, the next moment, I'm an innocent man who's been wrongfully imprisoned. Now *you* try to make sense out of that, because I'll be damned if *I* can! It is just too much!

"I think there are a number of conclusions that might be drawn about the criminal justice system from my experiences. First of all: the death penalty. I was far from the first, and I won't be the last innocent person that the State seeks to execute. It has happened before and it will happen again. And if it happened to me, it can happen to you! It can happen to *any*body! And if you are black and poor, and don't have the quality of lawyers that I've had, the chances are the State will be successful. And that penalty of death is final. It is irrevocable. And it is permanent!

"Secondly, and many of you may not wish to hear what I have to say about this, prisons are not country clubs. They are not vacation resorts. I know—I've just spent twenty years of my life there. And criminals are not coddled. Where is the proof of this? Just go sixty miles south of here to a place called Trenton, New Jersey and you will find a unit there called the Vroom Readjustment Unit, and I challenge any reporter to go to that building, to see the devastation, come back and report that to the people, and I guarantee you that that building will be torn down brick by brick before the sun goes down that day. What we have to understand and what we have to come to grips with is that brutal punishment in a totally hostile environment does nothing to alleviate crime. Absolutely nothing. If this society is serious about eliminating crime, and I can see little evidence of that being the case, then it should concentrate its energies on eradicating the causes, the roots of crime—the drugs, poverty, illiteracy, unemployment and racism. A simple-minded 'Lock-em-up and throw-away-the-key' approach ensures only that those who have already been condemned to a life of violence and despair are then punished further for it. If we are to have compassion for the victims of crime—and we must!—then we must include *all* victims. Because peace rules the day, only where reason rules the mind.

"Thirdly, there is far too much power invested in local prosecutors, and far too little, if any, accountability. The Passaic County prosecutors, who unfortunately are not atypical, were able to persecute John Artis and me for twenty-two years using the enormous resources of the state and constrained by no one. They were constrained neither by the truth, by the facts, nor by justice. And they are even now, in effect, legally immune from the consequences of their actions. Now that's what I would call unchecked and unbalanced.

"Fourthly, federal review of state court criminal proceedings, or what is known as habeas corpus, is absolutely vital and necessary. All too often state courts succumb to political considerations and local pressures that have nothing to do with justice. In our case, it took nineteen years before we could get out of the state court system and seek federal review—nineteen years! But once we did, it was a matter of only a few months before the federal court found that the state court convictions, and I am quoting now, were based on 'appeals to racism rather than reason, and concealment rather than disclosure.' The district court, in concluding that without these grave constitutional violations the jury would have found me innocent, ordered my immediate release. And all the federal courts, including the United States Supreme Court, agreed. . . .

"But even federal review is no real guarantee of justice. Because the most powerful enemy of justice is inertia, maintaining the status quo, or, let's not ruffle any feathers. And that's why I want to acknowledge here today, and sing the praises of Federal Court District Judge H. Lee Sarokin. His clarity, his wisdom and depth of understanding [are] incomparable. For he alone had the courage to face squarely an issue that the state courts for nineteen years had sidestepped—and that is that the poison of racism had permeated the state's entire case. To not throw out these convictions, so wrote Judge Sarokin, would be to commit a crime as heinous as those for which we were unjustly convicted. Now, ain't that saying a mouthful?

"The question invariably arises, it has before and it will again: 'Rubin, are you bitter?'

"And in answer to that I will say: after all that's been said and done—the fact that the most productive years of my life, between the ages of twenty-nine and fifty, have been stolen; the fact that I was deprived of seeing my children grow up—wouldn't you think I would have a right to be bitter? Wouldn't anyone under those circumstances have a right to be bitter? In fact, it would be very *easy* to be bitter. But it has never been my nature, or my lot, to do things the easy way. If I have learned nothing else in my life, I've learned that bitterness only consumes the vessel that contains it. And for me to permit bitterness to control or to infect my life in any way whatsoever, would be to allow those who imprisoned me to take even more than the twenty-two years they've already taken. Now, that would make me an accomplice to their crime—and if anyone believes that I'm going to fall for that . . . then they are green enough to stick in the ground and grow!

"Thank you."

It was an electrifying and moving speech, and after the applause the room was hushed, silent. For several moments not a person budged.

"I'll be happy to answer your questions now," said Rubin.

No one said a word. The press had been so enthralled, so caught up with what he was saying, they forgot for the moment they had come there to question him. Rubin was stunned too, as he looked in vain for a raised hand among the crowd. He chuckled and said, "No questions? Great!" and he feigned a move to leave. Laughter then broke the spell and the questions began. At the end of the press conference, Rubin was given a standing ovation.

After meeting the press *en masse,* Rubin gave his first one-on-one television interview to Carol Martin, a news-anchor of WCBS-TV in Manhattan. The next day, after he was interviewed by Charlie Gibson on ABC-TV's "Good Morning America," Rubin, Sam and Terry climbed into the reliable old Mercedes.

They headed north.

EPILOGUE

Some things change, some things never change.

Lesra received an Honours B.A. from the University of Toronto and a Master's Degree in Sociology from Dalhousie University in Halifax. Then, true to his youthful dream, Lesra did indeed become a lawyer. He graduated from Dalhousie Law School in 1997 and is now living in British Columbia.

Lesra's family in New York have not fared so well. In the late eighties, his parents, Earl and Alma Martin, died within a year of each other, Earl from cancer, Alma from medical neglect. Elston, the brother who was closest to Lesra in age and about whom he felt so guilty leaving, was shot without provocation on the streets of Brooklyn in 1995; he died in the arms of Leland, the second youngest Martin. Lesra's older brother, Fru, continues his life in and out of prison.

When Lesra first met the Canadians in 1979, one out of four young African-American men were under the control of the criminal justice system; today it is one out of three.

John Artis is now living in Virginia and counseling youthful offenders.

Sam Leslie, "The Rose," was freed from prison in May 1990, his conviction overturned as a direct result of the brief that Rubin Carter and his Canadian partners had written seven years earlier.

In the eighties, Alfred Patrick Bello was reputed to be living under an assumed identity in Albuquerque, New Mexico. His whereabouts today are unknown.

The real murderers of the three people in the Lafayette Bar in Paterson on June 17, 1966, were not found, nor were they pursued.

Former Assistant Prosecutor Ronald Marmo now presides on the Passaic County superior court, the bench from which Judge Bruno Leopizzi has retired. John Goceljak is still employed at the Passaic County prosecutor's office, as Deputy First Assistant Prosecutor.

Myron Beldock and Lewis Steel are still practicing criminal attorneys in New York City, as is Leon Friedman, who continues to teach at Hofstra University School of Law on Long Island.

Federal Judge H. Lee Sarokin, despite much opposition, granted a writ of habeas corpus to another prisoner at Rahway in 1990, James Landano, who had been unjustly convicted of killing a police officer and had served 13 years. Landano was found innocent in a subsequent trial. Judge Sarokin was elevated to the United States Court of Appeals for the Third Circuit Court in 1994. Two years later, at the age of sixty-seven, he resigned from the bench, concerned that his tenure had become too politicized, that his ability to render independent decisions and to serve effectively had been hampered by incessant political attacks. He had become one of the prime targets of a concerted right-wing campaign against federal judges who, by enforcing the Constitution, were perceived to be "soft on crime." In announcing his resignation, Judge Sarokin said that "to hold judges responsible for crime is like blaming doctors for disease."

In the 1990s new laws were passed and new court precedents set that have effectively curtailed prisoner access to habeas corpus. Today, if Rubin Carter were applying for a writ of habeas corpus, as Judge Sarokin testified at a hearing on habeas corpus before the Congressional Judiciary Subcommittee on Civil and Constitutional Rights, his petition would have to be denied. He had slipped through the eye of a needle and that eye is now shut.

After the events described in this book, Rubin Carter moved to

Canada, married Lisa, and made his home with the Canadians for a while. In a ceremony in Las Vegas in December 1993, Rubin was awarded the Championship Belt by the World Boxing Council, a lifetime honor never before bestowed on any man, but given to Hurricane Carter in the belief that his unjust incarceration had robbed him of the world middleweight title. The year before, Rubin nearly died from tuberculosis, which he had unknowingly contracted in a Rahway State Prison epidemic just before being freed. After lying dormant for several years, the TB attacked Rubin's blind right eye and attached itself to the stitches that had mistakenly been left there from the prison operation decades earlier. That eye had to be surgically removed and replaced with a prosthesis.

Rubin continues to speak out eloquently against the death penalty and on behalf of justice and literacy issues, testifying before Congress and lecturing at various legal forums, including the American Bar Association, and universities like Harvard and Yale. He is on the Board of Directors of the Southern Center for Human Rights in Atlanta and is Executive Director of the Association in the Defence of the Wrongly Convicted, a Toronto-based group that the Canadians helped found and that has been instrumental in clearing the names of a number of innocent men.

The Canadians, most of whom still live together in the Toronto area, continue their activities unabated. Most recently, they have been involved in a burgeoning private-label hat and urban apparel business named Big It Up with another young black man, Dameion Royes, who is the cousin of Paulene, Lesra's first girlfriend in Canada (she moved in with the Canadians in 1983 and never left).

A major Hollywood motion picture, *The Hurricane,* based on this book and *The Sixteenth Round,* has just completed filming under the direction of Academy Award winner Norman Jewison. To be distributed in North America by Universal, it stars Oscar-winning Denzel Washington as Rubin Carter and Vicellous Reon Shannon as Lesra, Deborah Unger as Lisa, Liev Schreiber as Sam and John Hannah as Terry. Rod Steiger plays Judge Sarokin.

Not everyone in New Jersey, however, is elated by the prospect of this movie. Sheriff Edwin J. Englehardt recently told the *Bergen Record* that, as Paterson's police commissioner, he had been one of the first people to arrive at the murder scene in 1966. He said it was "because of a technicality" that Carter was set free and called it "a disgrace to the system. . . . If the movie makes any money, the state should charge Carter $77 a day for the twenty years of free room and board he got while in prison." Sheriff Englehardt further vowed, "If I could do something to destroy the movie, I would."

Some things change, some things never change.

Toronto, 5 April 1999

APPENDIX A

Hurricane

Lyrics by Bob Dylan & Jacques Levy

1. Pistol shots ring out in the barroom night
   Enter Patty Valentine from the upper hall
   She sees the bartender in a pool of blood
   Cries out, "My God, they killed them all!"

   > *Here comes the story of the Hurricane*
   > *The man the authorities came to blame*
   > *For somethin' that he never done*
   > *Put in a prison cell, but one time he coulda been*
   > *The champion of the world.*

2. Three bodies lyin' there does Patty see
   And another man named Bello, movin' around mysteriously
   "I didn't do it," he says, and he throws up his hands
   "I was only robbin' the register, I hope you understand
   I saw them leavin'," he says, and he stops
   "One of us had better call up the cops"

And so Patty calls the cops
And they arrive on the scene with their red lights flashin'
In the hot New Jersey night

3. Meanwhile, far away in another part of town
Rubin Carter and a couple of friends are drivin' around
Number one contender for the middleweight crown
Had no idea what kinda shit was about to go down
When a cop pulled him over to the side of the road
Just like the time before and the time before that
In Paterson that's just the way things go
If you're black you might as well not show up on the street
'Less you wanta draw the heat

4. Alfred Bello had a partner and he had a rap for the cops
Him and Arthur Dexter Bradley were just out prowlin' around
He said, "I saw two men runnin' out, they looked like middle-
weights
They jumped into a white car with out-of-state plates"
And Miss Patty Valentine just nodded her head
Cop said, "Wait a minute boys, this one's not dead"
So they took him to the infirmary
And though this man could hardly see
They told him he could identify the guilty men

5. Four in the mornin' and they haul Rubin in
Take him to the hospital and they bring him upstairs
The wounded man looks up through his one dyin' eye
Says, "Wha'd you bring him in here for? He ain't the guy!"

> *Yes, here's the story of the Hurricane*
> *The man the authorities came to blame*
> *For somethin' that he never done*
> *Put in a prison cell, but one time he coulda been*
> *The champion of the world*

6. Four months later, the ghettos are in flame
Rubin's in South America, fightin' for his name

While Arthur Dexter Bradley's still in the robbery game
And the cops are puttin' the screws to him, lookin' for somebody
   to blame
"Remember that murder that happened in a bar?"
"Remember you said you saw the getaway car?"
"You think you'd like to play ball with the law?"
"Think it mighta been that fighter that you saw runnin' that
   night?"
"Don't forget that you are white"

7. Arthur Dexter Bradley said, "I'm really not sure"
   Cops said, "A poor boy like you can use a break
   We got you for the motel job and we're talkin' to your friend Bello
   Now you don't wanta have to go back to jail, be a nice fellow
   You'll be doin' society a favor
   That sonofabitch is brave and gettin' braver
   We want to put his ass in stir
   We want to pin this triple murder on him
   He ain't no Gentleman Jim"

8. Rubin could take a man out with just one punch
   But he never did like to talk about it all that much
   It's my work, he'd say, and I do it for pay
   And when it's all over I'd just as soon go on my way
   Up to some paradise
   Where the trout streams flow and the air is nice
   And ride a horse along a trail
   But then they took him to the jail house
   Where they tried to turn a man into a mouse

9. All of Rubin's cards were marked in advance
   The trial was a pig-circus, he never had a chance
   The judge made Rubin's witnesses drunkards from the slums
   To the white folks who watched he was a revolutionary bum
   And to the black folks he was just a crazy nigger
   No one doubted that he pulled the trigger
   And though they could not produce the gun

The D.A. said he was the one who did the deed
And the all-white jury agreed

10. Rubin Carter was falsely tried
The crime was murder "one," guess who testified?
Bello and Bradley and they both baldly lied
And the newspapers, they all went along for the ride
How can the life of such a man
Be in the palm of some fool's hand?
To see him obviously framed
Couldn't help but make me feel ashamed to live in a land
Where justice is a game

11. Now all the criminals in their coats and their ties
Are free to drink martinis and watch the sun rise
While Rubin sits like Buddha in a ten-foot cell,
An innocent man in a living hell

> *That's the story of the Hurricane*
> *But it won't be over till they clear his name*
> *And give him back the time he's done*
> *Put in a prison cell, but one time he coulda been*
> *The champion of the world*

APPENDIX B

The Carter Case—A Twenty-Two-Year Chronology

June 17, 1966—Two men and a woman are fatally shot at the Lafayette Bar and Grill in Paterson, N.J. Rubin Carter and John Artis are questioned by the police, are not identified by the surviving victims, pass lie-detector tests and are released. Police declare that Carter and Artis were never suspects.

June 29, 1966—Carter and Artis testify voluntarily before a Passaic County grand jury and are exonerated. Neither are they indicted by grand juries sitting in August, September and October.

October 14, 1966—Alfred Bello, a well-known local criminal and a suspect himself, gives the police a signed statement claiming he saw Carter and Artis at the murder scene. Carter and Artis are arrested and indicted for the triple murder.

May 27, 1967—An all-white jury convicts Carter and Artis. The prosecutor seeks the death penalty, but the jury recommends mercy. Carter and Artis are sentenced to three life terms.

July 1974—Carter files a federal suit against the state for illegally transferring him from Rahway State Prison to the Vroom Readjustment Unit (VRU) at the Trenton State Psychiatric Hospital. After a hearing, United States District Judge Clarkson S. Fisher orders Carter's immediate release from VRU detention.

September 1974—Carter's book, *The Sixteenth Round,* is published by Viking Press. Bello and Arthur Bradley, the only witnesses to claim Carter and Artis were at the scene, separately recant and state they were pressured by Paterson detectives to give false testimony; they were offered inducements of $10,000 in reward money and promises of lenient treatment in criminal charges pending against them.

December 8, 1975—Bob Dylan gives "Night of the Hurricane" benefit concert at Madison Square Garden.

March 17, 1976—The New Jersey Supreme Court unanimously overturns the convictions, ruling that the prosecution withheld evidence favorable to the defence, and orders a new trial. Carter and Artis are released on bail.

December 22, 1976—After a second trial in which the prosecution was allowed to argue for the first time that the murders were motivated by racial revenge, Carter and Artis are reconvicted; the same life sentences are imposed, and they are returned to prison.

December 22, 1981—Artis is released on parole, after serving fifteen years.

August 17, 1982—The New Jersey Supreme Court, in a 4-to-3 decision, rejects an appeal for a new trial.

February 17, 1983—Carter wins his suit against the state for his 1974 illegal detention in the Vroom Readjustment Unit. Federal District Judge Dickinson R. Debevoise issues an opinion granting Carter damages.

November 7, 1985—Judge H. Lee Sarokin of the United States District Court in Newark overturns the second trial convictions after finding that the prosecution committed "grave constitutional violations": the convictions were based on "racism rather than reason, and concealment rather than disclosure." Judge Sarokin advises the State, in the interests of justice and compassion, against seeking a third trial.

November 8, 1985—In the district court, the prosecutors argue that Carter is dangerous and should remain in prison pending the State's appeal. Finding no evidence of dangerousness, Judge Sarokin orders Carter freed without bail: "Human decency mandates his immediate release." Carter has served nineteen years.

December 19, 1985—The prosecutors assert to the United States Third Circuit Court of Appeals that Carter is a danger to the community and should be re-incarcerated pending appeal.

January 17, 1986—The United States Court of Appeals rejects the State's arguments, and Carter remains free.

August 21, 1987—The United States Court of Appeals upholds Judge Sarokin's decision throwing out the convictions.

January 11, 1988—The United States Supreme Court denies the State's appeal, thus affirming Judge Sarokin's rulings.

February 19, 1988—The Passaic County prosecutor's office announce they will not seek a third trial, and they file a motion to dismiss the 1966 indictments against Carter and Artis.

February 26, 1988—A Passaic County judge formally dismisses the indictments. The twenty-two-year saga is over.

INDEX

ABOUT THE AUTHORS

SAM CHAITON AND TERRY SWINTON were born in Canada. They were business partners in the 1970s before they and a group of friends adopted Lesra (Lazarus) Martin and subsequently fought for the release of Rubin Carter. Sam and Terry moved to New Jersey where they researched the voluminous record in the Carter case and wrote the factual portions of the briefs to the U.S. federal courts that succeeded in freeing the wronged ex-prizefighter. They later helped found the Toronto-based Association in Defence of the Wrongly Convicted, and now operate an urban apparel and hat company called Big It Up International. The Norman Jewison-directed Hollywood film starring Denzel Washington as "The Hurricane" also features actors Liev Schreiber and John Hannah as Sam and Terry.